Word ~~Pares~~, ~~Pears~~, Pairs

Margie Wakeman Wells

MARGIE
HOLDS
COURT
·PUBLISHING·

To order this publication, go to
margieholdscourt.com.

Word Pares, Pears, Pairs

Margie Holds Court Publishing
www.margieholdscourt.com

Eleventh Printing, December 2021

Email: mww@margieholdscourt.com

Follow Margie

- @MargieWW
- @MargieHoldsCourt
- @MargieHoldsCourt

ISBN 978-1-4675-6944-6

ISBN 978-1-4675-6944-6
53295>

9 781467 569446

INTRODUCTION

No matter what your purpose is in producing a written document in English -- Ph.D. thesis, letter to the editor, court reporting transcript, personal note to Aunt Mary, email to the boss -- the issue of how to spell different forms of the same word or words that sound similar is going to arise. You simply cannot communicate well in writing without a knowledge of word pairs: e.g. *flair/flare, born/borne, gentle/genteel, accelerate/exhilarate.* Whether they sound exactly alike or just similar, these words present a challenge. With this in mind, I created a class on these word pairs that I taught for many years and today have put together this book.

The need for such a book arises from the fact that the dictionary is of little value when you have a word in a context where it simply does not fit. You have *feral*; you know it means "beastly." You know that meaning does not fit in the sentence "The feral had slipped out of place, and the leg of the framework collapsed." How do you look up a word in a dictionary that is close to a certain sound but for which the spelling is unknown? You don't always do that easily. You have no means of finding the other word since you do not know exactly how it is spelled. Maybe you don't even know a similar word exists. Maybe it starts with an entirely different letter. (I will leave it to you to find the pairs for *feral.*)

My goal for this project was simple: Write a book that defines and explains and gives context samples of words that sound alike and/or words that sound similar. The result is Word ~~Pares, Pears,~~ *Pairs.*

As always in the writing of any book, there are many people to thank for the support and encouragement along the way. My dear husband, Adolphus, is my rock; my dear priest, Peter, is always in my corner; Scott and Tedd, my two sons, always have my back; my family and friends are ever a source of strength and joy in my life; Barbara, Christen, and Kathy were invaluable in taking care of the last-minute proofing and assembling of this work.

But this book is dedicated to my dear brother, John, and his "girls," Jezzibelle and Kahlua. In August of 2011, we formed Margie Holds Court Publishing and took over publication of my punctuation text and workbook. John has worked tirelessly to make this company run smoothly -- offering aid and support, calling me daily with ideas and solutions or just to chat, making phone calls and sending emails on my behalf, taking the operational work from my shoulders -- thus giving me time to write this book and teach seminars and teach classes and write a blog. Without his efforts for Margie Holds Court, this book would never have been written, and my life would be a whole lot crazier than it is now.

What a rich and varied language we have the privilege of speaking and using. Enjoy.

Margie Wakeman Wells
Culver City, California
March 2013

...in the time that remains...

PUBLICATIONS FOR PURCHASE
Court Reporting: Bad Grammar/Good Punctuation

CR: BG/GP Workbook

Practice Really DOES Make Perfect (Drill Books for Accuracy)

All Things English

AT MARGIEHOLDSCLASS.COM
Take online classes
Join Margie Rules
Subscribe to a monthly one-hour seminar – The SEMINAR
Join Margie's English Corner

Subscribe to the blog.

Follow Margie
@Margie WW on Twitter
Margie Holds Court on Facebook

For details on all purchases, go to
margieholdscourt.com..

ABOUT THE BOOK

In amassing the list of words and deciding which ones to include, I obviously had to make choices. I had no thought of trying to include every sound-alike/look-alike word in the language. I picked those I thought most common and/or most troublesome. Doesn't the *affect* and *effect* dilemma jump right up and beg to be explained? Do you take a "*new tack*" or a "*new tact*"? Is it "The *incidence* of crime in the city is rising" or "The *incidents* of crime in the city is rising"?

There was no intention to include every definition for every word. For example, rarely did I include medical words, nor did I include the more technical definitions for a given word. Also, there was no thought to giving a sample for every word. Some words are so common as not to need a sample, in my opinion. When there is both a noun and a verb meaning that is similar, I did not necessarily list both.

To make this book user friendly, I had to solve some issues: alphabetical order. Should I list every pair under each alphabetical choice? *Accede/exceed* under both *a* and *e*? *Kneed/need* under both *k* and *n*? No. Doing that would increase the size and cost of the book exponentially. Should there be alphabetical order within each pair? No. It just didn't always make sense to do that.

Another issue was do I include the exercises and make everything into one book? You know that I think you have to practice to make information really stick in your brain! Though I think practicing these words in order to really master the meanings is crucial, I know that some of you are not going to do that. So I made the two books separate. If you don't want to work the exercises, you are not forced into buying pages that you do not need. The exercise practice is a separate book, which becomes my next project.

When it came to dividing the pages, I wanted to keep the pairs together. Logistically it didn't always work. There are pages that are "short" and a few words that are out of alphabetical order -- all in an effort to make things fit on the pages. Do I add "filler" so that all the pages look uniform? No.

And, last, I had to decide how you were going to find the word you are looking for. Take *jealous/zealous* as an example. Since I didn't list it under both spellings, how was I going to make it easy to find? If you have *jealous* and know that is not correct, where do you look? My solution is an alphabetical listing of every word in the book and the page on which it is found. It is my belief that this makes it easy to find the word you are looking for: Look up the word you have, go to the page listed for it. You find the words that are the same or similar in sound.

And, of course, I use the word *pair* very loosely in referring to this text. There are obviously more than two entries for many of the "pairs."

By the way, I did proofread this book more than once and also had other people proof it. When you find a mistake, be gentle; but please let me know!

USING THE BOOK

What the book contains:

- The words are given alphabetically (with the disclaimer noted). Special word pairs like *principal* and *principle* and *passed* and *past* are included in the normal alphabetical order. Only *affect/effect* and *cite/sight/site* have their own pages.

- Some prefixes that form a pair -- e.g., *inter-* and *intra-* -- are included in the listings with only the briefest of definitions.

- There are a few concepts that have been given their own section: for example, the prefix *re-* that has to be hyphenated when we already have a solid word with a different meaning -- *resign* and *re-sign;* the article *a* as a separate word or a solid word -- *abridge* and *a bridge*.

- I have imported the one-word/two-word section from Chapter 29 of my punctuation textbook, *Court Reporting: Bad Grammar/Good Punctuation*, though a more complete explanation is available there.

- The basic information given for each word is this:

    Grammar information where appropriate: e.g., plurals, verb parts

    Part of speech

verb	VB	adverb	ADV
noun	N	preposition	PREP
pronoun	PRO	conjunction	CONJ
adjective	ADJ	interjection	INTERJ

    Definitions and samples

    Special indications: e.g., slang, foreign word

    Idioms and expressions, where appropriate

How to use the book:

Go to the alphabetical list of words, which is located in the back of the book. Find the word you are questioning. Go to the page that discusses that word, and you will find those words that sound like or close to the word you have. One of them is likely to fit into your sentence.

TABLE OF CONTENTS

Chapter 1
The Letter *A*

AB-　　　　　　Prefix meaning "away from" as in *abnormal* and *abstract*

AD-　　　　　　Prefix meaning "toward" as in *addict* and *adverse*

ABDUCT　　　　VB: carry off, move away from centerline
...attempted to abduct the child from the playground...

ADDUCT　　　　VB: move toward centerline
...adduct the two molecules...

ABDUCTION　　N: act of taking away from, removing
N: unlawful taking of someone from their home/family
...abduction of the Lindbergh baby in 1932...

ADDUCTION　　N: act of being drawn toward
...adduction of the feet as the toes turn in...

ABDUCTOR　　N: muscle that draws a part away from the median line or axis
...abductor muscles pull the arm away from the body...

ADDUCTOR　　N: muscle that draws a part toward the median line or axis
...adductor muscles pull the arm toward the body...

ABDOMINAL　　ADJ: relating to the middle of the body, the stomach
...suffered from abdominal pain...

ABOMINABLE　ADJ: causing disgust or hatred
...abominable behavior...

ABERRANT　　ADJ: straying from the right or normal way
...his aberrant behavior became frightening...

ABHORRENT　ADJ: hateful, repugnant, repulsive
...action was abhorrent even to the most hardened...

ABERRATION	N: deviation from a moral code or standard
	...behavior that night was an aberration...
ABRASION	N: scraping, wearing away, rubbing away
	...abrasions on his left side from the accident...
	...left abrasions on his extremities...
ACCEDE	Intransitive verb; it never has a direct object (usually followed by *to*)
	VB: give into, acquiesce
	...accede to the wishes of his father...
	...will accede to the demands of the job...
EXCEED	Transitive verb; it usually has a direct object
	VB: go beyond what is expected
	...exceed my fondest dreams...
	...will always exceed the limit...
ACCELERATE (-ATION)	VB/N: cause to go or happen faster
	...accelerate to the speed of 80...
	...rate of acceleration made me dizzy...
EXHILARATE (-ATION)	VB/N: stimulate, put into high spirits
	...felt exhilarated when he got a raise...
	...feeling of exhilaration upon hearing the news...
ACCEPT	VB: receive or take something offered
	...accept the award with gratitude...
	...did not want to accept the truth of the situation...
EXCEPT	VB: object, take exception to
	...I except. That is beyond the scope...
	PREP: leaving out, but, other than
	...everyone got it except him...
EXPECT	VB: anticipate, await
	...I expect a call at any moment...

acquiesce

ACCESS	VB/N: admittance, way of approach, passage *...gained access illegally to her account...*
EXCESS	N: beyond what is expected or desired *...in excess of what was expected...*
ASSESS	VB: put a value on something, judge the worth of something *...assess the house for $200,000 more than last year...*
AXIS	N: point around which something revolves *...earth revolves on its axis...*
ACCLAMATION	From the verb *to acclaim*: praise, laud, applaud N: plaudits, applause *...received the acclamation of the supportive crowd...*
ACCLIMATION	From the verb *to acclimate*: become accustomed, get used to N: becoming used to *...acclimation to a new environment takes time...*
ACCOMPLICE	N: someone who aids in the carrying out of something (often illegal) *...would not name his accomplice...*
ACCOMPLISH	VB: succeed in a task *...nothing left to accomplish...*
ACME	N: high point, peak, summit, zenith *...reached the acme of his career...* (Opposite is *nadir*: depth, bottom, low point)
ACNE	N: skin condition *...went to a dermatologist for the problem with acne...*
AD(S)	Short for *advertisement* Plural of *ad* N: announcement, notification
ADD(S)	Third person singular, present tense of *to add* VB: combine to form a sum *...all adds up to nothing...* Second spelling: *adz*
ADZE	N: cutting tool, used for shaping wood

Handwritten note next to ACCLAMATION: acclaim praise

Handwritten note next to ADZE: cutting tool

ADAPT	VB: adjust, make fit or suitable
	VB: modify or alter for a different purpose or situation
	(Refers to what you do with something you already own or have)
	...adapt his plan to our needs...
	...necessary to adapt to the new environment...
ADEPT	ADJ: very skillful, expert
	...very adept in the dance moves...
ADOPT	VB: take for one's own
	(Refers to taking on something you did not have before)
	...adopt a new plan for the company...
	...intend to adopt a child in the spring...
ADDICT	Pronounced /a-<u>dict</u>/
	VB: surrender excessively or obsessively
	...became addicted to playing the slots...
	Pronounced /<u>a</u>-dict/
	N: someone who is obsessively dependent on some habit
	...admitted to being an addict...
EDICT	Pronounced /<u>ee</u>-dict/
	N: order or command
	...issued an edict about overall performance...
ADDITION	N: act, process, or result of increasing; something added
	...second addition to the house...
	...addition of another member on the board...
EDITION	N: copies of a book, newspaper, or magazine -- all issued at the same time
	...latest edition of the book...
ADO	N: commotion, fuss
	...from Shakespeare's "Much Ado About Nothing"...
ADIEU	FRENCH: *good-bye*
	...bid adieu to our relatives returning to Australia...

command (handwritten annotation near EDICT)

ADVERSE	ADJ: unfriendly, unfavorable, harmful ...*adverse reaction to the drug*... ...*had adverse feelings toward his weird sister*...
AVERSE	ADJ: opposed, (unwilling) (Most often used after a form of the verb *to be*) ...*is averse to getting in the car with him because of his drinking*... ...*was averse to leaving his long-time position*...
ADVICE	N: opinion about what should be done ...*try never to give her advice*...
ADVISE	VB: tell others what they should do or say, offer advice, counsel ...*will advise her to vacate the office*... ...*advise her of the need to spend more time on it*...
AEGIS	N: within someone's sponsorship, under someone's protection ...*under the aegis of his company*...
AGE(S)	VB: get older ...*will age more quickly now that he is alone*... N: eras, years old, long time ...*haven't seen him for ages and ages*...
AREA	N: space ...*wants to move to a better area of the city*... ...*surrounded by an area of farmland*...
ARIA	N: operatic solo ...*aria by the soprano*...
AURA	N: subtle sensory stimulus ...*radiates an aura of contentment*... N: energy field that is said to emanate from a person ...*got an aura around her eyes before a major migraine*...

[handwritten note next to AEGIS/AGE(S): under sponsor or protection]

AERIE *(handwritten: nest on cliff)* N: nest of a bird on a cliff or mountain
...spotted the aerie from the road...

AIRY ADJ: fresh, light, open, spacious
...light and airy pastry...

EERIE ADJ: creepy, strange
...was eerie and quiet inside the cave...

ERIE N: canal, lake, town in Pennsylvania, tribe of Indians
(Acronym for the five Great Lakes -- HOMES:
Huron, Ontario, Michigan, Erie, Superior)

(See page 23 for a full explanation)

AFFECT VB: have an effect on, influence
...doesn't affect my life...

EFFECT VB: bring about, make happen
...will effect a change in her behavior...
N: outcome, result
...cause and effect relationship of the two views...
...has no effect on my life...

AFFECTATION *(handwritten: not real)* N: something which is not real or genuine
...affectation in the lilt of her speech...

AFFECTION N: liking, love
...genuine affection for animals...

AFFECTIVE *(handwritten: from feelings, emotion)* ADJ: arising from feelings or emotions
...had both cognitive and affective symptoms...
ADJ: expressing emotion
...affective response to the announcement...

EFFECTIVE ADJ: producing a decided, decisive, or desired outcome
...effective in making the child listen...
...effective means of getting the job done...
ADJ: operative
...tax law becomes effective in January...

AFFINITY N: liking, drawing toward, fondness, kinship
...has an affinity for anything with sugar...

INFINITY N: forever
...seems to stretch out to infinity...

AFFLUENCE	N: wealth *...affluence in that high-priced area of town...*
EFFLUENCE	N: flow, something flowing out *...odor emanating from the effluence...*
AFFLUENT	ADJ: wealthy N: people who are wealthy *...argues that the affluent need to pay more taxes...*
EFFLUENT	ADJ: out-flowing (usually used in the plural) N: sewage or liquid waste that flows out into a body of water *...effluents that harm the water in the canal...*
AID	VB/N: help or assist *...will aid in the rescue attempts...* *...came to his aid after the accident...*
AIDE	N: assistant, person who helps *...spoke with the aide for the patient...*
AIDS	ACRONYM: acquired immune deficiency syndrome
-ADE	SUFFIX: act or action as in *blockade* SUFFIX: product, especially a sweet drink as in *limeade*
AIL	VB: be ill *...always asks, "What ails you?"...*
ALE	N: type of beer *...spent the evening tasting several kinds of ale...*

Handwritten annotations: flow; outflowing (sewage)

AIR	N: earth's atmosphere
	...*overcome by the polluted air*...
	EXPRESSION
	put on airs = act stuck up and snobbish
HEIR	N: one who inherits
	...*one of the nine heirs of his rich uncle*...
E'ER	Short for *ever* (poetic)
ERE	Short for *before* (poetic)
	...*ere I saw her again*...
ERA	N: age, historical time period
	...*in a very different era from the present*...
ERR	Pronounced /er/, not /air/ (rhymes with *her*)
	VB: make a mistake
	...*need to err on the side of caution*...
	..."*To err is human; to forgive is divine*"...
AISLE	N: passageway between seats in a theater or other room
	...*so popular that there were people sitting in the aisle*...
I'LL	CONTRACTION: *I will*
ISLE	N: island
	...*stayed on a small isle in the Caribbean*...
ALIMENTARY	ADJ: relating to food
	...*problem is in the alimentary canal*...
ELEMENTARY	ADJ: basic
	...*seems elementary to me, but he finds it difficult*...
ALL	PRO/ADJ: entirety, the whole of, things without exception
	...*all people involved in such a worthy cause as ending hunger*...
AWL	N: pointed instrument used to pierce holes in leather
	...*used an awl to make an extra hole in his belt*...

[handwritten note: before]

ALLAY(S) *soothe reduce*   VB: soothe, subdue, reduce the intensity of
...*tried to allay her fear of flying*...

ALLEY(S)   N: narrow, back street

ALLY (-IES)   Pronounced /uh-<u>lie</u>/
VB: unite by formal agreement, treaty or alliance, side with
...*intends to ally himself with the underdog*...
...*always allies herself with her sister against her brother*...
Pronounced /<u>al</u>-eye/
N: person or nation united with another person or nation, friends
...*is an ally of our side of the argument*...
...*are allies of his point of view*...

ALLIES (-IED)   N: forces during World War II
...*Allies were led by Eisenhower*...
(The Allied Powers were Britain, France, Russia, and the
United States.
The Axis Powers were Japan, Italy, and Germany.)

ALLEGATION *accusation*   N: something asserted or brought forth by way of accusation
...*tried to refute the allegation*...

ALLOCATION   N: something apportioned
...*allocation of funds was insufficient to get the job done*...

ALLOT *assign a share*   VB: assign a share, allocate
...*allot three to each person*...

A LOT   Never, ever correct as one word!
N: piece of land
...*have a lot next to the lake*...
ADV: informal English for *many* or *much*
...*were a lot that were involved*...

ALLOW(ED)   Past tense and past participle of *to allow*
VB: permit
...*smoking not allowed inside the restaurant*...

ALOUD   ADV: spoken at an audible level
...*was not spoken aloud*...

ALLUDE *[handwritten: casual mention]*
VB: mention casually, refer to indirectly
...*did allude to his prior convictions*...

ELUDE *[handwritten: escape]*
VB: avoid or escape by cunning or quickness
...*suspect continued to hide out and elude police*...

A LEWD...
ADJ: obscene
...*made a lewd remark in front of the young children*...

ELIDE *[handwritten: sound]*
VB: squish out a medial sound
(Says "Come Monday" as "Comonday" as if there were just one *m*)
...*tends to elide the two consonants into one*...

ALLUSION *[handwritten: casual mention]*
N: passing, casual, or indirect reference
...*allusion to her checkered past*...

ILLUSION
N: something that deceives by producing a false impression
...*water in the road in the desert was an illusion*...

ELISION *[handwritten: omission]*
N: act or instance of omitting something in speech
...*says "mi hijo" as "mijo" as an elision in Spanish*...

ELYSIAN *[handwritten: blissful]*
ADJ: blissful, delightful
...*spring in the elysian fields*...

DELUSION
N: something that is falsely believed or propagated
...*had delusions of grandeur*...

ALLUSIVE *[handwritten: indirect mention]*
ADJ: pertaining to indirectly mentioning something
...*allusive comments about his sexual orientation*...

ELUSIVE *[handwritten: difficult to pin down]*
ADJ: difficult to pin down
...*trying to get a shot of the elusive figure*...

ILLUSIVE
Substandard form for *illusory*

ALTAR
N: raised structure used in religious ceremonies
...*homemade altar at home for the purpose of worship*...

ALTER
VB: vary, modify
...*tried to alter his appearance so he would not be recognized*...

ALTERATION	N: change *...had to make an alteration in the approach...*
ALTERCATION	N: controversy, minor fight *...witnessed the altercation between the two litigants...*
ALTERNATE	VB: perform by turns or in succession *...will alternate days with my partner...* VB: change from one to another repeatedly *...clouds alternate with sun...* VB: arrange one above or alongside the other *...will alternate boys and girls in each row...* N: one that substitutes for or with another *...alternate juror on the case...* ADJ: occurring or succeeding by turns *...time of alternate sadness and happiness...* ADJ: every other, every second one *...comes in on alternate days...* ADJ: substitute *...took an alternate route because of the traffic...*
ALTERNATIVE	N: choice between two or more things, only one of which may be chosen *...no alternative but to join him on the dais...* N: something which can be chosen instead *...picked an alternative to communal living...* ADJ: offering or expressing a choice ADJ: outside the established culture, social, or economic system *...chose an alternative lifestyle...* ADJ: different from the usual or conventional *...use of alternative fuels...*
ALTITUDE	N: height *...flew at an altitude of 38,000 feet...*
ATTITUDE	N: angle of flight in relation to level *...flew at a level attitude...* N: mental position or state *...had a bad attitude...*

ALUMNA ~~b~~   N: one female graduate
ALUMNAE ~~b~~   N: many female graduates
ALUMNI ~~m & b~~   N: many male graduates or many graduates both male and female
ALUMNUS ~~m~~   N: one male graduate
(The license frame that says "Alumni" is valid only with more than one graduate in the car; in other words, it is probably incorrect.)

AMATEUR   N: not a professional, not paid for performance
...amateur golfer who almost won the tournament...
ARMATURE ~~armor~~   N: armor

AMIABLE   ADJ: pleasant, agreeable
...found her to be amiable and easy to deal with...
AMICABLE   ADJ: friendly
...was amicable to our point of view...

AMPLE   ADJ: enough or more than enough, sufficient, plentiful
...ample food for the trip...
AMPULE   N: sealed glass capsule containing a single dose of medication
...carrying an ampule to inject...

ANDROGENOUS ~~m~~   ADJ: tending to produce male children
ANDROGYNOUS ~~both m & b~~   ADJ: having both male and female characteristics
...androgynous figure in the painting...

ANECDOTE   N: story usually told to support a point
...told an anecdote about his father...
ANTIDOTE   N: substance that works against poison
...antidote wasn't given in time to save her...
ANTEDATE ~~predate~~   VB: predate, precede in time

ANGEL   N: spiritual being, heavenly messenger
...was an angel who helped me through it...
ANGLE   N: geometric measurement of two intersecting lines
N: someone's point of view
...from his angle...

ANNALIST *(historian)*	N: writer of annals, historian *...annalist kept the historical records of the group...*
ANALYST	N: one who analyzes: i.e., people, stock market, financial *...wants to be a financial analyst...*
ANNALS	N: historical records (used in the plural) *...never before in the annals of time...*
ANNUAL	ADJ: yearly *...submitted her annual report...*
ANAL	ADJ: pertaining to the anus
ANNUL *(invalidate)*	VB: cancel, invalidate, abolish, void *...cannot annul the marriage after five years...*
ANT	N: pismire, insect
AUNT	N: relative, sister of one's mother or father
ANTE-	Prefix meaning "before" as in *antecedent* and *antebellum*
ANTI-	Prefix meaning "against" as in *antidote* and *antiseptic*
APPALLING	Present participle of *to appall* VB: horrify, disgust *...conditions would appall all of us...* ADJ: horrible, disgusting *...his appalling attitude toward minorities...*
APPEALING	Present participle of *to appeal* VB: plead *...appeal to her good nature to help him...* ADJ: pleasing *...gift is appealing to her flair for art...*
APPELLANT *(one that appeals)*	N: one that appeals (person who appeals) *...appellant in the action that is before the court...*
APPELLATE *(relating to appeals)*	ADJ: relating to appeals (court where something is appealed) ADJ: having the power to review the judgment of another *...sent to the appellate court...*

APPRAISE *(estimate value)*
VB: estimate the value or quality of an object, set the value
...appraise the ring for over $5,000...

APPRISE *(inform)*
VB: give notice, inform, to advise
...apprise us of the change in the train schedule...

APPROXIMATE
Pronounced /...mate/
VB: estimate
Pronounced /...muht/
ADJ: nearly correct, not quite exact, rough
...is an approximate amount, not exact...

PROXIMATE *(imminent)*
ADJ: resulting, imminent
...alcohol is a proximate cause of the accident...

ARC
VB/N: part of a circle, path of sun, electrical discharge
...electrical arc caused a power outage...

ARCH
VB/N: curved structure
...tended to arch his back when he was seated...

ARK
N: boat
...baby loves the story of Noah's ark...

ARRAIGN *(formally charge)*
VB: formally charge in a criminal case
...arraign him on a charge of murder...

ARRANGE
VB: order, fix, plan
...arrange it before I get there...

ARRAIGNMENT *(proceeding where charges are brought against accused)*
N: proceeding where charges are brought against an accused
...faces arraignment in Superior Court later today...

ARRANGEMENT
N: something made by putting parts together
...arrangement was made for him to come in on a Saturday...
N: adaptation of a musical composition by rescoring

ARTISTIC	ADJ: creative, imaginative
	...*does everything with an artistic flare*...
AUTISTIC	ADJ: relating to a disorder that causes one not to be able to interact with people
	...*program for autistic children*...
ASCENT *act of rising*	N: act of rising
	...*slow ascent up the side of the mountain*...
ASCEND *move upward*	VB: move gradually upward
	VB: go back in time or in order of genealogical succession
	VB: succeed to, occupy
	...*will ascend to the office of president*...
ASSENT *agreement*	N: agreement, act of giving consent
	...*gave his assent to the changes that were to be made*...
ACCENT	N: stress on a word
	N: dialectical speech
	...*speaks with a Spanish accent*...
	N: distinctive sign of flavor
	...*with a small accent of peppermint*...
ASEPSIS	(Prefix *a* means "not"; *sepsis* means "dirt")
	N: state of being clean, sterile, without disease
	...*asepsis in the OR*...
ASEPTIC	ADJ: without dirt, clean
	...*must live in aseptic conditions because of severe allergies*...
A SEPTIC... *dirty*	ADJ: dirty
	...*working close to a septic system*...
ANTISEPTIC	N/ADJ: works against dirt or infection
	...*used an antiseptic to clean the wound*...
ASSORTED	ADJ: varied
	...*came in assorted colors*...
A SORDID...	ADJ: dirty, ugly, lewd
	...*was a sordid affair that disgusted everyone*...

ASSAY
VB: evaluate, assess
...have an assay done of the ore...

ESSAY
N: theme
...used his essay as evidence in the trial...

ASSIMILATE
VB: take on as one's own
...was quickly assimilated into the culture...

SIMULATE
VB: feign, assume outward qualities
...simulates the feeling of weightlessness...

SIMULATOR
N: training device, as in pilot training
...spent the requisite hours in the simulator...

STIMULATE
VB: arouse, rouse to action
...need to stimulate his muscles to move more...

ASSISTANCE
N: process of giving aid or help
...offered my assistance to the stranded group...

ASSISTANT(S)
Plural of *assistant*
N: aides
...had several assistants working with her...

ATTENDANCE
N: presence, audience
...attendance was required for all those enrolled...

ATTENDANT(S)
Plural of *attendant*
N: those who assist
...seven bridal attendants...

ATTENUATE *make thinner*
VB: make thin or slender
...outfit tends to attenuate her already thin figure...

EXTENUATE *reduce seriousness*
VB: reduce the seriousness of, mitigate
...tends to extenuate her circumstances and gives her some leeway...

ATYPICAL	Prefix *a* means "not"
	ADJ: not typical, unusual, uncharacteristic
	...*is an atypical reaction to the antibiotic*...
A TYPICAL...	ADJ: ordinary
	...*was a typical reaction to the antibiotic*...
AUGER	N: tool for punching holes
AUGUR *foretell*	VB: foresee, foretell
	...*good test scores augur well for her success*...
AUGURER	N: person who does foretelling
	...*augurer of good fortune*...
	N: weatherman
OGRE	N: bad guy
	...*boss was a real ogre that no one liked*...
AUGHT *- zero*	N: cipher, zero
	...*used a .30-06 to shoot rabbits on the farm*...
	N: to any degree, anything whatever
	EXPRESSION
	for aught I care = I don't care
	(More commonly said "for all I care")
NAUGHT	N: nothing, zero
	...*all of our efforts came to naught*...
OUGHT	VB: must, should
	...*ought to pay more attention to her English class*...
	(Never has a helping verb; *had ought* is never correct)

AURICLE *[handwritten: atrium of heart]* N: atrium of the heart
...*damage was discovered in the auricle*...
N: angular or ear-shaped lobe, process, or appendage

ORACLE N: person through whom God speaks
...*thought to be an oracle by those in the church*...

[handwritten: Wise thought or person] N: person giving wise or authoritative decisions or opinions
N: authoritative or wise statement
...*received the oracle from the CEO*...

AVERSION N: hatred, loathing, distaste
...*had an aversion to citrus fruit*...

EVERSION *[handwritten: turn inside out]* N: act of turning inside out

AW INTERJ: expresses sympathy, mild disappointment
AWE(D) VB: wonder, fright
...*intended to awe her with his work*...
N: wonder
...*in awe of his achievements*...
ADJ: stunned, surprised, overwhelmed
...*was awed by what he was able to do*...

ODD ADJ: strange

AWAY ADV: from, gone, not here
...*got away from work too late to attend*...
...*time slipping away*...
...*put away in the closet*...
...*sound dying away*...
ADV: by a long distance or interval
...*gone away too far to turn back*...
ADJ: played on an opponent's grounds
...*was an away game*...

AWEIGH *[handwritten: just clear of bottom]* ADJ: raised just clear of the bottom as an anchor
...*anchors aweigh*...

AWFUL	ADJ: terrible
	...spent an awful night in the ER...
OFFAL	N: waste or byproduct of a process
	...dumped the offal into the receptacle...
	N: viscera and trimmings of a butchered animal
AXEL	N: figure skating jump
	...missed the triple axel...
AXLE	N: shaft upon which the wheel revolves
	...turned out to be a broken axle...
AXIAL	ADJ: forming an axis
AXES	Pronounced /<u>ax</u>-uhz/
	Plural of *ax* or *axe*
	N: tool used for cutting
	...broke several axes in trying to cut down the tree...
	Pronounced /<u>ax</u>-eez/
	Plural of *axis*
	N: line on which an object rotates
	...revolved on several axes...
AXIS	N: straight line on which a body rotates
	...earth spins on its axis...
AYE	N: in favor of
	...part of the aye vote in favor of the bill...
	(Opposite is *nay*)
EYE	VB: look at
	VB: study carefully
	...began to eye the medal she was holding...
	N: organ of sight
	...had an infection around the eye...
I	PRO: first person singular

Handwritten annotations: Waste ; skating jump ; forming axis ; in favor

A, THE ARTICLE?
A, PART OF THE WORD?

(NOTE: These represent only a few of the combinations in this category. There are many others.)

ABASE *lower in rank* VB: lower in rank or position
...activities that abase his standing in the community...

A BASE N: foundation
...needs a base to sit on...
N: one of the baseball stations at the four corners of the field
...took a base on the pass ball...

ABOUT PREP: concerning

A BOUT N: session
...had a bout with the flu...

ABRIDGE *abbreviate* VB: abbreviate, condense, curtail, decrease
...abridge the original version of the book...

A BRIDGE N: overpass, connection, link, span
...built a bridge over the wash...

ACCLAIM *praise* VB/N: praise, applaud
...book received the acclaim of the critics...

A CLAIM N: demand for something, right to something
...made a claim against the estate...

ACCORD *agreement* N: agreement
...reached accord on the contract...

A CORD N: piece of string or twine
...used a cord to tie the box...
N: electrical connector
N: measurement of amount of wood
...bought a cord of wood...

ACCOUNT	VB: give a report
	...*tried to account for his time*...
	N: record, statement
	...*tried to reconcile his business account*...
A COUNT	N: number, total
	...*need a count of the number of people*...
ACCRUE	VB: accumulate, amass
	...*tried to accrue more in the way of disposable income*...
A CREW	N: group that assists
	...*need a crew to clean up*...
ACROSS	ADV/PREP: opposite from, over, through
	...*moved in across the street*...
A CROSS	N: structure with an upright and cross beam
	...*has a cross to bear*...
AFFAIR	N: matter, concern
	...*involved in the affair at the stadium*...
	N: romantic attachment, liaison
	...*had to resign once the affair became known*...
A FAIR	N: exhibition
	...*went to a fair in the small town*...
	ADJ: equitable, even
	...*received a fair distribution from the estate*...
	ADJ: moderate
	...*got a fair number of responses to the ad*...
AGLOW	ADJ: glowing with light or enthusiasm
	...*aglow on her wedding day*...
A GLOW	N: gleaming, shining
	...*saw a glow from the lights*...

ALIKE	ADJ: same
	...alike in so many ways...
A LIKE	N: preference
	ADJ: similar
	...got a like amount from the estate...

without standards (handwritten annotation)

AMORAL	ADJ: without standards
	...deemed his conduct in office to be amoral...
A MORAL	N/ADJ: standard
	...is a moral to the story...
	...clung to a moral code that impinged on this life...

APPEAL	VB: plead, beg
	...tried to appeal to her soft side...
	N: legal proceeding moving a lawsuit to a higher court
	...filed an appeal immediately...
A PEAL (bell)	N: sound of a bell
	...heard a peal from the bell tower...

ARRAY	N: arrangement, display, assortment, collection
	...in a whole array of colors...
A RAY	N: beam of light
	...saw a ray of light from under the door...
	N: fish

AROUND	ADV/PREP: in the vicinity
	...hanging around the liquor store...
	ADV/PREP: on all sides
	...was seen all around town...
A ROUND	N: song sung in unison, each part continuously repeated
	...sang the song as a round in the large group...
	N: one game
	...played a round of golf with friends...

AFFECT VERSUS EFFECT
(Very much in need of a page of their own!)

This is not a problem because it is clearly pronounced with the short *a*.

AFFECT *(flat affect)* — Pronounced /a-fekt/ (rhymes with the *a* in *cat*)
N: look someone has that denotes how he is doing (used in psychiatry)
...*patient has a flat affect*...
...*from his affect, seemed overly animated and somewhat nervous*...

AFFECTATION — N: airs, unnatural speech or conduct, artificiality
...*French accent is an affectation*...

AFFECTED *(snobbish)* — ADJ: snobbish, pretentious
...*her affected ways were obnoxious*...

If it is a noun and is pronounced UH/fect, it is always *effect*.

EFFECT — N: outcome, result
...*had no effect on me*...
...*effect of the disease*...

EFFECTS — N: personal belongings
...*body was found with no personal effects*...

If it is a verb or verbal, is pronounced UH/fect, and the words "bring about" or "make happen" can be substituted into the sentence, it is *effect*.

EFFECT — VB: bring about, make happen
...*loss did effect changes in his attitude*...
...*legislature has to effect a new law immediately*...
...*did effect an alteration in his status*...

If it is a verb or verbal, is pronounced UH/fect, and the words "bring about" or "make happen" do NOT work in the sentence, it is *affect*.

AFFECT — VB: influence
VB: produce a response, touch, alter
...*her sadness does not affect me*...
...*did deeply affect my mother*...
...*will not affect my job*...

BRING ABOUT DOES NOT WORK

BAD
ADJ: evil
...was a bad influence on her...

BADE
Past tense of *to bid*
Pronounced /bad/ (rhymes with *sad*)
VB: compel to do
...bade him to comply with the regulations...
VB: say good-bye
...bade them good-bye at the door...

BAIL
VB: post money for someone to be released from jail
...posted his bail in time for him to be out for his mother's funeral...
VB: help someone out of a tough situation (used with *out*)
...had to bail him out financially once again...
VB: use a vessel to remove water from a flooded area
...needed help to bail the water from the basement...
N: security given to obtain release of a prisoner while awaiting trial
...tried to make bail...
EXPRESSION
    bail on someone/something = abandon, not carry through
    ...always bail on me when I really need them...

BALE
N: large, closely pressed package of merchandise
...seven bales of cotton sitting on the dock...
N: sorrow, woe
...he is the bale of her sad life...

BALEFUL
ADJ: sorrowful
...baleful after the death of her father...

SORROWFUL

BAIT

VB: harass, persecute with taunts, tease
...*bait her to the point of harassment*...
...*bait him until he was desperate*...
VB: entice, lure, tempt
...*tried to bait her into giving him money*...
N: something used to lure, especially to a hook or trap
...*used his daughter as bait to get him to the scene*...
...*cops set the bait to catch the robber in the act*...
N: harmful material placed where it will be eaten by pests
...*put out the bait in an effort to get rid of the roaches*...
EXPRESSIONS
    bait and switch = scheme use to attract buyers by advertising a
        low price, then telling them all the things wrong with the
        product and trying to sell them something at a higher price.
        (This practice is illegal in most states.)
    take the bait = fall for a scheme, fall into a trap
    ...*took the bait and paid the cash for the worthless stocks*...

BATE *— hold in*

VB: hold in, reduce, diminish, deduct, restrain

BATES STAMP

VB/N: date stamp traditionally used to mark exhibits
...*has a Bates stamp number of 54*...

BAIT(ED)

Past tense and past participle of *to bait*
VB/ADJ: lure, entice
...*baited him into action with her taunts*...

BATE(D)

Past tense and past participle of *to bate*
VB/ADJ: hold in
...*waiting with bated breath*...

BALD	ADJ: lacking hair on the top of the head
	...became prematurely bald after the surgery...
	ADJ: lacking a natural or usual covering
	...mountains were bald after the devastating fire...
BALD FACED	ADJ: unconcealed, undisguised, open
	...bald-faced lie about the cookies as sugar dripped from her mouth...
BARE FACED	ADJ: lacking in scruples
	...no qualms about telling the bare-faced lie...
BALL(ED)	Past tense and past participle of *to ball*
	VB/ADJ: formed into a ball
	...blood-stained T-shirt was balled up at the bottom of the hamper...
	EXPRESSIONS
	balled up = in a major mess
	...finances were balled up as a result of their incompetence...
	blackballed = voted out of an organization membership
	...blackballed during the McCarthy era...
BAWL(ED)	Past tense and past participle of *to bawl*
	VB/ADJ: cry loudly
	...bawled when she did not get her way...
BALL	VB: sexual activity
	N: spherical object
	...came toward us as a giant ball of fire...
	N: round, bouncy toy
	N: formal dance
	...was the belle of the ball...
	N: good time
	...had a ball with her old friends...
BAWL	VB: yell or cry loudly
	...continued to bawl about the ice cream she had dropped...
	...clear that he intended to bawl until he got his way...

BALLAD	N: romantic or sentimental song ...*sang a ballad in the middle of the loud rock concert*...
BALLET	N/ADJ: intricate group dance using pantomime and stylized movements ...*performed the ballet for a small group of devotees*... ...*danced with a famous ballet troupe*...
BALLOT	N: ticket or form by which a vote is registered ...*used an absentee ballot*... ...*cast his ballot in his home state*...
BALM	N: aromatic preparation, salve, healing agent ...*used a balm for her aching knees*... N: soothing restorative agent ...*needed a balm for her wounded soul*... ...*used music as a balm to quiet her nerves*...

BOMB	VB/N: explosive device
	...*tried to bomb the local abortion clinic*...
	...*discovered a bomb near the storage age*...
	EXPRESSION
	    drop a/the bomb = announce unexpected/controversial news
	    ...*dropped the bomb about her pregnancy during Christmas dinner*...

BOMBE	N: frozen dessert, usually made with ice cream ...*enjoyed the light bombe after dinner*...
BOMBAY	N: historical city in India (now Mumbai)

BAND	VB: form a group
	...need to band together to fight this bill...
	VB/N: something that constricts or binds
	...put a band around the package...
	...had a colorful band around the straw hat...
	N: musical group
	...in a successful all-girl band...
BAN(-NED)	Past tense and past participle of *to ban*
	VB/ADJ: outlaw, restrict
	...banned the man from returning to the bar...
	...banned the book from the school library...
	EXPRESSION
	banned in Boston = material that is salacious, objectionable, or
	sexually explicit
	...latest work will surely be banned in Boston...
BOND	VB/N: something that binds or restrains, uniting element
	...bond of friendship...
	N: amount of money used as a guarantee
	...put up a $10,000 bond to secure the goods...
	N: obligation made binding by having to forfeit money
	...posted a bond for release from jail...
	N: measurement of the quality of paper
	...paper is a high-quality bond...
BAND(ED)	Past tense and past participle of *to band*
	VB/ADJ: unite, join together
	...banded together to protect their property...
BOND(ED)	Past tense and past participle of *to bond*
licensed	VB/ADJ: license, authorize
	...hired bonded agents to transport the art...
	ADJ: brand put on whiskey

BANDY *[handwritten: argue form a bow as in bow-legged]*

VB: exchange words or argue back and forth
...could bandy that topic about for hours...
...bandy the ball across the net...
ADJ: forming a bow
EXPRESSION
    bandy legged = bowlegged
     ...small, bandy-legged man...

BANDIED

Past tense of *to bandy*
VB: argue back and forth
...bandied the idea about before making a decision...
...bandied the proposal for several hours...

BANTY *[handwritten: small rooster]*

Short for *bantam*
N: small rooster
N: person of diminutive stature and often combative disposition
ADJ: small, diminutive, pertly combative
...strutting around like a banty rooster...

[handwritten: mini] **BANTAM**
BANTAMWEIGHT

N: miniature of standard breed of small domestic fowls
N: boxer in a weight division with a maximum limit of 118 or 119 pounds
...moved up from the bantamweight division in May...

BAN(S)

Third person singular, present tense of *to ban*
VB/N: forbid, prohibit, outlaw
...bans literature containing graphic descriptions of rape...
...new legislation that bans smoking in any public place...

BANNS *[handwritten: announcement of marriage]*

N: public announcement of a proposed marriage
...banns posted in the local newspaper...

BARE

VB: uncover, unclothe, expose
...will bare the details of the crime on the stand...
...did bare her soul to him...
ADJ: naked, unadorned
ADJ: unfurnished or scantily supplied, empty
...room was bare except for a small cot...
ADJ: having nothing left over or added
...bare necessities of life...
ADV: merely
...barely made it...

BEAR

VB: hold up or support
...will bear the weight of the logs...
VB: has a feature or characteristic
...bear a striking resemblance to my sisters...
VB: give birth to, produce
...bear a child at the age of 40...
VB: put up with, endure
...could not bear her husband's obnoxious brother...
VB: call for as suitable or necessary
...condition will bear watching over time...
N: large heavy mammal having long shaggy hair
...found a bear wandering in the residential neighborhood...
N: surly, uncouth, or shambling person
...is a real bear before he has his coffee...
EXPRESSION
  bear false witness = lie
  bear in mind = remember
  bear left/right = keep left/right
  ...will want to bear left at the next corner...
  bear out = prove by evidence
  ...his behavior will bear this out...
  bear up = endure, hang in there
  bear with = don't leave, keep listening
  ...have to bear with me...

(Slightly out of alphabetical order to make it fit on the page!)

BAR
VB: stop, block, forbid, exclude
...will have to bar him from the meetings...
N: straight piece that obstructs or prevents passage or action
...was a bar across the door...
N: railing in the courtroom
...seated in the first row behind the bar...
N: whole body of lawyers qualified to practice law (often capped)
...member of the American Bar Association...
...admitted to the Bar...
N: establishment or counter where alcohol is served
...altercation that took place in a local bar...

BARRE
N: handrail used by ballet dancers

BARING
Present participle of *to bare*
VB/ADJ: exposing, showing
...baring her body for the camera...
...baring everything she knows about it...

BARRING
Present participle of *to bar*
VB/ADJ: blocking, forbidding entrance
...ended up barring the door so that she could not leave...
PREP: except for
...barring any unforeseen circumstances...

BEARING
Present participle of *to bear*
VB/ADJ: carrying, containing
...oil-bearing shale...
N: manner in which one behaves or comports oneself
...princess with a regal bearing...
N: comprehension of position or situation (usually used in the plural)
...need to get my bearings before starting out...
N: machine part in which another part turns or slides
N: support
...ordered to do no weight-bearing for six weeks...

BERING SEA/STRAITS
N: sea/straits near Alaska, separating Asia from North America

BARD *poet*
N: poet
...was hardly a bard with his two-line poems...

BARD
N: Shakespeare
...referred to as the "Bard of Avon"...

BAR(-RED)
Past tense and past participle of *to bar*
VB/ADJ: block
...barred the door from those wanting to enter...

BARE(D)
Past tense and past participle of *to bare*
VB/ADJ: reveal
...bared everything about that night...

BARON
N: nobleman
...descended from a baron...

BARON OF BEEF
N: cut of beef that is suited to roasting or braising

BARREN
ADJ: incapable of producing offspring
...results showed that his wife was barren...
ADJ: having little or no vegetation
...barren landscape...
ADJ: unprofitable, empty

BARRIO *neighborhood*
SPANISH: *neighborhood*, section of a city (usually low socioeconomic)
...lived in the barrio when he was young...

BARREL
VB: move at a high speed or without hesitation
...barrel down the highway without a thought for safety...
N: round cylinder
...several barrels designated for donations of food and clothes...
EXPRESSIONS
    barrel belly = large, round stomach
    has him over a barrel = under someone else's control
    ...has him over a barrel because of this DUI

BARROW *wheelbarrow*
N: framework
...using a wheelbarrow...
N: mound (used in the names of hills in England)

BORROW	VB: obtain something on loan
	...tried to borrow the expensive set of dishes for her party...
	VB: adopt or use as one's own
	...borrow her sister's way of dressing...
BOROUGH	N: self-governing town or administrative unit
	...happened in the borough of Queens...
	N: section of a city
	...small borough west of the main part of the town...
BURRO	N: small donkey
BURROW	VB: make a hole
	...squirrel tried to burrow into the ground around the tree...
	VB: hide out
	...will have to burrow in for a couple of days to finish his taxes...
	N: hole in the ground made by an animal for shelter
BUREAU	N: specialized administrative unit
	...for the Federal Bureau of Investigation...
	N: chest of drawers or writing desk
	...puts those things into the bureau in the corner...
BASAL	ADJ: forming a base; fundamental, minimal
	...low basal metabolism...
BASIL	N: aromatic herb
	...recipe called for sweet basil...
BASE	VB: use as a foundation, support
	...will base it on his years of experience...
	N: bottom, foundation
	...sitting on a marble base...
	...touch base before proceeding...
	ADJ: morally low
	...base act of stealing from his own mother...
BASS	Pronounced /bais/ (rhymes with *pace*)
	N: deep sound or tone, lowest male voice
	...played the bass clarinet...
BASS	N: fish
	Pronounced /bas/ (rhymes with *pass*)
	...caught three bass at the lake...
BAS-RELIEF	Pronounced /bah/ (rhymes with *ha*)
	N: type of sculpture

BASE(D)	Past tense and past participle of *to base*
	VB/ADJ: situate, establish upon, locate
	...company based in Arizona...
BASTE	VB: sew in loose stitches
	VB: moisten meat
	...baste the turkey while it is cooking...
BASE(S)	Third person singular, present tense of *to base*
	Pronounced /<u>bais</u>-uhz/
	VB: use as a foundation
	...bases it on his limited experience...
	Plural of *base*
	N: foundation
	...several believable bases for his reasoning...
	N: four corners of a baseball diamond
	...ran around the bases after hitting a homerun...
BASS(ES)	Pronounced /<u>bais</u>-uhz/
	N: low male voices
BASES	Plural of *basis*
	Pronounced /<u>bais</u>-eez/
	N: something on which something else is founded
	...all bases for his argument...
BASIS	N: source, origin
	...basis of the argument against it...
BAZAAR	N: marketplace, shop, or fair at which miscellaneous articles are sold
	...local bazaar sold Indian spices...
BIZARRE	ADJ: very strange, strikingly unconventional, odd
	...noticed his bizarre behavior right away...
BE	VB: exist
	...move that the meeting be adjourned...
BEE	N: insect
	...allergic to the sting of a bee...

BEACH	VB: run or drive ashore *...had to beach the yacht...* N: shore of an ocean, sea, or lake *...spent time at the beach...*
BEECH	N: tree

BEAT	VB: defeat, conquer
	...beat him in a fair fight...
	VB: strike repeatedly
	...beat on the door to try to rouse him...
	N: repeated sound or motion
	...tapping his toes with the beat...
	EXPRESSIONS
	    beat your own drum = sing your own praises
	    beat it = scram, leave
	    beat up = tattered, ragged, not in good condition

BEET	N: vegetable
BET	VB/N: wager *...placed his bet at the last minute...*
BEAUT	Short for *beautiful* N: used to indicate an extreme example of something *...black eye was a real beaut...*
BUTTE	N: isolated hill or mountain area with steep sides *...took place atop the butte...*
BEEN	Past participle of *to be*
BIN	N: container *...placed it in the bin...*
BEER	N: alcoholic drink made from malt and hops *...drank beer all afternoon...*
BIER	N: platform on which to put a coffin or the coffin itself *...resting precariously on the bier...*

(handwritten note next to BUTTE: mountain)

(handwritten note next to BIER: platform for a coffin)

BELL

N: hollow device that reverberates
...rang the bell to end the session...
...bell sounded before we even got started...

BELLE

N: popular and attractive girl
EXPRESSION
> *belle of the ball* = favorite
> *...was the belle of the ball on the project...*

BELLOW

VB: yell, holler
...would bellow out the orders...
N: bawl, roar
...heard the bellow of the cow...

BELLOWS

N: part of a pipe organ
...impressive bellows of the large organ...
N: tool that stokes a fire
...had to use the bellows to start the fire...

BILLOW

VB: rise or roll in waves and surges, bulge or swell out
...curtains billow in the wind...
N: great wave or surge, especially water
...watched the billow of the waves on the shore...
N: rolling mass of clouds or smoke resembling a wave
...billows of smoke from the fire...

BERRY

N: small juicy fruit, often with seeds
...had a lot of berries in the salad...

BURY

VB: place a body or an object into the earth or a tomb or obscure place
...tried to bury the mistake in a bunch of numbers...
...bury the body in a cemetery in his hometown...
EXPRESSION
> *bury the hatchet* = resolve differences, make peace
> *...decided to bury the hatchet and work together...*

(Slightly out of alphabetical order to make it fit on the page!)

BERM N: narrow shelf, path, or ledge at the top or bottom of a slope
...pulled onto the berm of the country road...
N: mound or wall of earth
..landscaped berm along the edge...
N: bump in the road to cause the cars to slow down, speed bump
...berm was so low as to be noneffective...

BURN VB: heat too much
VB: consume
...will burn through a lot of facts on this...
VB: become emotionally excited or agitated, yearn ardently
...will burn to tell the story...
VB: become very angry or disgusted
...remark made him burn...
VB: force or make a way to
...tried to burn her words into my heart...
VB: consume
...burn several calories...
VB: outdo, beat
...burn the cornerback with the pass...
N: area scarred by heat
...fire department doing a controlled burn...
N: abrasion on the skin
...got a nasty burn from the stove...
EXPRESSIONS
do a slow burn = increasing fury
...doing a slow burn over his expenditures...
burn through = use at a fast rate
...will burn through that money in a matter of months...

BERTH	N: place to sleep on a ship or train
	...*had an upper berth on the train*...
	N: place where ship docks
	...*came in at Berth 39*...
	N: job or position
	...*really wanted the berth in the university system*...
	EXPRESSION
	give wide berth to = allow freedom to make decisions
	...*gave wide berth of her artistic ideas in decorating*...
BIRTH	VB: give life to
	...*his hard work will birth more projects*...
	...*will birth her fifth child next month*...
	N: beginning
BESIDE	PREP: next to, at the side of
	...*sat beside her*...
BESIDES	PREP: in addition to
	...*no one besides her*...
	ADV/CONJ: other than, except
	...*besides, that is not true in this case*...
BETTER	VB: defeat
	... *better his opponent by ten seconds in the race*...
	ADJ: of higher quality
	...*better quality fabric*...
	ADJ: more successful
	...*ended in a better position*...
BETTOR	N: one who bets
	...*was always a losing bettor*...
BIANNUAL	ADJ: occurring twice a year
	...*biannual meetings in June and December*...
BIENNIAL	ADJ: occurring once every two years
	...*biennial meeting in May of this year and May two years from now*...

[handwritten annotation: 2x/year ; every 2 years]

BIBLIOGRAPHY	N: list of books or articles about a subject or person *...extensive bibliography about her family...* N: list of books used for reference *...omitted from the bibliography of the book...*
BIOGRAPHY	N: story of a person's life written by someone else *...his best-selling biography...*
AUTOBIOGRAPHY	N: story of a person's life written by the person himself (*Auto* means "self"; *bio* means "life"; *graph* means "write") *...read the autobiography of the President...*
BILE	N: alkaline fluid secreted by the liver *...bitter taste of bile...* N: anger, wrath, fury *...nothing but bile came out of his mouth about her...*
VIAL	N: small container for liquids *...small vial of liquid in her purse...*
VILE	ADJ: foul, disgusting, offensive *...vile comment...* *...found his behavior to be vile...*
BILL(ED)	Past tense and past participle of *to bill* VB: assess a charge *...billed for four visits...* N: notice for payment *...received a bill that had to incorrect...*
BUILD	VB: construct, make, or establish *...tried to build a good relationship...* *...build a new house near mine...* N: body form or mold *...had a great build because of hours in the gym...*

BIT	Past tense of *to bite*
	VB: seize with the jaws
	...bit into a piece of chocolate...
	N: small portion
	...bit of information...
	N: biting or cutting edge or part of a tool, replaceable part of a drill
	...need a different drill bit...
	N: unit of value equal to 1/8 of a dollar
	...gave just two bits for the piece of candy...
	N: binary unit (computer term)
	N: steel part of a bridle inserted in the mouth of a horse
	...inserted the bit in preparation to ride...
	N: short theatrical routine
	...corny comedy bit...
	N: aggregate of items, situations, or activities
	...rejected the whole bit about love and marriage...
	ADV: somewhat, rather
	...was a bit dull...
BITE	VB/N: seize with teeth or jaws
	...took a bite of the hot pizza...
	N: piece
	...had a bite or two left...
	EXPRESSION
	take a bite out of = reduce
	...measure intended to take a bite out of inflation...
	did not bite = wasn't fooled, didn't follow through
	...didn't bite on the real estate deal...
BIGHT	N: slack part or loop in a rope
	N: bend or curve in a river
	...crash occurred at the bight of the river...
BYTE	N: computer term (8 bits)
	...more than a gigabyte...

BLEU	FRENCH: color blue N: type of cheese *...prefer real Roquefort to bleu cheese...*
BLEW	Past tense of *to blow* VB: move air *...cold wind blew in off the ocean...* VB: drive, carry, propel *...whole plan blew up after he left...*
BLUE	N/ADJ: color *...bleeds Dodger blue...* ADJ: low in spirits *...feeling blue after she left...*
BLOC	N: group of persons united for a common purpose (usually political) *...represented the farm bloc...* N: political grouping *...always voted against the ultraconservative bloc...*

BLOCK	VB: obstruct or blockade
	...will have to block off the area...
	N:rectangular solid
	...sat on a block of ice to cool off...
	N: city square
	...walked around the block...
	EXPRESSION
	    blockhead = someone who is not acting smart
	    ...was a blockhead when it came to relationships...
	chip off the old block = child that is like a parent in looks or behavior

BLOND	ADJ: light-haired person *...blond and blue eyed...* (Sometimes a distinction is made: *blond,* male; *blonde,* female)
BLONDE	N: derogatory term synonymous with "airhead," said of a woman *...always telling blonde jokes...*

BOAR	N: male pig
	...attacked by a wild boar...
BOOR	N: clod, rude or insensitive person
	...was a boor in regard to her failures...
	...identified by all as a boor about her precarious position...
BOORISH	ADJ: insensitive
	...boorish behavior that hurt my feelings...
BORE	VB: drill a hole
	...tried to bore into the solid cement...
	(Can be used figuratively)
	...eyes bore into me...
	...bore a hole in the wall as he concentrated...
	Past tense of *to bear*
	VB: carry
	...bore up well under difficult circumstances...
	...bore the consequences of his bad decision...
	N: boring person
	...was a real bore at parties...
BORING	Present participle of *to bore*
	VB: make a hole
	...is boring the new holes for the artwork...
	ADJ: dull, not interesting
	...not a boring subject...
	...spent a boring afternoon in her company...
BOER(S)	N: South African of Dutch descent

(handwritten note next to BOOR: rude person)

(handwritten note next to BOER: Dutch)

BOARD	N: piece of wood
	N: meals provided for pay
	...could barely afford room and board...
	N/ADJ: group of persons managing a firm
	...member of the board with me...
	...obviously a board decision...
	EXPRESSIONS
	above board = on the up and up, honest
	...all of his actions are above board...
	across the board = for everyone
	...raise in effect across the board...
	on board = hired, agree
	...came on board the end of summer...
	overboard = gone too far
	...went overboard at the toy store...
	take the boards = exams
	...will take the boards this summer...
	tread the boards = act in the theatre
BORE(D)	Past tense and past participle of *to bore*
	ADJ: uninterested, wearied by something dull or tiresome
	...became bored very easily...
BOARDER	N: person who receives a room and meals regularly for a fee
	...decided to take in a boarder to make ends meet...
	...was such a helpful boarder...
BORDER	N: dividing line
	...moved across the border into the adjacent town...
	...crossed the border of good behavior when he took the first drink...
	VB/N: edge
	...behavior that does border on psychotic...

BODE	VB: foretell, presage
	...does not bode well for him...
BOW(ED)	Pronounced /bode/ (rhymes with *code*)
	Past tense and past participle of *to bow*
	VB/ADJ: shaped like a bow
	...bed bowed in the middle...
	Pronounced /boud/ (rhymes with *loud*)
	VB/ADJ: bent from the waist
	...bowed as the cross passed by...

BOLDER	ADJ: more forward, more courageous
	...bolder than he thought he could be...
BOULDER	N: large rock
	...needed to move the large boulder before construction began...

BOLE *treetrunk*	N: tree trunk
	...disease in the bole of the tree...
BOLL *pod*	N: pod or capsule of a plant
	...popped open the boll to look at the cotton...
BOLL WEEVIL	N: insect that infests the cotton plant
BOWL	VB/N: game with a ball and ten pins, played on an alley
	...wanted to bowl in two leagues a week...
	N: dish, rounded shape
	...drove the ATV around the bowl of sand...
	EXPRESSION
	bowl over = overwhelm, amaze
	...would bowl him over with her talent...
BOWEL	N: intestines
	...cancer had spread to the bowel...
	N: deep or remote parts (usually used in the plural)
	...searched the bowels of the ship...

BOLD   ADJ: daring, courageous
...his bold move saved the house from being completely destroyed...

BOWL(ED)   Past tense and past participle of *to bowl*
...bowled a perfect game just once...

BOO(S)   VB/N: negative cheers of a crowd
...loudly boos the play of his rival...
...boos started just two minutes into the game...

BOOZE   SLANG: liquor
...swore there was no booze at the party...

BORN   Form of the past participle of *to bear* (used only in relation to birth)
VB: bear
...was born on a Friday...
ADJ: untaught, natural
...child born with that ability...

BORNE   Form of the past participle of *to bear*
VB: give birth to
...has borne five children...
VB: carry, withstand
...has borne the burden for the family...

BOURN ~~stream~~   N: little stream or brook
...came across the bourn deep in the woods...

BOUILLON   N: soup, clear broth
...drank the chicken bouillon...

BULLION   N: gold bricks
...bullion stored at Fort Knox...

BOW	Pronounced /bo/ (rhymes with *toe*)
	VB: bend in an arc
	...bricks did not bow under pressure...
	N: anything curved or bent
	...bow in the middle of the shelf...
	N: device for shooting arrows
	...owned a custom-made bow...
	N: decorative knot with two or more loops
	...tied the ends into a bow...
BEAU	N: boyfriend
	...her latest beau...
BOW	Pronounced /bou/ (rhymes with *cow*)
	VB: bend from the waist to show respect
	...will bow as the Queen passes by...
	N: front part of a ship
	...standing on the bow of the ship...
	EXPRESSION
	bow down = pay homage
	bow out = quit, resign
	...decided to bow out of the project...
BOUGH	Pronounced /bou/ (rhymes with *cow*)
	N: branch of a tree or shrub
	...sat on the bough of the tree...
BOWER	N: attractive dwelling or retreat
	N: arbor
	...lovely flowers in the bower...
BOWIE	N: kind of knife (named for Jim Bowie)
BOY	N: male child
BUOY	VB: bolster, support
	...tried to buoy her confidence...
	N: marker in the water
	...tacked out past the buoy...

BRAKE	VB: slow down or stop *...able to brake the car in time...* *...put the brakes on inflation...* N: device for slowing or stopping a machine or vehicle *...applied the brakes too late to avoid the accident...*
BREAK	VB: separate into parts by force *...always tends to break away from the other horses...* VB: smash *...tried to break her favorite cup in a fit of anger...* N: opening or interruption *...need a break from the workload for a while...* *...break in the electrical line...*
BREACH	VB: break, make an opening by breaking something *...whales will breach the waves...* N: failure to observe the terms of a law or agreement *...breach of contract...* N: opening made by breaking something *...fired into the breach...*
BREECH	N: thick end of anything, buttocks *...breech birth...* N: part of a cannon where the ammo goes N: tight-fitting pants (usually used in the plural) *...wore breeches to the masquerade...*
BREAD	N: food made from flour or meal *...fed the bread crumbs to the ducks...* SLANG: money *...need bread to make the trip...*
BRED	Past tense and past participle of *to breed* VB: be the source, produce *...bred several varieties of wheat...*
WELL BRED	ADJ: reared with refinement

BREADTH	N: distance from side to side, width (Spelled with the same *dth* as *width*) *...looking at the depth and breadth of the situation...*
BREATH	N: air taken in and given out by the lungs *...took a deep breath...*
BREATHE	(Pronounced /breethe/ (rhymes with *seethe*) VB: inhale and exhale, take air in and let it out *...told me to breathe deeply...*
BREW(ED)	Past tense and past participle of *to brew* VB: concoct, loom, develop VB: prepare by steeping, boiling, or fermenting *...brewed a unique-tasting tea...*
BROOD	VB: meditate, worry, dwell on something longer than necessary *...going to brood about it for days...* N: young of an animal N: large number of children *...arrived with the whole brood at the ice cream store...*
BREW(S)	Third person singular, present tense of *to brew* VB: concoct, develop, loom *...storm brews in the area...* Plural of *brew* SLANG: beer
BRUISE	VB/N: injury resulting in a discoloration of the skin *...large bruise that covered most of her upper arm...*
BRIDAL	ADJ: pertaining to a bride or wedding *...had the typical bridal jitters...*
BRIDLE	VB: hold back, curb *...tried to bridle his temper...* VB: hold the head high to express scorn, anger, pride *...bridle in anger over the fiasco...* N: part of the harness that goes over the horse's head

BRITAIN	Short for *Great Britain*
BRITISH	N/ADJ: of or from Britain
	...with a British accent...
BRITON	N: person who lives in or is from Britain
	...sat with a Briton on the flight...
BRITTANY	N: region in northwest of France, southwest of Normandy
	...owns a Brittany spaniel...
BRETON	N: native or inhabitant of Brittany
BROACH	VB: pierce as a cask in order to draw the contents, tap
	VB: shape or enlarge a hole
	...needed to broach the hole to make this fit...
	VB: make known for the first time
	...intended to broach it after dinner...
	VB: open up a subject for discussion
	...decided it was time to broach the subject of his behavior...
	VB: break the surface from below
	N: any of various pointed or tapered tools, implements, or parts
	...used a broach...
	N: spit for roasting meat
	...meet turned on the broach...
	N: tool for tapping casks
BROOCH	N: ornament that is held by a pin or clasp and is worn at or near the neck
	...clearly a very expensive brooch...
BUCCAL	ADJ: of or relating to the cheek or inside the mouth
	...buccal surface of the tooth...
BUCKLE	VB: give way, collapse
	...knees buckled when she heard the news...
	N: fastener to join two loose ends
	...had several buckles that he wore for different occasions...
BUS	VB/N: transport
	...will bus the students across town...
	...rode on the bus...
BUSS	VB/N: kiss
	...buss on the cheek...

BUT	PREP: except
	...everyone but John...
	CONJ: otherwise, yet, only, just
	...on Friday but not Saturday...
BUTT	VB: thrust or strike against
	...will butt heads with his superiors...
	N: thick end of anything, stub or stump
	...hit him with the butt end of the gun...
	N: object of ridicule or criticism
	...butt of some very cruel jokes...
BUY	VB/N: purchase
	...great buy on that car...
BY	ADV/PREP: next to, near at hand, through the medium of
	...go by on my way home...
	...passed by his house...
BYE	(Historically transposed from "be with ye")
	N: word said at the time of leaving
	...said bye to everyone...
	N: week off in sports
	...get a little rest during our bye week...

CHAPTER 3
THE LETTER *C*

CABAL	N: faction, group
	...cabal of artists...
	N: group engaged in artifice and intrigue
	...cabal against the government...
CABALA	Variant of *kabbalah*
	N: theory of medieval and modern Jewish mysticism
CABLE	N: wire, rope, chain
	...tripped on the electric cable near the door...
	N: type of television reception
	...watched it on my tennis cable channel...
CACHE	N: hiding place, especially for concealing provisions or implements
	...looked into her cache for the supplies he needs...
	N: something hidden
	...cache of chocolate in her desk...
CASH	VB: turn into ready money
	...went in to cash the check...
	N: ready money
	...pay with a credit card as I have no cash...
	EXPRESSIONS
	cash in on = take advantage of
	cash out = quit playing

CACHET	Pronounced /ka-<u>shay</u>/
	N: seal used, especially as a mark of official approval
	...*Good Housekeeping cachet*...
	N: advertisement forming part of a postage meter impression
	N: motto or slogan included in a postal cancellation
	...*cachet had an American flag*...
	N: medicinal preparation for swallowing
	...*put the bad-tasting medicine into a cachet*...
SACHET	Pronounced /sa-<u>shay</u>/
	N: small bag containing a perfumed powder or potpourri
	...*sachet in her underwear drawer*...
SASHAY	VB: strut or move about in an ostentatious or conspicuous manner
	...*intended to sashay through the room*...
	N: square dance step
CADDIE	N: one who carries someone's golf clubs
	...*paid the caddie 10 percent of his earnings*...
CADDY	N: apparatus for holding or organizing things
	...*caddy always on the edge of his desk*...
CATTY	ADJ: malicious, hurtful
	...*several catty comments about her weight*...
CALENDAR	VB: schedule
	...*will calendar it for next Tuesday*...
	N: system for dividing time
	...*will put it on my calendar*...
	N: appointment
CALENDER	VB: press between rollers to smooth or glaze, make into thin sheets
	...*calender the sheets to add the glossy finish*...
	N: machine that uses rollers to smooth or glaze
	...*used a calender to create the fabric*...
COLANDER	N: strainer, perforated pan
	...*used a colander to drain the vegetables*...

CALIBER	N: measurement of a gun barrel *...a .45 caliber automatic...*
CALIPER	N: instrument for measuring *...used calipers to measure it...*
CALLER	N: one that calls *...mysterious caller at 2:00 every morning...*
CHOLER	N: ready disposition to irritation, irascibility, or anger *...reputation for choler in these situations...*
COLLAR	VB: seize by the neck, grab VB: arrest *...tried to collar him at the scene...* N: band, strip, or chain worn around the neck *...wore his clerical collar...* N: arrest, capture *...put the collar on him...*
CALLOUS	ADJ: lacking in pity or mercy, unfeeling, insensitive *...had a callous attitude toward his wayward sister...*
CALLUS	N: thick, hardened place on the skin *...had a callus on her thumb from using the machine...*
CALVARY	N: hill near Jerusalem, where Christ was crucified *...led them to Calvary...*
CAVALRY	N: mounted troops *...cavalry rode to the rescue...*
CAMBER	N: turning in at the bottom *...camber of the wheels on the car...*
CAMPER	N: one who lives outside *...ran across a lone camper off the trail...* N: truck/trailer used for the purpose of traveling/living outdoors *...huge 60-foot camper...*
CAMPHOR	N: compound used in insect repellent *...covered in camphor because he lived in the woods...*

CANAPÉ	N: appetizer or hors d'oeuvre, crackers with treat on the top
	...served canapés instead of a meal...
CANOPY	N: cloth covering, protective covering
	...kept out of the rain under the canopy...
CANCEL	VB: call off, stop
	...had to cancel the concert because of illness...
CHANCEL	N: space around the altar in a church
	...flooded the chancel area...
CANNON	N: large weapon of war, big gun
CANON	N: center or main part of law or body of law
	...not included in the canon of the organization...
	N: law or body of law of a church
	...goes against the canon of Catholicism...
	N: established standard, principle, or rule
	...according to the canon we observe...
CANYON	N: deep, narrow valley with steep walls
	...explore the canyon while we are there...
CAÑON	SPANISH: *canyon*
CANTER	VB/N: gait of a horse
	...kept him at a slow canter...
CANTOR	N: chief singer in a church or synagogue
	...haunting voice of the cantor...
CANVAS	N: strong cloth widely used to make sails, tents, and drop cloths
	...tent was made of light-weight canvas...
CANVASS	VB: search for something in a wide area
	...canvass the neighborhood for the missing boy...
	VB: go through a district or area soliciting votes or to sell or take orders
	...intended to canvass the area for their candidate...

CAPITAL	N: city where the government of a country or state is located ...*Sacramento, capital of California*... N: money or property a company uses in carrying on business ...*not enough capital to get the business started*... N: uppercase letter ADJ: punishment by death ...*on trial in a capital case*... ADJ: best of something ...*think that is a capital idea*...
CAPITOL	N: state or federal building in which a state or national legislature meets ...*up the steps of the capitol*...
CAPITOL	N: building in Washington, D.C. ...*met on Capitol Hill to decide*...
CARAT	N/ADJ: unit of weight for precious stones ...*wearing a five-carat diamond*...
KARAT	N: unit of fineness for gold equal to 1/24 part of pure gold in an alloy (Gold at 18 karats is as pure as is practical; otherwise, it is too soft) ...*wedding ring of 18-karat gold*...
CARET	N: proofreading mark (^) to show where something has been left out ...*inserted a caret for the word "an," which is missing*...
CARROT	N: vegetable
CARCASS	N: dead body, corpse ...*found the carcass of a large animal*...
CAUCUS	VB/N: small body that decides policy ...*Republican caucus blocked the vote*...
CARIES	N: dental decay (used only in the plural) ...*had multiple caries because of neglect*...
CARRY (-IES)	Third person singular, present tense of *to carry* VB: bear the load ...*carries heavy responsibilities for his family*...

CAROL	VB: sing in a joyful manner
	VB: go about outdoors with a group that is singing
	...join the group who will carol at the senior citizen home...
	VB: warble
	N: song of joy or mirth
	...lilting carol of the bird...
	N: popular song or ballad of religious joy
	...joined in singing the Christmas carol...
CARREL	N: table that is often partitioned or enclosed and is used for individual study, especially in the library
	...went straight for my usual carrel in the library...
CARRIER	N: one that carries
	...said to be a carrier of the disease...
COURIER	N: one who delivers, messenger
	...courier of bad news...
CURRIER	N: one who grooms horses
	...worked as a currier in the stables...
CURRIER	N: famous American lithographer (Currier and Ives)
CART	VB: take from one place to another, haul
	...had to cart him to all his activities...
	N: small device for transporting goods
	...moved it into place with a small handcart...
CARTE	FRENCH: *document*
	EXPRESSIONS
	carte blanche = free rein
	...has carte blanche to make changes...
	a la carte = pricing items separately
	...ordered a la carte from the menu...

CARTON	N: cardboard box *...drank milk straight from the carton...*
CARTOON	N: exaggerated, amusing sketch or line drawing
CAST	VB: throw or fling with a quick motion *...cast aside the model of our prototype...* VB: form in a mold or from plaster *...model that was cast from the set of tire tracks...* VB: put into a certain role *...cast as the lead in the school play...* N: players in a theatrical company *...cast went to dinner after the close of the play...* N: that which is formed in a mold or from plaster EXPRESSION *cast in stone* = unchangeable
CASTE	N: exclusive social system having class distinctions based on birth, rank, wealth, position *...caste system is fading in that society...*
CASUAL	ADJ: happening by chance *...casual encounter at the restaurant...* ADJ: offhand, careless, informal, negligent *...claims it was casual contact...* ADJ: occasional
CASUAL WATER	N: water standing where you wouldn't expect it to be *...slipped on casual water...*
CAUSAL	ADJ: bringing something about, effecting *...causal force behind these rantings...*
CATTLE	N: cows N: human beings en masse *...packed into the room like cattle...*
CHATTEL	N: article of personal property *...when women were considered chattel...*

CAUDAL	ADJ: relating to the tail
	ADJ: situated in or directed toward the hind part of the body
	...*caudal block for the surgery*...
CAUDLE	N: drink (as for invalids) usually of warm ale or wine mixed with bread or gruel, eggs, sugar, and spices (Yum!)
CODDLE	VB: cook (eggs) in liquid slowly and gently just below the boiling point
	...*will coddle the eggs because he likes them prepared that way*...
	VB: spoil, pamper, indulge
	...*can only coddle him so much*...
CUDDLE	VB: hold close for warmth or comfort or in affection
	...*will cuddle in the cold before the Rose Parade*...
	VB: lie close or snug
	...*decided to sit on the couch and cuddle with her baby for a while*...
CAUGHT	Past tense and past participle of *to catch*
	VB: entrap, discover, seize
	...*was caught red-handed*...
COT	N: small portable bed to sleep in
	...*slept on a small cot in the basement*...
CAUTERY	N: stanch the flow of blood
	...*in need of immediate cautery*...
COTERIE	N: select group of people
	...*coterie of hand-selected people*...

CEASE	VB: stop, discontinue
	...demanded that he cease the offensive activity...
SEIZE	VB: take hold of suddenly or violently
	...could seize at any moment because of the trauma...
	VB: take possession by force, confiscate
	...intended to seize the property...
	VB: grab
	...intended to seize the ring the first chance he got...
CEDE	VB: yield, grant
	...will cede the point...
	VB: formally give over in an agreement
	...will cede 100 acres of prime land in the settlement...
SEED	VB: sow
	...seed the field in the spring...
	VB: treat a cloud to induce precipitation
	...decided to seed the clouds in a desperate attempt to bring rain...
	VB/N: schedule tournament players or teams so that better ones will not meet in early rounds and eliminate each other
	...tournament will seed 16 places...
	N: competitor who has been rated in a tournament
	...was the top seed in the tournament...
	N: grains of plants used for sowing
	N: progeny

CEILING	N: top of a room
	...noticed a spiderweb on the ceiling...
	N: upper limit
	...put a ceiling on spending...
	N: vaulted area
	...carvings in the ceiling of the chapel...
	EXPRESSION
	glass ceiling = limit a woman can reach (lower than that of a man)
	...reached the glass ceiling in very little time with the company...
SEALING	Present participle of *to seal*
	VB: securing
	...sealing the envelope securely...
	ADJ: fastening or closing tightly
	...used a strong sealing agent...
CEL	N: one frame in a cartoon
	...pointed out the third cel in the sequence...
CELL	N: small bare room in a prison or convent
	...jail notorious for overcrowding in the cells...
	N: unit of living matter, building blocks of the body
	...disease penetrated to the cell level...
	N: small electric battery
	N: portable phone
	...always has her cell with her...
	N: small unit of a group, often subversive in nature
	...part of the Communist cell...
SELL	VB: exchange for money or other payment
	VB: exchange goods
	...had to sell stocks to go to school...
CELEBRATE (-TION)	VB/N: observe or commemorate a date or event
	...will celebrate his promotion...
CEREBRATE (-TION)	VB/N: think about, use the mind
	...sat alone to cerebrate...

CELLAR	N: underground room where goods are stored
	...*kept them in the cellar because it was colder there*...
SELLER	N: one who exchanges property or goods for payment
	...*seller bears the responsibility for collecting the money*...

CEMETERY	N: burial ground
SYMMETRY	N: balance, evenness
	...*liked the symmetry of the art piece*...

CENSER	N: incense burner, instrument used to dispense incense
	...*used a censer for the incense*...
CENSOR	VB: examine for objectionable or harmful material, edit, expurgate
	...*censor the movie because of nudity and violence*...
	N: person who reviews or examines materials for portions that could be deemed objectionable or harmful
	...*serves as a censor for children's television programming*...
SENSOR	N: device that responds to a physical stimulus
	...*signal picked up from the sensor*...
CENSURE	VB/N: formal process of condemnation or reprimand
	...*censured on the floor of the Senate for his behavior*...

CENSUS	N: official count of the population
	(done in the United States every ten years in the "zero" year)
	...*taking the census for the government*...
SENSES	N: functions of sight, smell, hearing, touch, and taste
	EXPRESSION
	come to one's senses = wake up and realize

CENT	N: coin, one penny
SCENT	N: odor, fragrance
	...*light scent of lavender in the room*...
SENT	Past tense and past participle of *to send*
	VB: mailed, dispatched, caused to go
	...*sent to boarding school*...

CENT(S)	Plural of *cent*
	N: more than one penny
SENSE	VB: notice, detect
	...sense something is wrong immediately...
	N: point or meaning of something
	...do not see the sense in this...
	N: ability to reason or think soundly; wisdom, sagacity
	...has no common sense...
SCENT(S)	Plural of *scent*
	N: smells, aromas
	...scents that penetrated the entire house...
SINCE	PREP/CONJ: from that time
	...have not seen her since Friday...
CENTURY	N: 100 years
	...massive changes in technology in that century...
SENTRY	N: guard
	...posted a sentry at each door...
CEREAL	N: food made from grain
SERIAL	N: story published or broadcast one part at a time at regular intervals
	...watched her soap opera serial every day...
	ADJ: at intervals, ongoing
	...identify a serial killer...
SURREAL	ADJ: weird or grotesque, beyond normal
	...circumstances seemed surreal...
CERTAIN	ADJ: sure, inevitable, without any doubt
	...has a certain future in this area...
CURTAIN	N: fabric that covers a window or conceals a stage
	...curtain falls without a resolution...

CERVICAL	ADJ: relating to the cervix ...*diagnosed with cervical cancer*...
SURGICAL	ADJ: relating to surgery ...*necessary to undergo a surgical procedure*...
CESSION	N: formal yielding, concession ...*cession of the land to the neighboring country*...
SESSION	N: meeting, series of meetings ...*discuss it in the court session this afternoon*... ...*have a session with her psychiatrist*...
CHAFE	VB: irritate or vex, feel irritation or discontent, fret ...*will chafe under the tight restrictions of the new regime*... ...*chafe at the restrictive desk job*... VB: warm by rubbing, especially with the hands ...*chafe his hands together*... VB: rub so as to wear away, abrade VB: make sore by or as if by rubbing ...*soap will chafe several areas on her underarms*... VB: rub and thereby cause wear or irritation ...*rough fabrics chafe her sensitive skin*... N: state of vexation, rage N: injury or wear caused by friction
CHAFF	VB: tease good naturedly, mock, joke ...*chaff his fellow students in the program*... N: seed coverings and other debris separated from the seed in threshing ...*separate the wheat from the chaff*... N: something comparatively worthless ...*get rid of the chaff*... N: material such as foil or clusters of fine wire ejected into the air for the purpose of reflecting radar waves to confuse an enemy's radar ...*chaff was released to confuse the other pilots*... N: light jesting talk, banter

CHAISE (LONGUE)	Pronounced /shaiz-lawnzh/ FRENCH: *long chair* *...rested in the chaise after the procedure...*
CHASE	VB/N: pursue, hunt *...chase them to the edge of the property...* *...dangerous police chase...*
CHEZ	FRENCH: *at the house of* Pronounced /shay/ *...welcome to Chez Jay...*

CHALK	VB: write or draw or cover with chalk
	...chalk the pool cue before he started to play...
	VB: sketch, plan
	...chalk the plan to share with the others...
	N: limestone marker or crayon
	...used chalk on the sidewalk to mark the boundaries...
	EXPRESSIONS
	chalk talk = instructional talk (used with chalk and a blackboard)
	    ...coach did a chalk talk of his second-half game plan...
	    chalk it up to = attain, credit
	    ...chalk it up to his inexperience...

CHOCK	VB: stop, brace
	...chock the barrels so that they do not roll around...
	N: brace
	...used a chock to hold it steady...
	EXPRESSION
	    chock-full = full to the limit
	    ...store was chock-full of tourists...

SHOCK	VB/N: upset, alarm, fright *...shock him with the details...* *...stunned by the shock of her death...* VB/N: pass an electric current through *...subjected him to electric shock treatments...*

CHAMP	VB: make biting or gnashing movements, bite
	Short for *champion*
	...was a real champ through the ordeal...
	EXPRESSION
	champ at the bit = be impatient about delay or restraint
	...champ at the bit to get the race started...
CHIMP	Short for *chimpanzee*
	...had a chimp at his house as a pet...
CHOMP	VB: crunch, munch, noisily bite
	...chomp on the bone...
CHUMP	N: sap, sucker, easy target
	...real chump when it came to supposed bargains...
CHANCE	N: opportunity, prospect, luck
	...took a chance on him...
CHANT(S)	Third person singular, present tense of *to chant*
	VB/N: recite, intone, song
	...chants as a part of his meditation practice...
CHARD	N: vegetable
	...not sure how best to prepare the chard...
CHAR(-RED)	Past tense and past participle of *to char*
	VB: burn, scorch
	...visited the charred remains of the burned-out house...
SHARD	N: fragment, splinter
	...shard of glass on the floor...
CHART	VB/N: have something mapped out, plan in detail
	...chart all the possibilities...
CHARTER	VB: hire or lease a vehicle
	...could charter a luxury yacht...
	N: document that establishes the rules
	...part of the original charter...

CHART(ED)	Past tense and past participle of the verb *to chart* VB: map out *...charted the route in detail...*
CHARTER(ED)	Past tense and past participle of the verb *to charter* VB: rent, lease *...chartered a limo for the prom...*
CHARY	ADJ: cautious, wary, mindful of *...chary in the face of her co-workers...*
CHEERY	ADJ: happy, joyful *...his cheery disposition...*
CHERRY	N: fruit *...had a black cherry-flavored drink...*
SHERRY	N: wine *...enjoyed a glass of sherry...*
CHASE(D)	Past tense and past participle of the verb *to chase* VB: run after or cause to run away *...chased it down the street...*
CHASTE	ADJ: virtuous, modest *...rather chaste attire for the interview...*
CHATTER	VB/N: babble, prattle, rant *...incessant chatter drove me nuts...*
SHATTER	VB: smash, break, explode *...will shatter into a million pieces...*
CHEAP	ADJ: not expensive, not worth much *...thought the price was cheap for what she was getting...* ADJ: despicable, stingy *...too cheap to buy me even a hamburger...*
CHEEP	VB/N: make a sound like a young bird *...cheep at 4:00 A.M. every morning...*

CHEEK	N: fleshy part of side of face
	...nasty cut on his cheek...
CHIC	Pronounced /sheek/ (rhymes with *seek*)
	ADJ: stylish, sophisticated
	...looked chic at the opera...
CHICK	N: small chicken
	SLANG: girl
	...saw a chick standing alone and approached her...
SHEIKH	Also spelled *sheik*
	Pronounced /sheek/ (rhymes with *sleek*)
	N: Arab chief
	...visited the sheikh at his palace...
CHERISH	VB: hold dear
	...will always cherish the last days I spent with her...
CHURLISH	ADJ: rude, boorish
	...churlish behavior made me sick...
CHEW(S)	Third person singular, present tense of *to chew*
	VB: masticate one's food
	...often chews with his mouth open...
CHOOSE	VB: select, pick out
	...choose the one on the left...
	VB: want, desire
	...did not choose to be a part of this...
CHOSE	Past tense of *to choose*
	VB: opt, pick, select
	...chose to ignore the warning signs...
SHOW(S)	Third person singular, present tense of *to show*
	VB: demonstrate
	...shows signs of failure...
	VB: reveal
	...dress shows a little too much skin...
	N: theatrical performance or move

CHIN	N: part of the lower jaw
	...cut on his chin...
SHIN	N: part of the leg between the knee and the ankle
	...scraped his shin on the cement step...
CHOIR	N: group of singers, most commonly in a church
	...joined the all-male choir...
QUIRE	N: set of 24 or 25 sheets of paper of the same size and stock
	...need a quire of that color...
QUERY	VB/N: ask a question or the question itself
	...query him regarding his whereabouts...
	...can no longer ignore the query...
CHORAL	ADJ: relating to any singing group
	...is a choral arrangement...
CORAL	N: skeletons of tiny sea creature that may form ridges
	...scraped his leg on the coral when he was diving...
	N: color
CORRAL	VB: round up, keep in one place
	...needs to corral her children...
	N: pen for animals
	...decided to meet at the corral on the far edge of the ranch...
CHORALE	N: group of singers with trained voices, singing long, complicated arrangements
	...sang with a master chorale...
CHORUS	N: something performed, sung, or uttered simultaneously by a number of persons or animals
	...sang with the school chorus...
	N: part of a song recurring at intervals
	...knows the words to the chorus but not the verses...
	N: supporting players in a production, members of a group
	...content to be a member of the chorus...
	N: unanimous utterance
	...part of the growing chorus of voices in favor of the bill...

CHORD	N: combination of musical notes in harmony
	...rather dissonant chord...
	N: emotional response
	...story strikes a sympathetic chord...
	N: straight line joining two points on a curve, part of a circle
	N: straight line joining the leading and trailing edges of an airfoil
CORD	N: anatomical structure resembling a rope
	...was a spinal cord injury...
	N: measure of wood cut for fuel
	...going to need more than a cord of wood this winter...
	N: small insulated electric wire fitted with a plug
	...spark from an electrical cord...
CORE(D)	Past tense and past participle of *to core*
	VB: remove the central part, as an apple
	...chewing on a cored apple...
CHOW	SLANG: food
	...grabbed some chow on the way out...
	N: breed of dog
	EXPRESSION
	chow down = eat a large quantity, usually quickly
CIAO	ITALIAN: *hello, good-bye*
CHRONIC	ADJ: constant, unceasing
	...debilitated with a chronic disease...
CLONIC	ADJ: relating to jerky movements of muscles, typical of some diseases
COLONIC	ADJ: relating to the colon
	...suffering from colonic problems...
CHURL	N: rude and surly person
	...acted like a churl every time I saw him...
CURL	VB/N: twist, coil, bend
	...would curl up into a ball when she was afraid...
	...decided to curl her hair for the occasion...

CHUTE	N: inclined passage to slide things down
	...put the refuse in the trash chute...
SHOOT	VB: let fly
	...let the water shoot out of the pipe...
	VB: motion of rapid propulsion or the firing of a gun or missile
	...suddenly began to randomly shoot at customers...
	VB/N: photograph, take pictures
	...did the shoot in the nearby park...
	N: young outgrowth from a shrub or tree
	...took a small shoot of the plant...
CINCH	VB: tighten
	...will cinch it in at the waist...
	VB: conclude, wrap up, assure
	...will cinch a place in the playoffs with a win on Saturday...
	N: easy task, sure thing
	...is a cinch to be one of the top five candidates...
CLINCH	VB: make final or irrefutable, settle
	...could clinch the argument with this new fact...
	VB: wrap up the victory in a game
	...Dodgers will clinch the pennant...
	VB/N: hold an opponent in boxing at close quarters with one or both arms
	...referee had to break up the clinch...
	VB: hold fast or firmly,
	VB: turn over or flatten the protruding pointed end of a nail, screw, bolt, rivet
	...will clinch the nails in order to avoid being scratched...
	N: embrace
	...found the teenagers in a tight clinch...
CLENCH	VB: hold fast
	...clench the steering wheel...
	...tried not to clench her teeth at night...
	...raise a clenched fist into the air...

CIRCUMCISE	VB: surgically remove the foreskin of the penis ...*will circumcise the baby before he leaves the hospital..*
CIRCUMSCRIBE	VB: restrict, limit, demarcate ...*circumscribe the number of entries in the contest...*

(More at page 95-96)

CITE	VB: make reference to ...*could not cite a reference to back up what he was saying...*
SIGHT	VB/N: see ...*regained his sight after the surgery...*
SITE	N: location ...*found the abandoned car at a site near town...*
INCITE	VB: stir up, arouse
INSIGHT	N: awareness
IN SIGHT	N: within one's field of vision
CLAMBER	VB: climb awkwardly ...*tried to clamber up the side of the hill...*
CLAMMER	N: one who digs clams ...*several clammers in Pismo Beach...*
CLAMOR	VB/N: shout, scream, yell ...*clamor for more help for the devastated region...*

CLAMP	VB/N: vise, device used to constrict
	...*used a clamp to keep it in place...*
	EXPRESSION
	    clamp down = impose restrictions
	    ...*police are going to clamp down on street racing...*

CRAMP	VB/N: involuntary muscle contraction ...*cramp behind her knee...*
CRIMP	VB/N: crease, tuck ...*decided to crimp her hair...* VB: restrict EXPRESSION *crimp her style* = get in the way of what she wants

CLAN	N: group with common interests
	...her native Scottish clan...
KLAN	Short for *Ku Klux Klan*
	...is a member of the Klan...
CLEAT	N: wedge-shaped piece fastened to something serving as a support or a check
	...up against the cleat...
	N: fitting with two projecting horns around which a rope is secured
	...wrapped the ship's ropes around the cleat...
	N: projecting piece, as on the bottom of shoes, that furnishes a grip
	...golf shoes equipped with metal cleats...
CLEEK	N: large hook as over a fireplace to hold a large pot
	...hung the pot on the cleek...
	N: four wood golf club
CLICK	VB: strike, move, or produce a sound
	...click her heels together in joy...
	VB: fit together, hit it off
	...did not click with me who she was until later...
	VB: function smoothly
	...plans are clicking along...
	VB: succeed
	...movie that does not click with the audience...
	N: slight sharp noise
	...heard the click as he turned the key in the lock...
	N: speech sound
KLICK	Short for *kilometer* (military)
	...160 klicks north of Saigon...
CLIQUE	N: closely knit, snobbish group, select group
	...joined the clique with the elite...
CLICHÉ	N: trite phrase or expression or the idea expressed by it
	...talks only in clichés...

(Slightly out of alphabetical order to make it fit on the page!)

CLAUSE

N: division of a sentence
N: group of words containing a subject and verb
...identifying the dependent clause in the sentence...
N: separate section of a formal document
...contains a clause that forbids contact between the two...

CLAW(S)

Third person singular, present tense of *to claw*
VB: scrape, scratch
...tried to claw his way into the cat food bag...
N: sharp, curved nails on an animal's toes
...sharp claws tore the edge of the carpet...

SANTA CLAUS

N: St. Nicholas

CLEAVER

N: large knife
...intended to use a meat cleaver...

CLEVER

ADJ: smart, quick witted
...clever solution to the problem...

CLEF

N: sign at the beginning of a musical staff that determines the pitch
...cannot read the notes on the bass clef...

CLEFT

N: fissure, crevice, gap
...born with a severe cleft palate...

CLIMACTIC

Adjective form of the word *climax*
ADJ: pertaining to the highest point
...collapsed at the climactic moment of the show...
ADJ: orgasmic

ANTICLIMACTIC

ADJ: describing an event strikingly less important than what precedes it
...anticlimactic measures after the law was passed...

CLIMATIC

Adjective form of the word *climate*
ADJ: pertaining to climate, weather
...under adverse climatic conditions...

CLIMB	VB: ascend, mount, scale
	...wants to climb Mount Everest in his lifetime...
	N: ascent, increase, advancement
	...most difficult climb up the face of the mountain...
CLIME	N: climate
CLOISTER	VB: seclude from the world
	...cloister her while she heals from this terrible tragedy...
	N: convent, monastery
	...lived in the cloister all her life...
CLUSTER	VB/N: bunch, group, collect, huddle
	...found a cluster of cancerous cells...
CLOSE	VB: come or bring to a conclusion
	...will close the door on these negotiations...
	ADJ: near
	...close to an agreement...
CLOTHES	N: wearing apparel
CLOTH(S)	N: fabrics
CLOSER	N: pitcher who comes in to preserve the win (baseball)
	ADJ: nearer
	...no closer to an agreement than they were...
CLOSURE	N: end, conclusion, finish
	...needs closure about the accident...
CLOTURE	N: limiting debate
	...called for a vote for cloture...
CLOT	VB/N: coagulate, thicken
	...formed a clot near the main artery...
CLOUT	N: influence, power
	...had no clout in that organization...

COAMING	N: raised frame to keep water out, as on a ship
	...breaks in the coaming near the doors...
COMBING	Present participle of *to comb*
	VB: run a comb through
	VB: go over thoroughly (usually used with *through*)
	...combing through the rubbish to find the lost ring...
COARSE	ADJ: unrefined, crude
	...coarse manner is not acceptable...
	ADJ: not fine in texture, rough
	...coarse fabric was rough against the skin...
COURSE	VB: run through
	...medication coursed through his veins...
	N: way, path, channel, or direction taken
	...took a different course...
	N: regular mode of action or development
	...second course of treatment...
	N: part of a meal
	...five-course meal...
	N: series of studies in school
COASTAL	ADJ: pertaining to the coast
	...enjoy the early morning coastal fog...
COSTAL	ADJ: pertaining to the rib
	...had an intercostal tear along right side...

COAT	VB: cover
	...will coat the surface with a layer of oil...
	N: outer garment
	...did not have a heavy enough coat for the weather...
	N: external growth on an animal
	...had a very heavy coat...
	N: layer of one substance covering another
	...added an extra coat of paint to the bathroom wall...
COTE	N: shed or coop for small domestic animals, especially doves and pigeons
CODE	VB: put into a system
	...attempting to code her myriad of books...
	N: body of laws
	...not part of the code...
	N: system of principles or rules
	...lived by a strict moral code...
	N: system of signals or symbols for communication, often secret
	...trying to decipher the complicated code...
COAT(ED)	Past tense and past participle of *to coat*
	ADJ: having a coat, covered
	...coated with sand after a day at the beach...
CODE(D)	Past tense and past participle of *to code*
	ADJ: written in a system of symbols
	...had to decipher the coded message...

COAX	Pronounced /cokes/ (rhymes with *pokes*)
	VB: urge
	...tried to coax her into the water...
COAX	Pronounced /<u>co</u>-ax/
	Short for *coaxial*
	N: kind of cable
COKE	Short for *cocaine*
	...ruined her health on coke...
	N: cola-type drink
	N: residue of coal left after distillation and used as fuel
COKE	N: beverages made by Coca Cola
COFFER	N: treasury, funds, valuables (often used in the plural)
	...open the coffers of the company to make the repairs...
COUGHER	N: person who coughs frequently
COIF	VB: style hair
	N: cap, hairstyle
	...had a new coif for the event...
QUAFF	VB: drink, usually beer, usually rapidly
	...quaff a few beers when he comes in from work...
COIFFURE	N: hairstyle
COIFFEUR	N: person who styles hair (male)
COIFFEUSE	N: person who styles hair (female)
COLA	N: soft drink
COLA	ACRONYM: cost of living adjustment
	N: used in contract negotiations

COLLABORATE (-TION)   VB/N: work together
...decided to collaborate on the project...
...need the collaboration of all parties involved...

CORROBORATE (-TION)   VB/N: confirm, support, back up
...three witnesses to corroborate her story...
...had no corroboration of the details...

COLLAGE   N: collection, hodgepodge
...collage of colors in the painting...

COLLEGE   N: higher education institution
...attended an out-of-state college...

COLLISION   N: violent contact, crash
...collision of two different lifestyles...

COLLUSION   N: secret understanding between people to cheat, defraud, damage others
N: conspiracy
...in collusion to defraud the company...

COLOMBIA(N)   N/ADJ: country in South America
COLUMBIA(N)   N: river in the Northwest United States

COLONEL   N: high-ranking Army officer
...met with the colonel and his commanding officer...

KERNEL   N: grain or seed
...problem caused by a popcorn kernel...
N: essential part
...not a kernel of truth to the story...

KENNEL   N: location to board dogs
CHANNEL   N: groove, passageway
...worked digging the channel for the river...

COMA   N: state of prolonged unconsciousness
COMMA   N: mark of punctuation
...really understands the rule for the comma in that sentence...

COMEDY

N: farce, satire, humor, joking, wit
...could do with a little less comedy and a little more work...

COMITY

N: social harmony, friendship
...in comity with each other...

   COMITY OF NATIONS

N: informal and voluntary recognition by one government of the laws of another, therefore allowing for extradition
...comity of nations...

COMICAL

ADJ: funny
...comical picture as the toddler tried to put on his dad's shoes...

CONICAL

ADJ: in the shape of a cone

COMMAND

VB: direct, order, be in control of
N: order, directive, authority, power, control
...in command of the unit...

COMMEND

VB: mention favorably, to praise
...commend him for his bravery in battle...

COMMENCE

VB: begin
...will commence the shutdown on Friday...

COMMENT(S)

Third person singular, present tense of *to comment*
VB: make a remark about something
...comments on all of the announcements from management...
Plural of *comment*
N: casual remark
...did not like the tone of his comment...

COMMUTE (-ATION)

VB/N: substitute, change a prison sentence to one that is less severe
...governor will commute the sentence...
...expecting a commutation at the last hour...

COMPUTE (-ATION)

VB/N: calculate
...need to compute the final sum I owe...
...computation was a bit off...

COMPARTMENT	N: section *...put it into the glove compartment for safekeeping...*
COMPORTMENT	N: behavior, attitude *...could use some work on her comportment in public...*
COMPLACENT	ADJ: satisfied, unworried, content *...had become complacent on the job...*
COMPLAISANT	ADJ: compliant, wanting to please *...willingness to be complaisant to the boss was over the top...*
COMPLEMENT	VB: complete *...scarf that will complement my blue outfit...* VB: supply a lack *...skills that complement the others' skills...* N: supplement, that which fills up or completes *...full complement of officers...*
COMPLIMENT	VB: praise, commend *...compliment him on the job he did...* N: praise or commendation *...received compliments on his performance...*
COMPLEMENTARY	ADJ: mutually supplying each other's lack *...skills complementary to hers...* ADJ: completing *...used complementary colors...*
COMPLIMENTARY	ADJ: flattering, praising *...comments on her book were complimentary...*

COMPOSE	VB: write, make up, create ...*will compose something for the occasion*...
COMPRISE	VB: include ...*comprise many parts*... VB: make up from many parts ...*United States comprises 50 states*...
COMPROMISE	VB: expose one's reputation to danger or suspicion ...*does not want to compromise his reputation by risking failure*... N: settlement in which each side makes concessions ...*reached a compromise*... N: result of a settlement
COMPREHENSIBLE	ADJ: understandable, intelligible ...*written in comprehensible language*...
COMPREHENSIVE	ADJ: large in scope, inclusive ...*comprehensive report of the recent activity*...
CONCEDE	VB: give up ...*will concede the argument*... VB: grant as a right or privilege VB: accept as true, valid, or accurate ...*did not concede that she is correct*... VB: make concessions ...*concede that he should have the money*...
CONCEIT	N: excessive appreciation of one's own worth ...*find her conceit contemptible*...
CONCEDE(D)	Past tense and past participle of *to concede* VB: give over, admit ...*conceded the game when it became impossible to win*...
CONCEIT(ED)	ADJ: stuck up, snobbish ...*was too conceited for me to have anything to do with*...

CONCENTRATE (-TION)	VB/N: think, focus, ponder, deliberate
	...*could not concentrate with all the noise*...
	VB/N: condense, gather
	...*concentrate his efforts on the houses at the end of the block*...
	...*concentration of young families in the neighborhood*...
CONSECRATE (-TION)	VB/N: make sacred
	...*consecrate the ground where she is to be buried*...
	...*carried out the consecration of the church building*...
CONCUR	VB: agree
	...*all sides concur that we must reach an agreement*...
CONQUER	VB: subjugate, overcome
	...*trying to conquer his fear of flying*...
CONFIDANT	N: one to whom secrets are entrusted
	N: trustworthy person -- male
	...*entrusted it to my confidant and his friend*...
CONFIDANTE	N: trustworthy person -- female
	...*entrusted it to my confidante and her friend*...
CONFIDENT	ADJ: assured, certain
	...*confident that we will win*...
CONFIDENTIAL	ADJ: classified, secret
	...*received confidential information about her status*...
CONFIDENTLY	ADV: with assurance
	...*went forward confidently and with self-assurance*...
CONFIDENTIALLY	ADV: in a classified or secret manner
	...*did it confidentially without anyone's knowledge*...

CONFIRM (-ATION)	VB/N: corroborate, verify *...will confirm the date of his arrival...* *...received confirmation of my appointment...*
CONFORM (-ATION)	VB/N: adapt, obey the rules *...will conform to the new management...*
CONFUSION	N: perplexity, puzzlement *...mass confusion when the Titanic hit the iceberg...*
CONTUSION	N: bruise *...came out with a large contusion on his right leg...*
CONGENIAL	ADJ: having a good, friendly attitude *...enjoyed her congenial manner...* ADJ: having the same nature, disposition, tastes *...three of them are congenial...*
CONGENITAL	ADJ: existing at or dating from birth *...report that it is a congenital defect...* ADJ: constituting an essential characteristic or nature
CONSCIENCE	N: inner sense of right and wrong *...will be on his conscience for a long time...*
CONSCIENTIOUS	ADJ: knowing the difference between right and wrong *...conscientious in fulfilling her obligations...* ADJ: feeling that one should do the right thing ADJ: exact, fastidious, prudent, responsible *...always conscientious on the job...*
CONSCIOUS	ADJ: being aware of, able to feel *...was conscious when I left...*

CONSCIENTIOUSLY	ADV: pertaining to knowing right from wrong *...do her job conscientiously...*
CONSCIOUSLY	ADV: pertaining to being awake and aware *...committed this act consciously...*
CONSERVE (-ATION)	VB/N: protect, preserve *...will conserve water use...* *...interested in conservation causes...*
CONVERSE (-ATION)	VB/N: talk *...converse with his friends...* *...had a serious conversation with his parents...*
CONSOLE	Pronounced /con-<u>sole</u>/ VB: make someone feel less sad or disappointed, comfort *...tried to console her after the accident...* Pronounced /<u>con</u>-sole/ N: cabinet *...was a console model...*
CONSUL	N: official appointed by a government to live in a foreign city and look after his or her country's business interests and citizens there *...gave it to the consul from Argentina...*
CONSULATE	N: residence or official premises of a consul *...took refuge at the American consulate...*
COUNCIL	N: group of people selected, appointed, or elected to make laws, settle questions, give advice *...spoke with members of the town council...* N: persons who run a governmental body (usually on the local level)
COUNSEL	VB: advise *...needed to counsel him on what to do...* N: attorney *...spoke with her counsel...*

CONSONANCE	N: agreement
CONSONANT(S)	Plural of *consonant*
	N: letters that are not vowels
	...has all consonants in his last name...
CONSTRICT(ION)	VB/N: narrow, compress
	...constrict the blood vessels...
	...area of constriction around the heart...
CONSTRUCT(ION)	VB/N: build
	...construct a new model of operation...
	...project is under construction...
CONSULAR	ADJ: pertaining to the consul
	...member of the consular corps...
COUNCILOR	Also spelled *councilor*
	N: person who sits on a city council, member of a council
	...councilor from my district...
COUNSELOR	N: one that gives advice in law and manages cases for clients in court
	...spoke to her counselor about the case...
	N: one who has supervisory duties (often working with kids at camp)
	...worked as a summer camp counselor...
CONTIGUOUS	ADJ: being in actual contact
	...measured only in the contiguous 48 states...
	ADJ: touching along a boundary or at a point
CONTINENCE	N: self-control, moderation, restraint
CONTINENT(S)	Plural of *continent*
	N: large land masses
COUNTENANCE	VB: permit, sanction, permit
	...will not countenance her stubborn behavior...
	N: look, expression, face
	...did not detect anything about it from her countenance...
	N: approval
	...gained enthusiasm with her countenance of it...

CONTINUAL	Adjective form of *to continue*
	ADJ: repeated often, happening over and over again
	...presented a continual problem in the classroom...
CONTINUOUS	Adjective form of *to continue*
	ADJ: happening without interruption, unceasing
	...had continuous rain for a week and flooding everywhere...
CONTINUANCE	N: continuation, succession
	N: postponement
	...asked for a continuance of the case...
COO	N: baby sound
	...continued to coo even after he went to sleep...
	N: cry of a dove or pigeon
COUP	Pronounced /koo/ (rhymes with *sue*)
	N: final blow, death blow or shot administered to end suffering of one mortally wounded
	N: decisive, finishing blow, act, or event
	N: overthrow of a government
	...don't believe there can be a peaceful coup in this situation...
	N: swift, decisive stroke
	...real coup for him in securing the job at the prestigious firm...
	N: Indian custom of touching the enemy and counting it as a victory
COOP	N: small building for housing poultry
	...collected the eggs from the chicken coop...
	N: confined area
	EXPRESSION
	cooped up = confined, restricted in movement
	...cooped up in the house because of the weather...
COUPE	N: type of car with two doors, smaller than a sedan
	...had never driven a coupe because he liked larger cars...
CO-OP	Shortened for *co-operate* ("operate together")
	N: place where monies or supplies are pooled
	...have always belonged to a food co-op...

(Slightly out of alphabetical order to make it fit on the page!)

COUP D'ÉTAT — N: strike against the state
N: sudden, decisive exercise of force in politics, especially the violent overthrow of a government by a small group
...military coup d'état in the small country...

COUP DE GRACE — N: blow of mercy, final straw
...coup de grace to the relationship...

COOPERATION — N: acting or working together
...worked in cooperation with management...

CORPORATION — N: type of business organization
...known to be a corrupt corporation...

COP(S) — Third person singular of *to cop*
EXPRESSION
 cops a plea = confesses and tries to get a plea deal
 cop-out = flimsy excuse
 ...her "I got lost" was a cop-out for her being late...
N: police officers
...cops arrived in the nick of time...

COPE(S) — Third person singular of *to cope*
VB: handles well
...copes well with difficulty...

COPSE — N: coppice, a thicket, grove, or growth of small trees
N: forest originating mainly from shoots or root suckers rather than seed
...deep within the copse near the road...

CORE	N: central or most important part
	...is a core issue for us...
CORE	ACRONYM: Congress of Racial Equality
CORPS	Singular and plural are spelled the same way
	Singular pronounced /core/
	Plural pronounced /corz/
	N: group of people having a common activity or occupation
	...joined the domestic Peace Corps...
	N: branch of the Armed Forces, having a specialized function
	...part of the Marine Corps...
CORP.	ABBREVIATION: *corporation*
CORPSE	N: dead body
	...lying near the corpse...
	N: human or animal body whether living or dead
CORRESPONDENCE	N: written communication
	...sent correspondence to everyone involved...
CORRESPONDENT(S)	Plural of *correspondent*
	N: person with whom one communicates
	...correspondents who reported from the war zone...
CORNER	N: bend, turn, angle
	...standing on the corner near the liquor store...
CORONER	N: officer who holds inquests into death
	...awaiting the results from the coroner...
CORPORAL	N: noncommissioned officer
	...reach the rank of corporal in a very short time...
	ADJ: relating to the body
	...does not believe in corporal punishment...
CORPOREAL	ADJ: physical, not spiritual

COSTUME	N: style of dress peculiar to a nation, class, or historical period or appropriate to a particular time or occasion ...*wore a period costume to the celebration on July 4...* N: garment worn on the stage or at a masquerade
CUSTOM	N: usual way of acting in given circumstances ...*his custom of starting every day with yoga...*
COUSIN	N: son/daughter of the sister of one's mother or father ...*have only one first cousin...*
COZEN	VB: cheat, trick ...*tried to cozen her into thinking she was at fault...*
COWARD	N: one who lacks courage
COWER(ED)	Past tense of *to cower* VB: shrink back, crouched and shivering with fear ...*cowered in the corner with his hands over his head...*
CREAK	VB: move with a harsh, squeaky, grating noise ...*stairs began to creak as I walked down them...* N: harsh noise
CREEK	N: small stream, somewhat larger than a brook
CRICK	N: painful spasm of muscles, as in the neck or back ...*woke up with a crick in her neck...*
CREDIBLE	ADJ: believable, reliable, trustworthy ...*no credible reason for doing that...*
CREDITABLE	ADJ: worthy of credit; honorable, respectable ...*did a creditable job on the reorganization of the office...*
CREVASSE	Pronounced /kri-<u>vas</u>/ N: deep crack, especially in ice ...*fell through the crevasse...*
CREVICE	Pronounced /<u>kre</u>-vuhs/ N: small crack or opening ...*hid the ring in a small crevice in the wall...*

CREW(ED)	Past tense and past participle of *to crew*
	VB: staffed a ship or plane
	...crewed on a flight from Seattle...
CRUDE	ADJ: coarse, uncouth
	...made a crude remark...
	ADJ: unrefined, unprocessed
	...worked with crude oil...
	ADJ: undeveloped, primitive, unsophisticated
	...crude tool for digging holes...
CREWEL	N/ADJ: stitchery
CRUEL	ADJ: mean, heartless
	...cruel and inhumane treatment...
CREW(S)	Third person singular of the verb *to crew*
	VB: work on a ship or plane
	...crews with three others on the catamaran...
	Plural of *crew*
	N: groups of people that work together
	...several cleaning crews were needed to do the job...
CRUISE	VB: take a trip on a ship
	...will cruise to Alaska this summer...
	VB: move randomly from place to place
	...cruise through the shops at the mall...
	VB: drive around
	...cruise the boulevard...
	N: journey by ship
	...took an Alaskan cruise with her family...
CRUSE	N: earthen pot used for holding a liquid
	...stir the contents of the cruse...

CRITIC	N: someone who analyzes or rates *...critic did not like the movie...*
CRITIQUE	VB/N: analyze, evaluate, account *...will critique her work as a part of the evaluation...*
CROCK	N: earthenware pot *...cooked it in the crock...* SLANG: bunk, falsehood, lie *...story he told was a crock...*
CROOK	N: criminal *...was known to be a crook...*
CROTCH	N: angle formed by the parting of two things *...caught the crotch of his pants on the fence as he went over...*
CRUTCH	N: aid, prop, support *...used her as a crutch to help him avoid having to work...*
CLUTCH	VB: hold, grasp, grab *...began to clutch her purse as she felt it being grabbed...* N: small handbag that can be held in one hand *...carried a clutch with only the essentials in it...*
CRONE	N: ugly old woman, virago *...told her she was acting like a crone...*
CRONY	N: long-time friend, companion *...sat with his crony and discussed it...*
CRUMBLE	VB: break into small pieces (and cannot be restored) *...will crumble as soon as you touch it...* *...brick buildings will crumble in the earthquake...*
CRUMPLE	VB: wad up, collapse (but can be restored) *...will crumple up the divorce papers...* *...crumpled to the floor when she heard the news...*

CUE	VB: hint, remind or prompt
	...will cue the actors from backstage...
	N: stick used to play pool or billiards
	N: on time, signal
	...came in right on cue...
QUEUE	VB: get in line
	...queue up early for the movie...
	N: waiting line
	...waiting in the queue...
	N: list of messages waiting to be processed or printed by a computer
	...four files in the print queue...
	N: braid of hair
	...queue down her back...
CURB	VB: control, reduce
	...tried to curb his appetite...
	N: edge of the sidewalk that goes into the street
	...tripped on the curb and fell...
CURVE	VB/N: arc, bend, bow
	...too fast around the curve...
CURIOS	N: tchotchkes, trinkets
	...bought curios at every stop on the trip...
CURIOUS	ADJ: inquisitive, questioning
	...curious about how that is done...
	ADJ: strange
	...curious outcome of the tests...
CURRANT	N: berry
CURRENT	ADJ: now in progress, currently ongoing
	...current edition of the magazine...
	ADJ: up to date
	...current on my payments...
	N: body of water flowing in a definite direction
	...strong rip current...

COURANTE	N: dance, third movement in a suite
KORAN	N: Muslim holy book (one of the spellings)
QUR'AN	N: Muslim holy book (one of the spellings)
CYMBAL	N: musical instrument in the shape of a plate
	...played the cymbals in the marching band...
SYMBOL	N: token of identity
	N: visible sign
	...inaction is a symbol of his cowardice...

CITE, SIGHT, SITE
INCITE, IN SIGHT, INSIGHT

CITE

VB: call upon officially or authoritatively to appear before a court
...could cite him for speeding...
VB: quote as an authority
...cite prior cases in an attempt to sway the jury...
VB: mention as an example
...did cite her bravery under fire...
VB: mention formally in commendation, name in a citation
...will cite his military record...
N: reference
...has a cite to a similar case...

SIGHT

VB: get or catch sight of
...intending to sight whales off the coast...
VB: aim
...sight him as the target...
N: one of the five senses -- eyesight
N: something seen or worth seeing
...take in the sights of the city...
...go sight-seeing...
N: something/someone disorderly in appearance
...was a real sight as he came off the bus from camp...
N: great deal, a lot
...far sight better...
...not by a damn sight...
N: device for guiding the eye as in aiming a firearm
...needed to adjust the sight on the rifle...
EXPRESSIONS
    sight unseen = without ever having seen something
sight for sore eyes = see someone you have wanted/needed to see

SIGHT-READ

VB: perform without previous preparation or study
VB: perform music by simply looking at the notes
...tried to sight-read the text...

SITE VB: place at a location
...site the new construction at the corner of Elm and Main...
N: seat or scene of any specific thing
...site where the crime took place...
N: location of a building
...site of the construction...

INCITE VB: rile up, stir up
...tried to incite the crowd to action with his rhetoric...
...charged with incite to riot...

INSIGHT N: mental or spiritual perception, mental viewpoint, judgment
...has insight into how this is going to work...
...counted on him for insight into her character...

IN SIGHT N: within vision
...kept the kids in sight at all times...

CHAPTER 4
THE LETTER D

DAB

VB: pat gently
...dab at her eyes during the sad part of the play...
...dab at the sore to keep it from seeping...

DAUB

VB: plaster, paint unskillfully
...daub at the canvas in an attempt to create something...
...will do no more than daub with the watercolors...

DAIRY

N/ADJ: place where milk products are kept, stored, produced, or sold
...got our milk fresh from a dairy...

DIARY

N: periodic written account of what one has felt, thought, or experienced
   and the book in which this account is written
...kept a diary of her travel experiences...

DAL

Also spelled *dahl*
N: dried Indian legumes
...very tasty dal...

DOLL

N: child's toy
...dressed the baby in doll clothes...

DAM(-MED)

VB: build a barrier across a watercourse
...beavers dammed the river at that point...
N: barrier built across a watercourse
...visited the dam that has created Lake Cachuma...

DAMN(ED)

VB/INTERJ: curse
...said, "Damn," when he dropped it...
VB: condemn to a punishment
...could damn his cause...

DARING	Present participle of *to dare* VB: challenge *...is daring her to follow up on her threat...* N/ADJ: boldness, bravery, courage *...showed his daring in attempting the climb...*
DERRING-DO	N: deeds of daring *...his derring-do in the face of danger...*
DARK	N/ADJ: without light ADJ: gloomy, mysterious *...was in a dark mood the morning of the incident...*
DART	VB: dash from place to place *...would dart about, trying to keep everyone happy...* N: pointed missile *...threw the dart at the target...*
DAWN	N: break of day, first light *...dawn's early light...*
DON	VB: put on, as clothes *...will don his best suit for the occasion...*
DAY(S)	Plural of *day* N: several 24-hour periods *...had a fever for five days...*
DAZE	VB/N: dazzle, stupefy *...in a daze as he walked away from her bedside...*
DAIS	N: raised platform in a hall or large room *...stood at the dais as she spoke...* N: hustings, an election platform
DEAR	ADJ: beloved *...always been such a dear man...* ADJ: expensive *...too dear for my tastes...*
DEER	N: animal

DECADE   N: ten years
...took a decade to complete...

DECAY(ED)   VB/N: rot, spoil
...had decayed to the point that it was useless...

DECEASE(D)   N/ADJ: dead person
...came upon the body of the deceased in an alley...

DISEASE(D)   N/ADJ: sick, unhealthy
...tree that was diseased...

DESIST   VB: cease to exist, discontinue, renounce
...filed a cease and desist order against them...

DECEDENT   N: deceased person
...following the will of the decedent...

DESCENDANT   N: one descended from another or from a common stock
...descendant of George Washington...

DECENT   ADJ: proper, right, in good taste
ADJ: respectable
...makes a decent wage...

DESCENT   N: coming/going down from a higher to a lower place
...treacherous descent down the mountain...

    DESCEND   VB: come down, go down

DISSENT   VB: differ in belief or opinion, disagree
...felt he had to dissent on this topic...
N: disagreement
...dissent among the members of the House...

DECANT   VB: pour from one vessel to another
...will decant the wine...

    DECANTER   N: vessel used to decant or to receive decanted liquids
N: ornamental glass bottle used for serving wines

DESCANT   N: line of harmony sung over the melody
...lilting sound of the descant...

DEFECT(ION)
VB/N: desert, abandon
...intended to defect to the rival company...
...his defection was a blow to all of us...

DEFLECT(ION)
VB/N: turn aside
...deflect the personal questions...
...deflection of the bullet saved his life...

DETECT(ION)
VB/N: notice, sense, perceive
...could detect a faint odor...
...high-quality detection equipment...

DEFECTIVE
ADJ: flawed
...software was defective...

DETECTIVE
N/ADJ: investigator
...did detective work to uncover the real truth...

DEFECTOR
N: deserter
...defector was caught before he could divulge state secrets...

DETECTOR
N: device that senses electromagnetic waves
...smoke detector did not function...

DEFER(-RED)
VB: put off to a future time, delay
...has to defer his decision until she returns...
VB: yield courteously to the wish or judgment of another (used with *to*)
...tried to always defer to her wishes...
...deferred to her every wish...

DEFERMENT
N: official postponement of military service
...received a deferment in order to go to school...

DIFFER(ED)
VB: vary or disagree
...her view will always differ from his...
...differed in every way from each other...

DEFERENCE
N: courteous yielding to the wishes of someone else
...did it in deference to his position...

DIFFERENCE
N: state of being different, unalike, dissimilar
...no visible difference in the twins...

DEFERENTIAL	ADJ: showing or expressing deference *...received deferential treatment...*
DIFFERENTIAL	N: gear system in a car *...problem with the differential...* N: distinguishing, based on or resulting from a difference *...standard differential in the two values...*
DEFINITE	ADJ: clear, explicit *...set a definite date...*
DEFINITIVE	ADJ: ultimate, perfect, best *...discovered the definitive cause of the fire...*
DEFUSE	VB: make less harmful or potent *...her presence will defuse the tense situation...*
DIFFUSE	VB: scatter, distribute widely *...diffuse the smoke in the room...*
DEFY	VB: disobey, resist, disregard *...seems to defy logic...*
DEIFY	VB: make into a god *...tended to deify his English teacher!!...*
DELEGATE	VB: hand over, farm out, pass on *...always tried to delegate the hard jobs...* N: representative *...delegate to the convention...*
DELICATE	ADJ: fragile *...did delicate work on the watch...*
DELETERIOUS	ADJ: having a harmful effect, injurious *...medication had a deleterious effect on her vision...*
DILATORY	ADJ: intended to delay, postpone, slow *...dilatory in her efforts to complete the project...*

DELUDE(D)	VB: take someone away from legitimate thought, trick someone *...tried to delude her into thinking she could finish...* *...deluded by her parents...*
DILUTE(D)	VB: water down *...needed to dilute the solution...* *...diluted the dye so that the color would not be so bright...*
DEMUR	VB: take exception, object (often used with *to*) *...attorney will demur to that statement...* N: hesitation, as in doing or accepting, usually based on doubt of the acceptability of something offered or proposed
DEMURE	ADJ: shy, innocent, affectedly modest, reserved *...demure young lady...*
DEMURRER	N: response in a court proceeding in which the defendant does not dispute the truth of the allegation but claims it is not sufficient grounds to justify legal action, facts do not sustain the contention *...filed a demurrer after listening to the evidence presented...*
DEN	N: nest, cave, casual room *...wandered into a den of thieves...*
DIN	N: hubbub, racket, uproar *...could not be heard over the din of voices...*
DINE	VB: eat *...will dine with a few friends for his birthday...*
DENT	VB/N: depression *...could dent the hood when he backed up...* *...sustained only a minor dent on the door...*
DINT	N: power, force *...succeeded by dint of hard work...*

DENSE	ADJ: having a lot of material to be penetrated *...lost in the dense trees...*
DENT(S)	Plural of *dent* N: depression made by a blow or by pressure *...several dents in the side of his car...*
DUNCE	N/ADJ: one who is slow witted or stupid
DEPENDENCE	N: reliance, trust, addiction *...dependence on alcohol...*
DEPENDENT(S)	Plural of *dependent* N: those who need support *...claimed three dependents on his taxes...*
DEPOSE(D)	VB: oust, topple, overthrow *...depose the despotic king...*
DISPOSE(D)	VB: get rid of, eliminate *...need to dispose of the body...* VB: incline, arrange *...disposed to complaining...*
DEPRAVE(-ATION)	VB/N: corrupt, ruin, lead astray *...was depraved by years on the streets...* *...depravation of the man charged with the crimes...*
DEPRIVE(-ATION)	VB/N: rob, take away, withdraw *...deprive him of his privileges because of his defiance...* *...deprivation of the children living on the streets...*
DEPRECATE (-TION)	VB/N: express disapproval *...will deprecate his efforts...* *...constant deprecation of his fellow workers...* VB/N: belittle *...always tried to deprecate him in front of his friends...*
DEPRECIATE (-TION)	VB/N: lower in value *...car will depreciate rapidly...* *...depreciation rate is very high on new cars...*

DESERT	Pronounced /<u>dez</u>-ert/
	N/ADJ: dry, barren, sandy, treeless region
	...enjoys the dry desert climate...
	Pronounced /de-<u>zert</u>/
	VB: abandon, leave behind
	...will desert her to spend time with his kids...
	EXPRESSION
	got his just deserts = got what he had coming (usually negative)
DESSERT	N: course served at the end of a meal
	...enjoyed a light dessert...
DESPERATE	ADJ: frantic, worried, distressed
	...was desperate to get a job...
DISPARATE	ADJ: unequal, unlike, dissimilar
	...of such disparate tastes...
DETERRENCE	N: act of deterring
	...threat of prison did not seem to be a deterrence...
DETERRENT(S)	Plural of *deterrent*
	N: things that deter
	...had no deterrents to his bad behavior...
DETRACT(ION)	VB/N: take away, diminish, reduce
	...is going to detract from her real purpose...
	...not a detraction from her overall intelligence...
DISTRACT(ION)	VB/N: sidetrack, divert
	...tends to distract me when I am trying to practice...
	...served as a distraction for him during a time of major stress...
DEVICE	N: machine, piece of mechanical apparatus
	...complicated device...
DEVISE	VB: plan, invent, think out
	...needs to devise a plan for it...

DEW	N: moisture that condenses during the night
	...sidewalks were slippery because of the dew...
DO	VB: carry out, perform
	...have to do this before I leave...
	Short for *hairdo*
	N: hairstyle
	...has a new do...
DUE	ADJ: owed (as a debt or school essay)
	...payment due on Friday...
	...philosophy paper due in two weeks...
	ADJ: expected by a certain date
	...went two weeks past her due date...
	PREP: owing to, because of (used with *to*)
	...delay is due to a malfunction of the lights...
DUO	N: two or a pair
	...Mary and Annette make a great duo...
DIABETIC	N/ADJ: person with diabetes, relating to diabetes
	...went into a diabetic coma...
DIETETIC	ADJ: relating to nutrition
	...changed her morning meal for dietetic reasons...
DIURETIC	N: something used to increase urine flow
	...took a diuretic for the bloating...
DIAGRAM	VB/N: drawing, illustration
	...needed a diagram of the rooms on that floor...
	...detailed diagram of the system...
DIAPHRAGM	N: muscle separating the chest and the abdomen
	...stab wound just below the diaphragm...

DIE	N: tool or device for stamping, cutting, molding, or shaping *...job as a tool and die maker...* VB: stop living, cease being viable *...let the project die...*
DYE	VB: change the color of anything by saturating it with a coloring substance N/ADJ: any substance used to color fabric, hair *...had a bad dye job...*
DIED/DYING	Past tense and past participle/present participle of *to die* *...died during the war...* *...small family restaurant is dying...*
DYED/DYEING	Past tense and past participle/present participle of *to dye* *...dyed to match her skirt...* *...dyeing the fabric the same color...*
DIFFIDENT	ADJ: hesitant in acting or speaking through lack of self-confidence *...acted in a diffident manner around him...*
DISSIDENT	N: person who dissents, disagrees, differs *...dissidents were gathered in protest...*
DIVIDEND	N: individual share of something distributed *...received a monthly dividend from the policy...* N: share in a pro rata distribution of profits to stockholders N: reward *...one of the dividends of her loyalty to him...*
DILATE	VB: make bigger or wider *...need to dilate the eyes to check for glaucoma...*
DILUTE	VB: make thinner or less potent *...dilute the strength to make it more palatable...*
DINER	N: one that dines N: small restaurant *...stopped at a small roadside diner...*
DINNER	N: principal meal of the day *...ate dinner at 7:00...*

DINGHY	N: small boat *...took a dinghy out to the yacht...*
DINGY	Pronounced /<u>din</u>-jee/ ADJ: drab, dirty, not white *...don't see how she lives in that dingy apartment...* Pronounced /<u>ding</u>-ee/ ADJ: be a little wacky or nuts *...really dingy when it comes to numbers...*
DIPLOMAT	N: one skilled in diplomacy *...diplomat from France...*
DIPLOMATE	N: one with a diploma, usually a physician *...recognized as a diplomate...*
DISAPPROVE	VB: dislike, consider wrong, reject *...disapprove of her behavior with men...* *...disapprove the ballot measure...*
DISPROVE	VB: prove that something is false or incorrect *...disprove her theory about the children's behavior...*
DISASSEMBLE	VB: take apart *...grandstand had to be disassembled after the parade...*
DISSEMBLE	VB: beat around the bush, fake, take on a false appearance *...began to dissemble when he thought he would be caught...*
DISBURSE	VB: pay out, expend *...need to disburse the funds before the end of the month...*
DISPERSE	VB: break up and scatter in all directions, distribute widely *...disperse leaflets in the neighborhood...* *...winds disperse the leaves...*

DISBURSEMENT	N: act of paying out, funds paid out
	...disbursement of the assets in the estate...
DISPERSION	N: act or process of scattering
	...dispersion of the clouds...
DISCREET	ADJ: showing good judgment, confidentiality
	...discreet about the amount of the inheritance...
DISCRETE	ADJ: separate and distinct
	...divides into discrete parts...
DISCUSS(ED)	Past tense and past participle of *to discuss*
	VB: talk or write about
	...discussed it at length...
DISGUST	VB: sicken, revile
	...behavior did disgust me...
	N: sickening distaste or dislike, revulsion
	...regard the child molester with disgust...
DISILLUSION	VB: rob someone of dreams
	...would disillusion me if I were in his shoes...
DISSOLUTION	N: termination or destruction by breaking down, disrupting, or dispersing
	N: divorce
	...regret the dissolution of the marriage...
DISINTERESTED	ADJ: unbiased, impartial
	...court reporter is a disinterested party...
UNINTERESTED	ADJ: not interested
	...am simply uninterested in that topic...
DISPLACE	VB: shift, move, take the place of
	...will displace the workers because of budget cuts...
DISPLAY(S)	Third person singular, present tense of *to display*
	VB/N: show, exhibit
	...displays his product at the convention...

DISSIDENCE	N: disagreement *...dissidence was a problem among the staff...*
DISSIDENT(S)	Plural of *dissident* N: those who do not agree *...several dissidents in the crowd...* *...interviewed some of the dissidents...*
DISTILL	VB: filter *...need to distill the water...*
DISTAL	ADJ: far end, farther away, far from the point of attachment or origin *...distal end of a bone...*
DOE	N: female deer *..."doe, a deer, a female deer"...*
DOE	N: with *John* or *Jane*, name for a person who has not been identified *...brought in a John Doe...*
DOUGH	N: mixture stiff enough to knead, made of flour and a liquid *...bread dough needs to rise...* SLANG: *money* *...don't have the dough to do it...*
DOER	N: one who participates, takes an active role *...is a doer that really accomplishes a lot...*
DOUR	Pronounced /<u>doo</u>-er/ (rhymes with *tour*) ADJ: stern, sullen *...had a dour look as she entered the meeting...*
DOWER	Pronounced /<u>dow</u>-er/ (rhymes with *tower*) N: widow's share of her husband's estate *...significant dower when she married...*

DOES	Pronounced /doz/ (rhymes with *toes*)
	Alternate plural of *doe*; accepted plural is *doe*
	N: deer
	Pronounced /duz/ (rhymes with *was*)
	Third person singular, present tense of *to do*
	...*does not remember the name*...
DOSE	N: portion of medicine
	...*small dose in the morning*...
	EXPRESSION
	dose of his own medicine = has to take what he dishes out
DOZE	VB: nap, sleep
	...*tried not to doze off during the lecture*...
DONE	Past participle of the verb *to do*
	VB: completed or ended
	...*done in high fashion*...
	ADJ: sufficiently cooked
	...*likes his steak well done*...
DUN	VB/N: ask a debtor repeatedly for payment
	...*had to dun him for the money*...
	N/ADJ: neutral, slightly brownish, dark-gray color
	N: horse having a grayish yellow coat with black mane and tail
	...*rode a dun in the race*...
	ADJ: marked by dullness and drabness
	...*hate the dun colors throughout the house*...
DOWEL	Pronounced /<u>dow</u>-uhl/ (rhymes with *towel*)
	N: rod or pin that is inserted into a hole to help hold something in place
	...*put a small piece of dowel to hold it*...
DOLE	VB: give out in small segments (usually used with *out*)
	...*dole out his stash of chocolate*...
	EXPRESSION
	on the dole = getting charitable money/assistance
	...*criticized for being on the dole*...

DRIBBLE	VB: flow in small amounts, trickle
	...facts of the accident will dribble out...
	VB: bounce a basketball
	...would dribble the basketball for hours...
DRIVEL	VB: drool
	N: meaningless talk
	...what she said seemed to be just drivel...
DRIFTER	N: wanderer, vagabond, hobo
	...realized he did not want the job and would always be a drifter...
GRIFTER	N: swindler, con man
	...taken by a grifter and left with no money...
DUAL	ADJ: having or composed of two parts
	...had a dual role in the play...
	...car had dual exhaust pipes...
DUEL	VB: fight, compete strenuously
	...duel until midnight at the tennis match...
	...challenged him to a duel...
	N: contest fought between two persons
	...a five-hour duel in the finals of the tournament...

DUCK	VB: thrust under water
	...duck his head under water...
	VB: lower quickly, bow
	...had to duck to keep from getting hit...
	VB: avoid, evade
	...duck behind a curtain to hide...
	VB: back out
	...tried to duck out on paying the bill...
	N: swimming bird
	N: durable, closely woven, usually cotton fabric
	...sail was made of heavy duck...
DUCK(ED)	Past tense and past participle of the verb *to duck*
	...ducked his head in shame...
DUCT	N: tube or pipe as in electrical, plumbing, or human body
	...stuck in the heating duct...
	N/ADJ: kind of tape
	...used duct tape on the cord...
DUSK	N: darker part of twilight at night, sunset
	...accident occurred right at dusk...
DUST	VB: remove particles from
	...need to dust the book shelves...
	VB: sprinkle with a powdery substance
	...dust the cookies with powdered sugar...
	...dust the crops with chemicals...
	N: fine, dry particles of earth or pulverized matter
	...fine layer of dust on everything...
	EXPRESSIONS
	dust back = pitch the ball very close to the batter (baseball)
	...tried to dust back the opponent's best hitter...
	dust off = restore to use
	...dust off last winter's coat...
	leave in the dust = leave far behind
	...left the competition in the dust...
	when the dust settles = when things settle down
	...wait to deal with that when the dust settles...

CHAPTER 5
THE LETTER *E*

EARN	VB: receive as return for effort, especially for work done or services rendered ...*attempt to earn the respect of his elders*...
URN	N: container N: vessel that is typically an ornamental vase on a pedestal and that is used for various purposes, often preserving the ashes of the dead ...*placed the ashes in a very ornate urn*...
ERNE	N: long-winged sea eagle
EARTHLY	ADV: pertaining to the earth ...*claimed to be an earthly being*...
EARTHY	ADJ: simple, basic, crude ...*had an earthy smell to it*...
EAVE	N: lower border of the roof that overhangs the wall ...*hard to paint up under the eaves*... N: projecting edge
EVE	N: evening or day before a special day ...*nervous on the eve of his college graduation*...
ECLIPSE	VB/N: hide, conceal, cover ...*accomplishments that eclipse all else he has done*...
ELLIPSE	N: even oval shape ...*in the form of an ellipse*...
ELLIPSIS	N: punctuation mark (three dots) that indicate an omission ...*uses an ellipsis to show the witness trailed off*...
ELLIPSES	Pronounced /...seez/ Plural of *ellipsis*

EEK	INTERJ: exclamation of surprise ...*Eek! A mouse!*...
EKE	VB: manage against great odds or with great difficulty (used with *out*) ...*trying to eke out a living while in college*...
EGG	N: ovum ...*will fix an egg dish to take to the party*...
YEGG	N: thug ...*acted the part of the yegg*...
EITHER	PRO/ADJ/ADV/CONJ: one of two ...*don't like either one*... ...*either with him or without him*...
ETHER	N: gas used as anesthesia ...*sick from the ether*...
ELDER	N: senior of the two ...*Rich, the elder of the two brothers*... N: leader ...*elder in the church*...
OLDER	ADJ: greater age ...*drives an older car*...
ELEGY	N: sad, serious poem ...*wrote an elegy to her deceased friend*...
EULOGY	N: words said in praise of a person ...*wrote the eulogy for his father*...
ELICIT	VB: draw forth ...*attempted to elicit details of the crime*...
ILLICIT	ADJ: forbidden by law, improper ...*carried on an illicit affair for three years*...

ELIGIBLE	ADJ: available
	...eligible for a raise at the end of the year...
LEGIBLE	ADJ: readable
	...handwriting is barely legible...
ELIMINATE (-TION)	VB/N: cast out or get rid of, remove, eradicate
	...need to eliminate hunger in the country...
	...elimination of six positions...
	VB/N: set aside as unimportant, ignore
	...eliminate her contributions from consideration...
	VB/N: expel as waste from the human body
ILLUMINATE (-TION)	VB/N: supply or brighten with light
	...enough to illuminate the entire room...
	...not enough illumination in the area...
	VB/N: enlighten spiritually or intellectually
	...sermons illuminate the passage for me...
	VB/N: make clear; elucidate
	...illuminate the ideas for him...
EMIGRANT	N: person departing from a country to settle elsewhere
	...emigrant from France...
IMMIGRANT	N: person coming into a country to take up residence
	...took immigrant status in his new country...
EMIGRATE (-TION)	(Used when referring to the place one is leaving)
	VB/N: leave one's residence or country to live elsewhere
	...emigrate from Mexico to the United States...
	...makes emigration from China almost impossible...
IMMIGRATE (-TION)	(Used when referring to the place where one is arriving)
	VB/N: come into a country of which one is not a native for residence
	...decided to immigrate to a new country to have a better life...
	...need immigration policies that are practical...

EMINENCE	N: someone or something distinguished, prominent, or well known
	...*spoke with* **IMMINENCE** N: state of something that is about to happen
	...*imminence of the bad weather...*
EMINENT	ADJ: distinguished, important, exalted, noteworthy
	...*listened to the eminent speaker...*
IMMINENT	ADJ: likely or about to happen
	...*rain was imminent by the looks of the sky...*
IMMANENT	ADJ: inherent, having existence or effect only within the mind or consciousness
	...*God is immanent in the world...*
EMANATE	VB: flow forth from a source
	...*infection has to emanate from some source...*
EMULATE	VB: copy, follow, imitate, model, pattern
	...*did not want him to emulate his father's behavior...*
IMMOLATE	VB: offer in sacrifice, kill as a sacrifice, kill, destroy (usually by fire)
	...*desire to immolate himself for the cause of freedom...*
EMIT	VB: give off, release
	...*emit a strange odor...*
OMIT	VB: leave out
	...*omit the gory details...*
EMPATHIZE	VB: identify with, sympathize
	...*empathize with their loss...*
EMPHASIZE	VB: stress, highlight
	...*emphasize her strong points...*

ENDEMIC	ADJ: native, restricted to one locality
	...plant is endemic to this region...
EPIDEMIC	N/ADJ: widespread contagion
	...epidemic has spread to the outlying areas...
	...flu has reached epidemic proportions...
PANDEMIC	N/ADJ: occurring over wide area affecting high proportions of people
	(more serious than an epidemic)
	...AIDS has become pandemic...

ENDURE	VB: last, continue to be
	...will endure beyond the job itself...
INURE	VB: become accustomed to (usually to something unpleasant)
	...inure himself to the harsh conditions...
	...has become inured to his anger...

ENERVATE(D)	VB: lessen vitality or strength
	(take energy away from)
	...enervated by the long hike...
INNERVATE(D)	VB: excite, become enthusiastic
	(bring energy into)
	...innervated by the high quality and outstanding leadership...
INNOVATE(D)	VB: do something in a new way, introduce as new
	...tried to innovate with some ideas about the methods...

ENSURE	VB: make sure, guarantee
	...ensure that everyone gets a seat...
INSURE	VB: protect against
	...insure the house against loss by fire...
ASSURE	VB: give confidence to
	...assure you we will deliver it...

ENTER	VB: go into *...intends to enter the field of astrophysics...*
INTER	Pronounced /in-<u>tur</u>/ VB: bury, deposit a dead body into the earth or in a tomb *...will inter the body on Friday...*
INTERN	Pronounced /in-<u>turn</u>/ VB: impound, confine (wartime) *...intern the Japanese during World War II...* Pronounced /<u>in</u>-turn/ VB: work for nothing to learn a skill *...will intern at the local hospital...* N: person who works for nothing in order to learn a trade or profession *...intern with the company for a year...*
ENTOMOLOGY	N: study of insects *...majored in entomology...*
ETYMOLOGY	N: history of a word *...looked at the etymology of the word...*
ENTRÉE	N: main dish *...did not offer a vegetarian entrée...*
ENTRY	N: access *...point of entry into the community...* *...his entry into the contest was a surprise...*
ENVELOP	VB: wrap up or cover, surround completely *...fog will envelop the coastline...*
ENVELOPE	N: wrapper or covering, folded paper container for letters *...envelope was mutilated when it arrived...*

EPIC	N: long narrative poem of the deeds of a legendary or historical hero ...*recognized as an epic poem*... ADJ: extending beyond the usual or ordinary in size or scope ...*epic movie about the Industrial Revolution*... ADJ: heroic ...*epic efforts to save her from the burning building*...
EPOCH	N: event or time marked by an occurrence that begins a new period ...*developed during that epoch*... N: memorable event or date N: historical period ...*occurred during the epoch of the American Revolution*...
EPITAPH	N: message on a tombstone ...*cryptic epitaph that I tried to decipher*...
EPITHET	N: abusive term ...*string of epithets when he smashed his finger*...
EQUABLE	ADJ: marked by lack of variation or change or inequality ...*easy to live with because of his equable personality*... ADJ: uniform, equal ...*equable climate of the tropics*...
EQUITABLE	ADJ: having or exhibiting equity ADJ: dealing fairly and equally with all concerned ...*admired for his equitable treatment of his employees*...
ERA	N: historical period distinguished by certain important or unusual happenings ...*in the era of the flapper*... ...*era of high interest rates*... N: period of time starting from some significant happening or date N: one of five extensive periods in the development of the earth ...*during the Pleistocene Era*...
ERROR	N: mistake ...*five errors in one sentence*...

ERASABLE	ADJ: able to be erased *...erasable surface...*
IRASCIBLE	ADJ: easily provoked to anger, hot tempered *...had to deal with the irascible old man...*
ERRAND	N: short trip taken to deliver a message or perform a task *...had to run errands before I could get to work...*
ERRANT	ADJ: roving, wandering *...errant pitch that went into the stands...* ADJ: straying from the proper standards *...errant behavior...*
ARRANT	ADJ: complete or thorough, out and out notorious *...was an arrant rogue with women...*
ERRATIC	ADJ: irregular, variable *...cited for erratic driving...*
EROTIC	ADJ: pertaining to sexual love *...erotic picture of her that was posted...*
ETHIC	N: moral principles or values (often used in the plural) *...lived by very strict ethics...*
ETHNIC	ADJ: racial group, sometimes minority *...part of his ethnic background...*
ETIOLOGY	N: cause, source *...disease of unknown etiology...*
IDEOLOGY	N: body of concepts *...don't understand the ideology of that method...*
EVALUATION	N: assessment *...received a good evaluation his first semester...*
VALUATION	N: value placed on something *...assessed valuation of the property...*

EVOKE VB: call forth
...evoke the history of his family...

INVOKE VB: call for help or protection
...invoke the name of God...

EWE N: female sheep

YEW N: evergreen tree or shrub
...bark of the yew has medicinal benefits...

YOU PRO: second person singular or plural

EXACERBATE VB: make worse
...weather will exacerbate the problems with her arthritis...

EXAGGERATE VB: overstate, overstress
...did not exaggerate the seriousness of the situation...

EXASPERATE VB: frustrate, madden
...continues to exasperate her...

EXALT(ED) VB: raise high or elevate
...exalted position of President...
VB: praise or glorify
...exalt the accomplishment achieved against all odds...

EXULT(ED) VB: rejoice
...exult in the victory...

EXALTATION N: act of praising
...exaltation of the deity...
N: increase in degree or intensity

EXULTATION N: act of rejoicing
...experienced the exultation of the moment...

EXHALATION N: something exhaled or given off, emanation
...inhalation and exhalation...

EXAMPLE	N: model, paradigm
EXEMPLAR	N: pattern, archetype, something worthy of imitating
	...need an exemplar of his handwriting...
EXCEPTIONABLE	ADJ: debatable, objectionable
	...exceptionable actions in front of the children...
EXCEPTIONAL	ADJ: uncommon, extraordinary
	...exceptional nature of this award...
	...does exceptional work for the organization...
EXECUTIONER	N: one who carries out a death sentence
	...felt as if he were my executioner...
EXECUTOR	N: person named in a will to carry out the provisions of the will
	...named the executor of the will...
EXERCISE	VB/N: use
	...exercise his right to vote...
	VB/N: exert oneself
	...exercise at the gym left him exhausted...
EXORCISE	VB: expel evil spirits
	...needed to exorcise his demons...
EXHORT	VB: encourage, urge
	...exhort him to finish the race...
EXTORT	VB: obtain by threats or force
	...extort the money from his own family...
EXPAND(ED)	VB: make larger
	...expand the width of the room...
EXPEND(ED)	VB: use up, spend
	...tends to expend too much energy...
EXPOUND(ED)	VB: set forth, explain
	...expounded upon his ideas for a better workplace...

EXPANSIVE	ADJ: having a free and generous nature
	...feeling expansive with his friends...
	ADJ: sympathetic, demonstrative
	...expansive in his care for his grandmother...
	ADJ: broad, extensive, comprehensive
	...has an expansive knowledge of the subject matter...
EXPENSIVE	ADJ: high priced, costly
	...likes expensive cars...

EXPLICIT	ADJ: clearly stated, definite, unreserved, outspoken
	...explicit in his directions to the babysitter...
	ADJ: leaving nothing out, unequivocal
	...explicit statement to the press...
IMPLICIT	ADJ: suggested, not plainly expressed, implied
	...implicit agreement because he said nothing...
	ADJ: unquestioning, absolute
	...implicit trust in his father...

EXTANT	ADJ: still in existence
	...two extant copies of the original will...
EXTENT	N: area, scope, range, size, space, length, amount
	...help to the extent he is able...
EXTINCT	ADJ: no longer in existence
	...discovered a species thought to be extinct...

EXTRUDE	VB: force out, press out
	...extrude the material in a ropelike form...
EXUDE	VB: give off, convey
	...always exude charm...

CHAPTER 6
THE LETTER *F*

FACE

VB: confront
...face her opponent straight on...
N: front part of the human head
N: front, upper, or outer surface
...on the face of the mountain...
N: countenance
...would know that face anywhere...
N: facial expression
...make a face at her...
N: outward appearance
...on the face of it...
EXPRESSIONS
 maintain a firm face = keep your composure and dignity
 ...maintained a firm face in spite of being embarrassed...
 lose face = lose dignity or prestige
 ...lose face because of his involvement in the scheme...
 save face = save dignity or prestige
 ...tried to save face in front of his friends...
 put your face on = put on makeup
 put on a happy face = smile even when you don't feel like it
 ...put on a happy face for her daughter...

FAZE

VB: cause to be disconcerted; intimidate, daunt
...nothing seemed to faze her...

PHASE

VB: adjust, synchronize
...wanted to phase it together with her project...
N: stage in a process
...in the early phase of the process...
N: point, part
...knows just one phase of the operation...

FACET	N: one of the small, polished surfaces of a cut gem *...light reflected off the facets of the diamond...* N: phase or aspect *...just one facet of his interesting personality...*
FAUCET	N: device controlling the flow of water from a pipe *...wasted water from the dripping faucet...*
FACETIOUS	ADJ: joking in a clumsy and inappropriate manner *...claimed he was being facetious when his attempt at humor fell flat...*
FACTITIOUS	ADJ: passes as fact but not true ADJ: produced by man rather than by natural forces *...factitious product with no natural parts...* ADJ: sham, created by spreading rumors *...factitious story about his involvement...*
FICTITIOUS	ADJ: not true, false *...gave a fictitious name to the police...*
FACIAL	ADJ: pertaining to the face *...had a severe facial tic...*
FASCIAL	ADJ: pertaining to the connective tissue *...problem in the fascial area of the knee...*
FACILE	ADJ: too easy, superficial *...appeared to be a facile job...*
FACILITATE (-TION)	VB/N: make something easy or easier, lessen the labor of *...tried to facilitate a reconciliation between the two...*
FACILITATOR	N: catalyst, one who aids two sides to meet in the middle *...acted as a facilitator...*
FELICITATE (-TION)	VB/N: express good wishes formally, congratulate *...received the felicitations of the guests...*

FACTION	N: section, block, division ...*several warring factions within the group*...
FRACTION	N: small part ...*accomplished only a fraction of the whole job*...
FACTIOUS	ADJ: relating to factions, sections, groups ...*factious dissension in the larger group*...
FRACTIOUS	ADJ: irritable, restless, touchy ...*fractious behavior in the class was disruptive*...
FACTS	Plural of *fact* N: details, specifics, particulars, data ...*seemed to have his facts confused*...
FAX	Short for *facsimile* VB/N: duplicate, exact copy ...*need to send a fax immediately*...
FAINT	VB/N: lose consciousness temporarily ...*would faint upon hearing the news*... ...*went into a dead faint*... ADJ: not clear ...*writing was too faint to make out*... ADJ: without strength ...*feel faint from the heat*...
FEINT	VB: deliver a pretended blow N: movement intended to deceive, pretended blow ...*staged a feint at the liquor store to draw the police from the bank*...
FEIGN	VB: give a false appearance of, pretend ...*tried to feign sleep when he came into the room*...
FIEND	N: person of great wickedness ...*was a fiend around young girls*... N: addict ...*was a dope fiend*...

FAIR	N: festival at which goods and livestock are displayed
	...met at the county fair...
	ADJ: impartial
	...just not a fair decision that he made...
	...judge must make a fair settlement in the case...
	ADJ: reasonable
	...not fair that she has been left out...
	ADJ: light, clear, beautiful
	...fair complexion...
FARE	VB: get along
	...did not fare well on the exam...
	N: sum of money paid for travel
	...fare has gone up significantly...
	N: range of food
	...fine fare in that restaurant...
FAIRY	N: mythical being of folklore, elf
	...Cinderella and her fairy godmother...
FERRY	VB/N: carry by boat over a body of water
	...needed to ferry them across the swollen river...
	N/ADJ: type of boat
	...took the ferry to the island...
	...large ferry system around Seattle...
FALLOW	ADJ: plowed land that is left unplanted
	...passed several fallow fields...
FELLOW	N: guy, man
	...seemed like a nice fellow...
	N: member of a prestigious group
	...Fellow of the Academy of Scientists...

FARTHER (-EST) Comparison/superlative form of *far*
(Refers to something that is physically measurable)
ADJ/ADV: at or to a greater distance or more advanced point
...to a farther point on the map...
ADJ/ADV: to a greater degree or extent, beyond
...cannot drive any farther tonight...
...walked farther into the canyon...

FURTHER (-EST) Comparison/superlative form of *far*
(Refers to something that is not physically measurable)
ADJ/ADV: at or to a greater distance or more advanced point
...to a further level of competence...
ADJ/ADV: to a greater degree or extent, beyond
...relationship can go no further...
...no further discussion...
VB: advance
...further his career plans with this move...

FATAL ADJ: deadly, causing death
...often fatal results from drinking and driving...

FETAL ADJ: referring to an unborn child
...wore a fetal monitor the last month of the pregnancy...
...doubled over into the fetal position...

FATE N: destiny
...ultimate fate is unknown...

FETE Pronounced /fait/ (rhymes with *hate*)
VB: celebrate an honor with festivities
...will fete her accomplishments at the gala...
N: festival, especially one held out of doors
...attended the fete with his family...

FATED	ADJ: destined, meant, intended *...fated to be successful in his field...*
FETED	Past tense and past participle of *to fete* VB/ADJ: celebrated, honored *...feted for his work with the homeless...*
FETID	ADJ: having a foul odor *...fetid smell coming from the trash chute...*
FATEFUL	ADJ: momentous, significant, critical *...on that fateful day...*
FAITHFUL	ADJ: loyal, accurate, truthful *...was faithful to his word...*
FAUX	Pronounced /foe/ (rhymes with *toe*) ADJ: fake *...wore faux pearls to the event...*
FOE	N: enemy, opponent *...formidable foe...*
FEAR(S)	Third person singular, present tense of *to fear* VB: dread, anticipate with alarm *...fears the consequences of his actions...* Plural of *fear* N: worry, doubt *...has no fear of water at all...*
FIERCE	ADJ: violent, stern, severe *...fierce competitor...*

FEAT	N: act showing great daring, skill, ingenuity *...incredible feat of strength as he lifted the box...*
FEET	Plural of *foot* N: terminal part of the leg *...having trouble standing on her feet...* N: measurement *...several feet of concrete...*
FEEBLE	ADJ: weak, frail, delicate, shabby *...made a feeble attempt to explain himself...*
FOIBLE	N: shortcoming, idiosyncrasy *...typical foible of an old man...*
FERAL	ADJ: beastly, untamed, uncultivated *...feral attack on him...*
FERRULE	N: metal ring or cap *...put a ferrule over the hinge to hold it...*
FERULE	N: paddle for children *...refused to use the ferule...*
FERMENT	VB: undergo an enzymatic change *...liquid was allowed to ferment...* VB/N: agitation, activity, tumult, uproar *...period of great ferment...*
FOMENT	VB: stimulate, stir up *...tried to foment dissension within the group...*

FERTILITY	N: fruitfulness, fecundity, productivity ...*decided to take fertility treatments*...
FUTILITY	N: ineffectiveness, pointlessness ...*futility of continuing to probe*...
FEUDAL	ADJ: referring to a period in the early Middle Ages ...*lived under a feudal system*...
FUTILE	ADJ: useless, serving no purpose ...*futile attempt to rescue her*...
FIANCÉ	N: man engaged to be married
FIANCÉE	N: woman engaged to be married
FINANCE	VB: provide money ...*needs to finance her studies with loans*... N: funds, capital, money ...*majoring in finance*...
FICHE	Short for *microfiche* N: sheet of microfilm containing data
FISH	VB/N: angle, trawl. search ...*trying to fish for clues on her whereabouts*...
PHISH	VB: try to get financial information from the internet by using subterfuge ...*email that intended to phish for information*...
FICTION	N: not real, made up ...*enjoys reading historical fiction*...
FRICTION	N: resistance, chafing, abrasion ...*too much friction caused it to snap*...
FINAL	N/ADJ: last exam, ultimate ...*studying for the final*... ...*was the final test of his loyalty*...
FINALE	N: last part of a piece of music or a play ...*interrupted the finale of the piece*...

FINALLY	ADV: at last
	...finally got to meet her...
FINELY	ADV: delicately, elegantly
	...finely crafted jewelry...
	ADV: in very small pieces
	...finely chopped onions...
FIND	VB: discover
	...finally able to find the right combination of drugs...
	N: something discovered
	...second-hand chair was a great find...
FINE(D)	Past tense and past participle of *to fine*
	VB: require to pay a sum of money as punishment for an offense
	...was fined over $500 for the ticket...
FIR	N: type of evergreen tree
	...some type of fir in the yard...
FUR	N: skin and hair of an animal, garment made of such skins
	...lush fur of the chinchilla...
FISCAL	ADJ: pertaining to money, financial matters
	...according to their fiscal policy...
	ADJ: pertaining to the business year
	...fiscal year ends in June...
PHYSICAL	ADJ: referring to the body
	...very little physical strength...
	ADJ: having material existence
	...found physical evidence that pointed to his guilt...
CYCLICAL	ADJ: in a cycle, recurring
	...headaches seem to be cyclical...
PSYCHICAL	ADJ: referring to the mind or psyche
	...psychical phenomenon...

FISHER	N: one who fishes
	N: animal similar to but much larger than a weasel that eats porcupine
FISSURE	N: crack in a wall or rock
	...large fissure in the wall after the earthquake...
FISSION	N: process of splitting into parts
	...atomic fission...
FUSION	N: synthesis, union, combination
	...fusion of the two bones...
FLACK(S)	Plural of *flack*
	N: one who provides publicity
	...used a flack to get the information out...
FLAK	N: criticism, condemnation, aggravation
	...gave him flak about his attitude...
	...took a lot of flak from his fellow workers because of his clothes...
	N: explosion of ammunition from antiaircraft guns
	...planes flew safely through the flak on their way to the target...
FLAX	N/ADJ: genus of herb
	...took the oil of the flaxseed...
PLAQUE	N: fatty material that clogs artery walls
	...found plaque in the coronary artery...
	N: flat plate for mounting on a wall
	...received a plaque for his contribution to the cause...
FLAGRANT	ADJ: outrageous, scandalous, notorious, glaring
	...flagrant violation of the ethics code...
FRAGRANT	ADJ: having a pleasing odor, sweet smelling
	...enjoyed the fragrant smells in the garden...

FLAIR	N: natural talent or aptitude
	...real flair for the dramatic...
	...shows a flair for art...
FLARE	VB: burn unsteadily
	...fire will flare in the late afternoon wind...
	VB/N: express strong emotion
	...temper began to flare...
	...had a flare of his chronic problem over the weekend...
	N: incendiary device
	...put out a flare to warn of the stalled car...
FLAUNT	VB: wave or display gaudily or ostentatiously, show off
	...intends to flaunt her new diamond...
FLOUT	VB: treat contemptuously, show contempt for, scorn, scoff
	...would always flout traffic laws...
	...had a lifetime to flout the laws on integration...
FLEA(S)	Plural of *flea*
	N: small parasitic jumping insect
	...infested with fleas...
FLEE(S)	Third person singular, present tense of *to flee*
	VB: run away
	...suspected that he would flee if given the chance...
FLEECE	VB: swindle, con, cheat
	...intending to fleece the senior citizens...
	N: sheep's wool
FLECK(S)	Plural of *fleck*
	N: small spots or streaks
	...flecks of paint on the floor...
FLEX	VB: bend, tighten muscles
	...tried to flex the muscles of her leg...
	...decided to flex his power over her...

FLEW	Past tense of *to fly*
	VB: pass through the air
	VB: pass quickly
	...time flew by as we enjoyed the vacation...
FLU	Short for *influenza*
	N: virus
	...very dangerous flu for the elderly...
FLUE	N: pipe for conveying smoke
	...flue was clogged with debris...
FLOE(S)	N: floating ice formed in a large sheet
	...ship was hit by a large floe...
FLOW(S)	VB: issue or move in a stream
	...flow of water trickled to a few drops...
	VB: proceed smoothly and readily
	...work will flow smoothly with the new plan...
	VB: derive from a source
	N: smooth uninterrupted movement, stream
	...steady flow of information from her...
	N: mass of material which has flowed when molten
	...lava flow continues...
	N: menstruation
FLO	Short for *Florence*
FLORESCENT	ADJ: flourishing, as with flowers
	...florescent garden...
FLUORESCENT	N/ADJ: bright or glowing as a result of emitting electromagnetic radiation
	...put in fluorescent lighting...

FLOUNDER	VB: hesitate, falter, have difficulty ...*began to flounder in the class when it involved math*... N: type of fish
FOUNDER	VB: break down, fail, fall through ...*caused the plan to founder*... N: person who establishes a group, creator, originator ...*recognized as the founder of the organization*...
FLOUR	N: ground grain used in baking ...*called for whole-grain flour*...
FLOWER	VB: come of age, mature ... *beginning to flower on the job*... N: bloom of a plant ...*smell like a flower in spring*...
FLUKE	VB: show a whale's tail as he breaks the surface ...*saw him fluke several times from the whale-watching boat*... N: one of the lobes of a whale's tail N: flatfish N: type of worm N: part of an anchor ...*fluke was tangled in a massive bed of seaweed*... N: stroke of luck ...*discovery was a fluke*...
FLUTE	VB: form into ridges ...*flute the pie crust*... N: musical instrument N: tall slender wineglass ...*two crystal flutes for the champagne*... N: rounded groove, one of the vertical parallel grooves on a classical architectural column ...*rather ornate flutes on that column*...

FOAL(ED)	Past tense of *to foal*
	VB: give birth to a foal
	...mare will foal in the spring...
FOAL	N: young of an animal of the horse family especially under one year
FOLD	VB: incorporate into a mixture by repeated gentle turning over without stirring or beating
	...fold in the beaten eggs...
	VB: concede defeat by withdrawing one's cards from play as in poker
	...had to fold because he just didn't have the cards...
	VB: fail completely, collapse
	...business will fold at the end of the month...
	VB/N: double or lay one part over another
	...had to fold the sheets to suit him...
	N: group of people or institutions that share a common faith, belief, activity, or enthusiasm
	...group brought him into the fold...
	...left the fold to strike out on his own...
FOGGY	ADJ: filled with a vapor of fine particles of water
	...very foggy as we landed at the airport near the ocean...
	ADJ: covered or made opaque by moisture
	...mirror was too foggy to use to apply the makeup...
	ADJ: blurred or obscured
	...foggy memory about the date...
FOGY	N: person with old-fashioned ideas
	...acting like an old fogy...
FONDLING	Present participle of *to fondle*
	VB: caress, pet
	...was fondling the wad of money in his pocket...
FOUNDLING	N: child that has no parents
	...looking for a permanent home for the foundling...

FONT	N: basin, often used for baptism
	N: kind of type
	...used a flashy font to attract attention...
FOUNT	N: source, fountain, spring
	...fount of knowledge for the whole company...
FOR	PREP: indicates purpose, intended goal; object or recipient of a perception, desire, or activity, et cetera
	...intended for her...
	...longing for the good old days...
	CONJ: because
	...leaving now, for I have much to do...
FORE	N: front, toward the beginning
	...came to the fore in the investigation...
	N: front part of the ship
	INTERJ: warning of an errant shot that might hit someone (golf)
	...yelled, "Fore," after he hit the errant shot...
FOUR	N/ADJ: number after three and before five
	...will turn four next month...
FORAY	N: raid
	...foray into the local village...
FRAY	VB: wear down by rubbing
	...so old that it has begun to fray...
	VB: strain, irritate
	...tempers began to fray at the end of the long session...
	N: fight or brawl
	...jumped into the fray...
	N: raveled place or worn spot
AFFRAY	N: fighting in a public place
	...called the police because of the affray...

FRAY(S)	Third person singular, present tense of *to fray* VB: unravel, strain *...always frays around the outer edges...*

PHRASE	VB: state something in a certain manner
	...needs to phrase it differently...
	N: saying, axiom
	...his final phrase keeps repeating in my head...
	N: short musical thought
	...had trouble with the timing of the phrase...
	EXPRESSION
	    turn of phrase = way of saying something
	    ...turn of phrase that really explains it well...

FRAISE	N: obstacle of stakes driven into the ramparts of a fortification in a horizontal or inclined position *...fraise around the castle...*
FORBEAR	VB: hold back, refrain *...need to forbear until things improve...*
FOREBEAR	N: ancestor (often used in the plural) *...forebears that came from Ireland...*
FORGO	VB: give up *...will forgo dessert because I am stuffed...*
FOREGO	N: precede *...is a foregone conclusion...*
FOREWORD	N: introduction or preface *...foreword explained the author's point of view...*
FORWARD	ADJ: toward the front *...in the forward section of the train car...* ADV: at or near the front *...marched forward into the streets...*

FORMALLY	ADV: in accordance with rules, forms, procedures, regulations *...formally withdraw from the organization...*
FORMERLY	ADV: in the past, some time ago *...formerly belonged to the organization...*
FORT	N: fortified building for defense *...boys built a fort in the backyard...*
FORTE	Pronounced /*fort*/ (rhymes with *port*) (Incorrectly pronounced as two syllables) N: something at which a person excels *...his forte is music...* N: part of a sword blade that is between the middle and the hilt and that is the strongest part of the blade *...accidentally grabbed it by the forte...* Pronounced /<u>for</u> tay/ ADJ: musical term meaning in a loud and forceful way *...to be played forte...*
FORTH	ADV: forward, onward *...go forth into the world...*
FOURTH	ADJ: preceded by three others in a series *...fourth in line...*
FOUGHT	Past tense and past participle of *to fight* VB: brawl, crash, struggle, battle *...constantly fought with his siblings...*
FRAUGHT	ADJ: full of (used with *with*) *...situation was fraught with danger...*
WROUGHT	Past tense form of *to work* (alternate form) VB: worked into shape with artistry and effort *...carefully wrought letters...* VB/ADJ: deeply stirred, excited *...wrought up over the change in the work conditions...* ADJ: hammered, bent, shaped, twisted *...wrought iron fence...*

FOUL	N/ADJ: out of bounds (baseball)
	...hit several balls foul before the home run...
	ADJ: disgusting
	...foul odor emanating from the sewer...
	ADJ: unfair
	...workers cried foul after the announcement...
FOWL	N: bird used for food
FREE(S)	Third person singular, present tense of *to free*
	VB: let go, liberate
	...frees innocent men and women to do other things...
FREEZE	VB: congeal with ice
	N: weather marked by temperature below the freezing point
	...Midwest is in the midst of a deep freeze...
FRIEZE	N: richly ornamented band (architecture)
	...delicate frieze at the top of the column...
	N: pile rug surface of uncut loops or of patterned cut and uncut loops
FRIAR	N: monk
	...with the friar in the monastery...
FRYER	N: young chicken suitable for frying
	N: deep utensil for frying foods
	...thought use of the deep fryer was not healthful...
FRIABLE	ADJ: easily crumbled
	...examination of the liver showed it was friable...
FRYABLE	ADJ: suitable for frying
FUNERAL	N: burial ceremony
	...decided not to have a funeral...
FUNEREAL	ADJ: relating to a funeral, somber
	...marched to the funereal dirge...

FURNACE   N: machine for heating
                     ...explosion caused by a faulty furnace...

FURNISH   VB: supply, provide, equip
                     ...will furnish the necessary information...

FURRY   ADJ: having fur
                     ...rather scary little furry creature that ran across the floor...

FURY   N: anger
                     ...reacted with fury to the shocking news...

CHAPTER 7
THE LETTER *G*

GAFF
VB: strike or secure with a spear
...tried to gaff the fish...
VB: deceive, trick, fleece
VB: fix for the purpose of cheating
...intended to gaff the dice...
N: hook for holding or lifting heavy fish
...used a gaff to spear the fish...
N: butcher's hook
...used a gaff to hang the ham to cure it...
N: large iron pin or its steel point used by a telephone lineman
...climbed the pole with the use of a gaff...
N: spar on which the head of a fore-and-aft sail is extended
...broken gaff on the ship...
N: hoax, fraud, gimmick, or trick
N: something painful or difficult to bear, ordeal
...could not stand the gaff...

GAFFE
N: blunder, social error
...his gaffe in mentioning her husband, who had just left her...

GAFFER
N: Originally, the gaffer was the man who walked the streets at dusk and lit the gaslights with his gaff, a long pole with a curved end. Today the gaffer is the electrician in charge of lighting for TV and movie sets.

GAIT
N: manner of walking or running
...knee injury affected his gait...
N: various movements of a horse
...perfect gait during the dressage...

GATE
N: movable structure across an entrance or exit
...put a gate across the driveway...
N: total admission money paid by spectators
...gate was more than $60,000...

GALLERY	N: building used to display art
	...displaying her art at a new gallery...
GALLEY	N: kitchen on a plane or ship
	...assigned to work in the galley during the flight...
GAMBIT	N: strategy, maneuver, ploy
	...used the gambit to win the match...
GAMUT	N: whole series
	EXPRESSION
	run the gamut = do the whole thing
	...run the gamut of emotions during the movie...
GAMBLE	VB/N: bet, wager
	...took the gamble on the property...
	...will not gamble with her life...
GAMBOL	VB: skip about in play
	...children gambol on the lawn...
GAMBREL	N: roof with two slopes on each side
GARBLE	VB: mix up, mangle, distort, confuse
	...poor quality speakers that will garble the sound...
GARGLE	VB: gurgle liquid in the throat
	...tried to gargle often to help his sore throat...
GARGOYLE	N: grotesque figure
GARNER	VB: gather, acquire, collect
	...garner support for his run for office...
GARTER	N: band to hold up socks
	...wore a fancy black garter...
GIRDER	N: beam, strut
	...used steel girders to reinforce the bridge...

GARISH	ADJ: gaudy, showy, loud, bright *...always wore garish colors...*
GARNISH	VB: take money from wages to pay a debt *...garnish his wages to pay his child support...* VB/N: decorate food *...added parsley as a garnish...*
GELD	VB: deprive of a natural or essential part, castrate *...always intended to geld the animal...*
GELDING	N: castrated male horse
GELT	YIDDISH: *money* *...wanted to spend his Chanukah gelt...*
GENE(S)	Plural of *gene* N: part of the germ plasma having a specific function in inheritance that is determined by DNA and RNA molecules *...researching a problem with the genes...* N: determiner of the traits of the individual person *...behavior seems to be in his genes...* N: genetic units
JEANS	N: pants made of denim *...wearing a pair of high-priced jeans...*
GENIAL	ADJ: pleasant, friendly *...had a genial chat with her about it...*
GENITAL	ADJ: relating to reproduction
GENIUS	N: exceptional gifts, strongly marking capacity or aptitude *...math skills that approach genius...*
GENUS	N: class, kind, sort *...falls into a genus that is little known...*

GENTEEL	ADJ: pretentiously polite, well bred, refined, elegant *...admire his genteel tastes...*
GENTILE	N: not Jewish, not Mormon *...made welcome the Gentiles in Palestine...*
GENTLE	ADJ: soft, not hard *...had a very gentle manner...*
GERMAN	N/ADJ: person from Germany *...spoke English with a German accent...*
GERMANE	ADJ: relevant, connected *...not germane to our discussion here...*
GESTURE	VB: indicate *...gesture toward the door just before it opened...* N: movement of the body or limbs that expresses or emphasizes an idea, sentiment, or attitude *...gesture that showed his contempt...* *...flowers were such a kind gesture...* N: use of motions of the limbs or body as a means of communication *...gesture to indicate the presence of the intruder...* N: something said or done by way of formality or courtesy or as a symbol or token or for its effect on the attitudes of other *...political gesture to draw popular support...*
JESTER	N: fool, one given to joking *...played the role of the court jester...* *...always acted as a jester...*
GHASTLY	ADJ: dreadful, appalling, horrid *...ghastly accident scene...*
GHOSTLY	N: vaporous, indistinct, eerie *...ghostly appearance after her long illness...*

GIB	N: metal plate that holds parts in place
JIB	VB: cause a sail to swing from one side of a ship to the other
	...sail began to jib...
	VB: refuse to proceed further, balk
	...caused him to jib...
	N: triangular sail set on a stay
	...set the jib...
	N: projecting arm of a crane
	...jib hit the edge of the building as the crane fell...
	N: derrick boom

GIBE	VB: make taunting, heckling, or jeering remarks; ridicule, deride
	...felt he needed to gibe her...
	N: derisive remark
	...got in a gibe about her job...

JIBE	VB: shift suddenly and forcibly from one side to the other
	...sail began to jibe in the wind...
	VB: change a vessel's course when sailing with the wind
	VB: be in accord, agree
	...does not jibe with the facts...

JIVE	VB: tease, cajole, kid
	...figured he was just trying to jive me...
	N: swing music or the dancing performed to it
	...performed a perfect jive in the competition...
	N: glib, deceptive, or foolish talk
	N: jargon of hipsters
	...talking jive...
	N/ADJ: special jargon of difficult or slang terms
	...full of that jive talk...
	SLANG: *phony*
	...that's just jive...

GIG	VB: goad, provoke
	N: something that whirls or is whirled, as with a helicopter
	N: rowboat designed for speed rather than for work
	...*took the gig to the island...*
	N: job usually for a specified time, entertainer's engagement
	...*had a gig at a jazz club...*
	N: military demerit
	...*gig against his record...*
	Short for *gigabyte*
	...*needed more than a gig of memory...*
JIG	VB: move with rapid jerky motions
	N: lively springy dance, music for such a dance
	...*danced the Irish jig...*
	N: fishing device that is jerked up and down or drawn through the water
	...*used a jig to attract the fish...*
	EXPRESSION
	the jig is up = game/trick is over
	in jig time = quickly, in a very short time
	...*finished it in jig time...*
GILD	VB: overlay with a thin covering of gold
	...*intends to gild the edges of the porcelain plates...*
GUILD	N: association of persons with similar pursuits, union
	...*belonged to the carpenter's guild...*
GILT	N: thin layer of gold
	...*covered with gilt...*
GUILT	N: state of having committed a wrong
	...*filled with guilt after the theft...*
GIST	N: point of the matter
	...*gave me just the gist of the conversation...*
	...*don't understand the gist...*
JEST	VB/N: joke
	...*try not to jest about this...*

GLEAM	VB/N: shine, glitter, sparkle ...*diamond tends to gleam in the sunlight*...
GLEAN	VB: garner, collect, scrape together ...*all I could glean from the little information that was offered*...
GLUTEN	N: protein substance ...*following a gluten-free diet*...
GLUTTON	N: person who eats a large amount, gourmand ...*glutton when he ate*... EXPRESSION *glutton for punishment* = someone who invites or takes on negativity
GOFER	N: person who does the bidding of another ...*just a gofer for whatever he needs*...
GOPHER	N: rodent ...*had a gopher in the yard*...
GOLFER	N: person who plays the game of golf ...*scratch golfer*...
GORILLA	N: large ape ...*gorilla at the zoo*...
GUERRILLA	N: one who engages in irregular warfare especially as a member of an independent unit carrying out harassment and sabotage N/ADJ: combatants in a small war ...*part of the guerrilla band in the mountains*...
GORE(D)	Past tense and past participle of *to gore* VB: pierce with an animal horn ...*gored when he ran with the bulls in Pamplona*...
GOURD	N: climbing or trailing plant, including pumpkin, cucumber, squash ...*dried gourds used as vases*...

GRADE	VB: make level
	...need to grade the surface before proceeding...
	VB: assign a numeric value
	...papers to grade...
	N: angle of ascent or descent
	...lost control on the steep grade...
	N: mark of achievement or quality
	...tried to make the grade...
	...high grade of meat...
GRAY(ED)	Past tense and past participle of *to gray*
	...has grayed since he has been in office...
GRATE	VB: have an unpleasant effect upon
	...really began to grate on my nerves...
	VB: grind into small pieces
	...recipe calls for you to grate the cheese finely...
	N: framework of iron bars to hold fire logs
	...use an ornamental grate in front of the fireplace...
GREAT	ADJ: large, important
	...passing up a great opportunity...
GRADER	N: person who scores tests
	...volunteered to be a grader for the test...
	N: machine used for leveling land
	...used a road grader...
GRATER	N: utensil for grating cheese
	...caught his thumb on the grater and tore the nail...
GREATER	ADJ: degree of good; larger, more wonderful in scope
	...greater than I expected...

GRADING	Present participle of *to grade* VB/N: leveling off to a smooth horizontal or sloping surface ...*continue grading the hillside*... ADJ: arranging in levels
GRATING	N: lattice used to close any of various openings ...*grating to cover the hole*...
GRAFT	VB: splice together ...*have to graft the two ends*... VB: add something N: illegal gain ...*proved there to be massive graft in the city government*...
GRAPH(ED)	VB/N: chart or diagram ...*produced a graph of the results*... ...*intended to graph the figures as a means of explanation*...
GRAM	N: unit of measure ...*several grams of cocaine*...
GRAHAM	N/ADJ: made of wheat flour ...*prefer graham crackers*...
GRANDER	ADJ: more impressive ...*grander than I remember*...
GRANDEUR	N: splendor, majesty, opulence ...*celebrate the grandeur of the occasion*...
GRANITE	N: kind of very hard rock ...*granite counters in her kitchen*...

GRANT(ED)	Past tense and past participle of *to grant*
	VB: allow, contribute
	...*was granted money to continue his research*...
	EXPRESSION
	    take for granted = assume something/someone to be acquiescent
	      ...*always took her for granted*...

GRAY(S)	Third person singular, present tense of *to gray*
	VB: make neither black nor white; become dingy
	...will gray over time...
	N: Confederate army (usually capped)
	...the Blue and the Gray...
	N/ADJ: series of neutral colors ranging between black and white
	...hair has turned gray...
	ADJ: lacking cheer or brightness in mood, outlook, style, or flavor
	...everything seemed to fade to gray for him...
	ADJ: dismal, gloomy
	...really a gray day with all the fog...
	ADJ: prosaically ordinary, dull, uninteresting
	...sees everything in shades of gray...
	ADJ: having an intermediate and often vaguely defined position, condition, or character
	...an ethically gray area...
	EXPRESSIONS
	gray matter = brains
	gray water = reused water
	...used gray water on the plants...
	gray ladies = women who work in a hospital
	graying of = having proportionally more older people
	...discussion of the graying of America...
	graybeard = old man
GREY(S)	Second and less preferable (British) spelling of *gray(s)*
GRAZE	VB: feed on growing foliage
	...cattle could graze on that land...
	VB: eat a little of this and a little of that
	...decided to graze rather than eat a full meal...
	VB: abrade or scratch
	VB: touch lightly in passing
	...bullet did graze the side of his ear...
GREIGE	Pronounced /grayzh/
	ADJ: being in an unbleached, undyed state, as taken from a loom
	...purchased the greige goods from the factory...

GREASE	VB: lubricate
	...*need to grease the pan*...
	N: fat, oil
	...*used too much grease*...
	EXPRESSION
	    grease someone's palms = pay someone illegally for something
	      ...*had to grease a lot of palms to get that*...

GREECE	N: country ...*Olympics held in Greece*...
GRIFT	VB/N: obtain money illicitly as in a confidence game ...*tried to grift his friends with the scheme*...
GRIFTER	N: one who obtains money illicitly
GRIST	N: grain for grinding N: matter of interest that serves as the basis of a story ...*just added more grist for the gossip*... EXPRESSION *grist for the mill* = something needed or turned to one's advantage
GRILL	VB: broil on a grill ...*decided to grill steaks after swimming*... VB: question intensely ...*police will grill the suspect until he talks*... N: cooking device on which food is exposed to heat ...*would use the grill to cook*... N: informal restaurant or dining room ...*ate with our friends at the grill*...
GRILLE	N: grating forming a barrier or screen, lattice, framework ...*tried to avoid walking on the grille over the vents*... N: ornamental barrier or screen at the front end of a car ...*grille had several ornamental figures on it*...

GRIMACE(D)
Past tense and past participle of *to grimace*
VB/N: facial expression usually of disgust or disapproval
...grimaced as the dentist began working...

GRIMMEST
ADJ: most harsh, most severe
...grimmest crime scene I have seen...

GRIP
VB: seize or hold firmly
...tried to grip the slippery handle...
VB: strongly hold the interest of
...story that will grip the readers...
N: firm tenacious hold typically giving control, mastery, or understanding; mental grasp
...has a good grip on what is expected of him...
...does not have a good grip on the gravity of the situation...
N: handle
...grip on the computer case is defective...
N: suitcase
...take my grip with me...
N: stagehand
...talk to the grip about the problem...
N/ADJ: strong or tenacious grasp
...grip strength of the rope...
EXPRESSION
   get a grip = control yourself

GRIPPE
N: acute febrile, contagious viral disease, influenza
...has the grippe and cannot get out of bed...

GRIPE
VB: complain with grumbling
...always has to gripe about his sister...
VB/N: afflict, distress, irritate, vex
...his comments really gripe me...
...have a legitimate gripe about that...

GRIPED/GRIPING	Past tense and past participle/present participle of *to gripe*
	...griped incessantly...
	...really tired of his griping...
GRIPPED/GRIPPING	Past tense and past participle/present participle of *to grip*
	...gripped with fear about the future...
	...extremely gripping story...
GRISLY	ADJ: inspiring horror, dread, fear
	...bared the grisly details of the crime...
GRISTLY	ADJ: containing gristle
	...gristly meat...
GRIZZLY	N: gray (bear)
	...came face to face with a grizzly on the camping trip...
	ADJ: have hair that is silver tipped
	...grizzly look to his hair as he began to turn gray...
GROAN	VB/N: utter a sound expressing pain, distress, or disapproval
	...will groan with every move as he lifts the weights...
	VB/N: make a creaking or grating sound as from great strain
	...building seemed to groan in the strong wind...
GROWN	Past participle of *to grow*
	VB: increase in size and develop toward maturity
	...weeds have grown up around the porch...
	ADJ: developed, mature
	...full grown before I saw her again...
GROSS	N: twelve dozen
	...ordered a gross of the flowers for the shop...
	N: before deductions
	...made over $10,000 gross on the deal...
GROUSE	VB: complain
	...always had to grouse about the conditions...

GROWING	Present participle of *to grow* VB: become larger, increase in size *...growing into a fine young man...*
GROIN	N: fold or depression marking the juncture of the lower abdomen and the inner part of the thigh *...injury to the groin...*
GUARANTEE	VB/N: assure, promise, pledge *...guarantee him I will be at the event...* *...gave him a guarantee...*
GUARANTY	N: thing offered as a guarantee, deposit, security *...offered the bonds as a guaranty for the loan...*
GUESS(ED)	Past tense and past participle of *to guess* VB: form a judgment or estimate of something without actual knowledge *...might have guessed he would not help us...*
GUEST	N/ADJ: person entertained at the home of another, visitor *...was a guest in our home...* *...made a guest appearance on the show...*
GUIDE	VB/N: steer, lead, direct *...needed him to guide me toward the right career...*
GUY(ED)	Past tense of *to guy* VB: stabilize *...has guyed the tower with heavier wires...*

GUISE
N: form or style of dress
N: external appearance, form of deception
...*under the guise of a police officer*...

GUY(S)
Plural of the word *guy*
N: fellows, persons
...*several guys were misbehaving*...
N: used to refer to members of a group without regard to sex
...*all the guys in the class have to do it*...
N/ADJ: ropes, chains, rods, or wires attached to something as a brace or guide
...*guy wires were cut*...
...*supported the tower with guys*...

HAIL	VB: greet, call loudly to *...needed to hail a cab in a hurry...* VB/N: sleet, frozen rain *...began to hail as the temperature dropped...* *...hail the size of quarters for more than a half hour...*
HALE	VB: compel to come or go, summons to court, call *...decided to hale him into court...* ADJ: strong, healthy *...feeling hale and hearty...*

HAIR	N: threadlike outgrowth of the epidermis
	...baby had a full head of hair...
	EXPRESSION
	    do something by a hair = barely do something
	     ...won the race by a hair...

HARE	N: rabbit *...story of the tortoise and the hare...*
HAIRY	ADJ: having a lot of hair, hirsute *...described a hairy monster with three eyes...*
HARRY	VB: harass, annoy *...nothing seemed to harry her when she was painting...*
HARRY	N: proper name
HARE (KRISHNA)	N: religious sect
HOARY	ADJ: white with age, snowy, old *...hoary frost...*

HALF	N: one of two equal parts
	...reduced the amount by half...
HALVE	VB: divide into two equal parts
	...will halve the estate of their parents...
HAVE	VB: hold or maintain as a possession
	...will want to have a copy of the document...
HALVE(S)	Third person singular, present tense of *to halve*
	...halves the orange between the two...
HAVE(S)	Plural of *have*
	N: those who are doing well and own possessions
	...the haves and the have-nots...
HALL	N: passageway or corridor
	N: large room for gatherings
	...congregation will meet in the hall...
HAUL	VB: move goods by wagon, truck, et cetera
	...will haul away the trash...
	N: distance over which something is transported
	...long haul from California to Florida...
	N: large amount gained at one time
	...made a haul in Las Vegas...
	EXPRESSION
	in it for the long haul = in it until the end
	...told him I am in it for the long haul...
HALLOW	VB: revere, set apart as holy
	...hallow the ground where she died...
HOLLOW	ADJ: empty, unfilled, vacant
	...hollow sound coming from the empty tube...
HALO	N: circle of light, corona, aura
	...deserved a halo for the care he gave his elderly mother...
HELLO	N: greeting
	...said hello to everyone in the place...

HAMMOCK	N: hanging bed *...took a nap in the hammock in the yard...*
HUMMOCK	N: hill, mound *...hummock made by the gopher...*
HANGAR	N: storage for airplanes *...had to be put into the hangar for repairs...*
HANGER	N: one who hangs something *...worked as an apprentice to a paperhanger...* N: thing on which something is hung *...put it on a wooden hanger...*
HANG	Principal parts: *hang, hanged, hanged* VB: put to death, suspended by the neck *...hanged for his crime...*
HUNG	Principal parts: *hang, hung, hung* VB: suspend, fasten *...hung the picture over the fireplace...*
HARDY	ADJ: refers to living things that are able to withstand adversity, robust *...from very hardy stock...* *...cactus is a hardy plant...*
HEARTY	ADJ: giving unqualified support, genuine, sincere *...his hearty support of the project...* ADJ: exhibiting vigorous good health *...feeling hale and hearty...* ADJ: abundant, nourishing *...ate a hearty meal...* *...enjoyed a hearty beef stew...* ADJ: warm, thorough *...gave him a hearty welcome...* *...lent our hearty support...*
HAUGHTY	ADJ: blatantly and disdainfully proud *...haughty attitude made him very unpopular...*

HART	N: male deer, stag
HEART	N: muscular organ
	N: center or essential part of something
	...at the heart of the problem...
	N: playing card in the suit of hearts
	...played the five of hearts...
	N: generous disposition, compassion
	...has a lot of heart as he faces the adversity...
	N: one's innermost character, feelings, or inclinations
	...man after my own heart...
	EXPRESSIONS
	learn by heart = memorize
	...learned the entire text by heart...
	take to heart = consider seriously
	...took to heart the doctor's warning...
HEARTH	N: fireplace
	...sat near the hearth to keep warm...
HAY	N: grass used for feeding livestock
HEY	INTERJ: call attention, express surprise or exultation
HEAL	VB: bring back to health
	...sore is beginning to heal...
	VB: mend, patch up
	...tried to heal the division between the sisters...
HEEL	N: part of the foot or shoe
	N: contemptible person
	...always acts like a real heel with her...
	N: crusty end of a loaf of bread
	N: bottom portion
	EXPRESSION
	well heeled = rich, well to do
	(From a time when only rich people could afford to put new soles and heels on their shoes.)
HE'LL	CONTRACTION: *he will*

HEALTHFUL	ADJ: good for the health, contributing to being hale or sound, beneficial to health of body or mind ...*follows a healthful diet*... ...*healthful exercise regimen*...
HEALTHY	ADJ: having or showing good health, well ADJ: enjoying health or vigor of body, mind, or spirit ...*mentally healthy outlook*... ...*feels healthy after battling pneumonia for a month*...
HEAR	VB: perceive with the ear ...*does not hear well*... EXPRESSION *will not hear of it* = will not tolerate it or accept it
HERE	ADV: in this place
HEARD	Past tense and past participle of *to hear* ...*have heard about her tantrums*...
HERD	N: group of animals ...*herd of buffalo on the prairie*...
HEARSAY	N/ADJ: rumor (what you "heard said") ...*would not accept the hearsay evidence*...
HERESY	N: sacrilege, dissent, unorthodoxy ...*could not believe the heresy coming out of his mouth*...
HEAVY	ADJ: weighty ...*too heavy for the chair*... ADJ: deep, important ...*heavy topic for the evening discussion*...
HEFTY	ADJ: robust, sturdy, rugged ...*hefty project to take on*...

HE'D	CONTRACTION: *he had* or *he would*
HEED	VB: pay attention to, notice, regard
	...need to heed the warning...
HEIST	N: robbery, holdup
	...involved in the heist at the bank...
HOIST	VB/N: lift, raise
	...hoist the bundle onto the rack...
	...used a hoist to lift the bales of hay...
HEROIN	N: drug
	...addicted to heroin...
HEROINE	N: female hero
	...playing the heroine in the play...
HETERO-	Prefix meaning "different" as in *heterosexual* and *heteromorphy*
HOMO-	Prefix meaning "same" as in *homogenized* and *homonym*
HEW	VB: cut with an ax or knife
	...continued to hew the wood carving...
HUE	N: particular color
	...different hue in the daylight than in the twilight...
	EXPRESSION
	hue and cry = loud outcry, hubbub
	...hue and cry about the rise in prices...
HUGH	N: proper name

HI	N: greeting
HIE	VB: hasten, go quickly
	...hie for cover when the rain begins...
HIGH	ADJ: of greater degree, amount, cost
	...consistently high prices...
	ADJ: advanced toward the most active or culminating period
	...high season in the desert in the winter...
	ADJ: exalted in character, noble
	...set out on the mission with high purpose...
	ADJ: very serious, grave
	...accused of high crimes...
	ADJ: critical, climactic
	...high point of the story...
	ADV: taller/bigger, farther
	...high up on the wall...
	SLANG: drunk, drugged
	...get high every night of the week...
HEIGH-HO	N: used typically to express boredom, weariness, or sadness or sometimes as cry of encouragement
	...heigh-ho of the seven dwarfs...
HIE(D)	Past tense and past participle of *to hie*
	VB: hurry
	...hied for cover as the shooting began...
HIDE	VB: conceal
	...tried to hide from the police...
	N: animal skin
HIGH(ER)	ADJ: farther up; loftier as in elevation, cost, et cetera
	...gasoline prices keep going higher...
HIRE	VB: employ
	...trying to hire new workers for the job...
	N: payment for the temporary use of something
	...looking for a cab for hire...

HIM	Objective case of the third person, singular, masculine pronoun
HYMN	N: song in praise or honor of God
	...sang her favorite hymns at the funeral...
HIPPIE	N: nonconformist
	...is a hippie from the 60's...
HIPPY	ADJ: having big hips
	...even she looked hippy with the horizontal stripes of the fabric...
HIS	PRO/ADJ: third person singular, masculine, possessive form
HISS	VB/N: murmur, shush, jeer, mock
	...hear the hiss of the crowd...
HISTORICAL	ADJ: providing evidence for a fact of history
	...following the historical facts...
	ADJ: based on people or events of the past
	...need the historical perspective...
HYSTERICAL	ADJ: wildly excited, subject to uncontrollable fits of laughter or crying
	...was hysterical upon hearing news of his death...
HO(S)	INTERJ: used especially to attract attention to something specified
	...land ho...
	INTERJ: what Santa Claus says
HOE(S)	VB: cultivate
	...intends to hoe the plot to prepare it for planting...
	N: tool used in gardening
HOEDOWN	N: square dance (From "Put your hoe down and dance")
HOECAKE	N: small cake made of cornmeal
HOSE	N: flexible tube for conveying fluid
	...major leak in the hose...
	N: outer covering for the legs, nylons
	...not really wearing hose anymore...

HOARD	VB: save greedily, store away *...tends to hoard things in the cupboards...*
HORDE	N: overwhelming number of people or things *...horde of shoppers for the sale...*
WHORE(D)	Past tense and past participle of *to whore* VB/N: pursue a faithless, unworthy, or idolatrous desire *...whored himself in pursuit of the position in the firm...*
HOARSE	ADJ: sounding rough and deep *...hoarse from shouting at the game...*

HORSE	N: four-legged animal
	N: basketball game
	EXPRESSIONS
	    horse around = play, roughhouse
	    eat like a horse = eat a lot

HOLD UP	VB: rob at gun point *...intended to hold up the shipment for lack of payment...* VB: call attention to *...will hold up the registration for them to see...*
HOLDUP	N: robbery *...was a holdup at the bank...*
HOLE UP	VB: take refuge or shelter in *...hole up while the cops are still looking for him...*

(Slightly out of alphabetical order to make it fit on the page!)

HOLD
VB: grab onto
...tried to take hold of the rope...
N: full comprehension
...get hold of exactly what is happening...
N: interior of a ship below decks, especially where cargo is stowed
...stored in the hold of the ship...
EXPRESSIONS

not hold a candle to = is not so good
...it did not hold a candle to her sister's performance...
doesn't hold water = argument that isn't valid
get hold of = obtain, grasp, understand
...cannot get hold of the math...
hold one's own = withstand, equal to
...tried to hold her own with her older brother...
hold the fort = take care of things
...will hold the fort while I am away...
hold court = exclaim, explain, talk in front of people
...Margie Holds Court...
hold out = resist
...will hold out for more money...
hold one's horses = stop
hold one's tongue = don't say something bad
...try to hold my tongue about her behavior...
left holding the bag = left to pay for someone else's problems
on hold = waiting

HOLE(D)
Past tense and past participle of *to hole*
VB: make a hole in
VB: drive into a hole (golf)
...holed the ball from 40 yards...

HOLE	N: open, hollow place
WHOLE	N: entire thing
	...parts of the whole...
	ADJ: having all its parts, complete
	...need to make it whole again...
HOLEY	ADJ: having holes in it
	...socks were holey...
HOLLY	N: kind of tree or shrub
HOLY	ADJ: sacred
	...consider it holy space...
WHOLLY	ADV: entirely
	...cannot be wholly sure of it...
HOME	N: abode, house
	...makes his home on the island...
	EXPRESSION
	home in on = go toward an objective
	...is homing in on her whereabouts...
HONE	VB: sharpen, perfect
	...hone his skill in carpentry in order to enter the workforce...
HOMELY	ADJ: not attractive, plain
	...said to be homely...
HOMEY	ADJ: comfy
	...homey feeling about his apartment...

HOOP(S)	N: ring, circular strip
	...large hoop earrings...
	EXPRESSION
	play hoops = play basketball
WHOOP(S)	VB/N: loud yell
	...let out a whoop of joy...
WHOOPING COUGH	N: disease marked by a very loud cough
OOPS	INTERJ: said when one has made a mistake
	...Oops. I didn't mean to say that...
HOSPITABLE	ADJ: giving welcome, food, or shelter to guests or strangers
	...was very hospitable to the guests...
	ADJ: favorable, receptive
	...hospitable environment for the success we were seeking...
HOSPITAL	N: place where sick or injured people or animals are cared for
	...entered the hospital for the infection...
HOSTEL	N: inexpensive hotel
	N: supervised lodging for young travelers
	...stayed in the youth hostels...
HOSTILE	ADJ: of or relating to an enemy, unfriendly
	...always acting hostile to his parents...
HOUR(S)	N: 60 minutes
	...in the ER an hour before they saw us...
	...seemed like hours before she came out...
OUR(S)	First person plural, objective case, possessive adjective/pronoun
	...cannot tell their house from ours...
	...our story needs to be told...
HUMAN	N: person
	ADJ: having forms and qualities characteristic of people or human beings
	...seemed to have a human form...
HUMANE	ADJ: kind, merciful, compassionate, sympathetic
	...promoting the humane treatment of prisoners...

HUMERUS	N: long bone in the upper arm *...clean break of the humerus...*
HUMOROUS	ADJ: funny, entertaining *...humorous look at the situation...*
HUMIDITY	N: dampness, amount of moisture in the air *...humidity in Florida was unbearable...*
HUMILITY	N: modest sense of one's own importance *...accepted the award with great humility...*
HURDLE	VB: jump over a barrier *...tried to hurdle the gate with disastrous results...* N: barrier, obstacle *...put a hurdle in his path...*
HURTLE	VB: hurl, fling *...hurtle the ball through the air...*
HURL	VB: throw *...hurl the bottle into the mirror...* SLANG: vomit
HYBRID	N: offspring of two animals or plants of different races, breeds, varieties *...comes from a hybrid fruit...* N: composite, mix, fusion N: car that runs partly on electricity and partly on gasoline *...drives a hybrid to save on gas...*
HIGH BRED	ADJ: of aristocratic blood *...clear from her behavior that she is high bred...*
HYPER-	Prefix meaning "over, above" as in *hypertension* and *hypersensitive*
HYPO-	Prefix meaning "below, under" as in *hypoglycemia* and *hypoallergenic*

CHAPTER 9
THE LETTER *I*

IDEAL N/ADJ: standard of perfection, beauty, or excellence
...location is ideal for what we need...
...represents the ideal for this type of endeavor...

IDLE VB: lay off
...will idle more than 100 workers...
ADJ: doing nothing, not busy
...plant is idle during the strike...
ADJ: lazy

IDOL N: any object worshipped as a god
...is an idol to all the youngsters...

IDYLL N: simple descriptive work in poetry or prose that deals with rustic life, pastoral scenes, or suggests a mood of peace
...wrote an idyll for the new book of poetry...

ILEUM N: part of the small intestine
...blockage was discovered in the ileum...

ILIUM N: bone of the pelvis
...stress on the ilium because of the surgery...

ILLEGIBLE ADJ: undecipherable, very hard or impossible to read
...illegible signature...

INELIGIBLE ADJ: not suitable, not qualified
...is ineligible for the team...

IMMEASURABLE ADJ: incapable of being measured, indefinitely extensive
...love for him is immeasurable...

UNMEASURABLE ADJ: physical distance that is incapable of being measured
...distance is unmeasurable because of the obstacles...

IMMORAL	ADJ: having no standards, corrupt, dishonest *...immoral conduct in office...*
IMMORTAL	ADJ: capable of living forever *...immortal character in "Miracle on 34th Street"...*
IMMUNITY	N: protection from disease *...has an immunity against malaria...*
IMPUNITY	N: protection from prosecution *...received impunity from prosecution...*
IMPLICATION	Noun form of *to imply* (something done by speakers and writers) N: suggestion without stating directly *...was an implication in the book that she would expose his past...*
INFERENCE	Noun form of *to infer* (something done by readers and listeners) N: conclusion from evidence presented *...inference I drew from what she said...*
IMPLY	VB: suggest without stating, express indirectly (something done by speakers and writers) *...email seems to imply that he will not be back with us...*
INFER	VB: deduce, conclude from evidence (something done by readers and listeners) *...did infer from what I had read that she was ill...*
IMPOTENT	ADJ: lacking power, strength, or vitality *...felt impotent in the face of such a formidable force...* ADJ: unable to get an erection
IMPRUDENT	ADJ: lacking in wisdom *...would be imprudent to invest that money right now...*
IMPUDENT	ADJ: lacking modesty ADJ: marked by contemptuous or cocky boldness or disregard for others *...impudent behavior around his parents...*

IN	PREP: indicates inclusion, location, or position within limits
	...in the lake...
	...in the summer months...
	...wounded in the leg...
INN	N: hotel
INANE	ADJ: nonsensical, silly
	...his inane comment about her magnificent performance...
INSANE	ADJ: crazy
	...driving at an insane speed...
	...admitted to an institution for the criminally insane...
INCIDENCE	N: rate of occurrence
	...high incidence of robbery in the area...
INCIDENT(S)	Plural of *incident*
	N: happening, event
	...several incidents of robbery last year...
INCITE	VB: urge to action, arouse
	...incite the crowd to storm the building...
	EXPRESSION
	incite to riot = rile up a crowd to commit an illegal act
INSIGHT	N: ability to see and understand clearly the nature of things
	...seems to have insight into those issues...
IN SIGHT	PREP PHRASE: in view, within one's range of vision
	...keep the children in sight at all times...
INCREDIBLE	ADJ: too unusual or improbable to be possible, unbelievable
	...incredible to think it has been five years...
INCREDULOUS	ADJ: unwilling or unable to believe, doubting, skeptical
	...remain incredulous that she could accomplish that alone...

INCUBATE (-TION)	VB/N: keep warm, hatch, nurture
	...incubate the eggs before they hatch...
	...have to wait for the incubation period...
INTUBATE (-TION)	N: insert of a tube
	...tried unsuccessfully to intubate the patient...
	...insisted there be no intubation...

INDEPENDENCE	N: freedom
	...worked hard for his independence...
INDEPENDENT(S)	Plural of *independent*
	N: those not under the control of someone else
	N: those not of any political party
	...independents could sway this election...

INDICT	VB: charge with an offense, accuse
	...will indict him on the charge of murder...
INDICTMENT	N: action or legal process of charging someone with a crime
	N: formal written statement framed by a prosecuting authority and affirmed by a jury, charging a person with an offense
	...indictment handed down on Friday...
INDITE	VB: compose, write, put into words
	...was going to indite a lovely poem for her...

INDIGENOUS	ADJ: having originated in and being produced, growing, living, or occurring naturally in a particular region or environment
	...plant is indigenous to the arid land...
INDIGENT	ADJ: poor, needy, destitute
	...found herself indigent and alone...
	N: person at a level of poverty in which real hardship and deprivation are suffered and comforts in life are wholly lacking
	...spoke with an indigent person in need of help...
INDIGNANT	ADJ: feeling or expressing anger or scorn
	...indignant over the circumstances of the firing...

INDUCE	VB: cause to happen
	...induce her labor...
	...induce her to talk with us about what happened...
INDUCT	VB: take in as a member, install
	...will induct him into the Baseball Hall of Fame...
	...will induct her into a scholastic society...
	VB: enroll for military training or service
	...induct him into the Marines...
INDUSTRIAL	ADJ: pertaining to manufacturing industries
	...part of the industrial complex in the center of the city...
INDUSTRIOUS	ADJ: hardworking
	...industrious young man has accomplished much...
INFARCTION	N: heart attack that leaves an area of the heart dead
	...suffered an infarction at work...
INFRACTION	N: violation of a law
	...charged with an infraction...
INFECT(ED)	VB: contaminate, corrupt
	...will infect the whole area...
INFEST(ED)	VB: spread or swarm in or over in a troublesome manner
	...slum is infested with crime...
	...kitchen infested with ants...
	...shark-infested waters...
INFLECT	VB: add an ending to a word to show its characteristics
	...inflect an s to show the plural...
INFLICT	N: impose, wreak, cause
	...inflict the harsh measures upon the lowest employees...

INFECTION	N: contamination, illness *...infection centered in the gut...*
INFLECTION	N: change in the timbre of the voice *...anger showed in the inflection of her voice...*
INFLICTION	N: blow that causes suffering *...infliction of bodily harm...*
INGENIOUS	ADJ: clever, skillful at inventing, resourceful, cleverly made and planned *...ingenious contraption that he build...*
INGENUOUS	ADJ: sincere, open, honest, naive *...ingenuous young boy without any wile...* ADJ: natural
INGÉNUE	N: native girl or young woman N: young actress *...ingénue stole the show from the veterans...*
INGEST	VB: take something into the body *...ingest some form of poison...*
INJECT	VB: introduce, instill, insert *...need to inject new energy into the project...*
IN JEST	PREP PHRASE: jokingly *...said it in jest...*
INHABIT	VB: live in, reside in *...residence too big to inhabit by one family...*
INHIBIT	VB: restrain, hinder *...presence of the boss does not inhibit them...*
INHUMAN	ADJ: brutal, ruthless, heartless *...efforts seemed inhuman...*
INHUMANE	ADJ: cruel, sadistic *...subjected to inhumane treatment...*

INNOCENCE	N: virtue, purity, blamelessness *...proclaimed his innocence to all...*
INNOCENT(S)	Plural of *innocent* N: those without sin or guilt *...law was to protect the innocents...*
INSOLENT	ADJ: insulting, contemptuous in speech or conduct, overbearing *...insolent behavior of the rebellious young man toward his teachers...*
INSULIN	N: pancreatic hormone used in the treatment and control of diabetes *...tests showed an insulin imbalance...*
INSOLUBLE	ADJ: does not dissolve *...oil is insoluble in water...*
INSOLVABLE	ADJ: not capable of being solved *...insolvable problem between the warring parties...*
INSOLVENT	ADJ: cannot pay debts *...financially insolvent and cannot pay the bills...*
INTELLIGENT	ADJ: having intelligence, able to learn quickly, alert, wise *...seems to be intelligent and very capable...*
INTELLIGIBLE	ADJ: capable of being understood *...intelligible words on the tape...*
INTENSE	ADJ: to an extreme degree *...intense negotiations between the two sides...*
INTENT(S)	N: purposes, meanings *...for all intents and purposes...*
IN TENTS	PREP PHRASE: in a portable shelter *...living in tents after the disaster...*
INTER-	Prefix meaning "between" as in *interactive* and *intersperse*
INTRA-	Prefix meaning "within" as in *intrastate* and *intracellular*

INTER	Pronounced /in-<u>tur</u>/
	VB: bury, deposit a dead body into the earth or in a tomb
	...will inter the body on Friday...
INTERN	Pronounced /in-<u>turn</u>/
	VB: impound, confine (wartime)
	...intern the Japanese during World War II...
	Pronounced /<u>in</u>-turn/
	VB: work for nothing to learn a skill
	...will intern at the local hospital...
	N: one who works for nothing in order to learn a trade or profession
	...was an intern with the company for a year...
INTERNIST	N: specialist in internal medicine
ENTER	VB: go into
	...intends to enter the field of astrophysics...
INTERRED	Past tense and past participle of *to inter*
	...interred in a cemetery on the edge of town...
INTERNED	Past tense and past participle of *to intern*
	...interned with us for a year...
ENTERED	Past tense and past participle of *to enter*
	...entered the hospital through the ER...
INTERCESSION	N: pleading on behalf of someone else
	...his intercession on her behalf with her parents...
INTERSESSION	N: period between semesters
	...took an intersession class...
INTERSTATE	ADJ: existing between states
	...ICC regulates interstate traffic among the Northeastern states...
INTRASTATE	ADJ: existing within a single state
	...intrastate traffic within Indiana...
INTESTATE	ADV: having made no valid will
	...died intestate, which led to a huge family fight...

INVADE	VB: enter by force, intrude *...tried to invade my space...*
INVEIGH(ED)	Past tense and past participle of *to inveigh* VB: protest, complain, scorn *...inveighed against the unfairness of the tax code...*
IRRELEVANT	ADJ: not relevant, inapplicable *...that statement is irrelevant to your argument...*
IRREVERENT	ADJ: lacking proper respect or seriousness *...showed an irreverent attitude toward my beliefs...*
IRRIGATE	VB: supply with water *...need to irrigate the fields...*
IRRITATE	VB: vex, annoy *...will irritate the rash even more...*
ITS	ADJ: possessive form of *it* *...had its origins in the 18th century...*
IT'S	CONTRACTION: *it is* *...it's going to be fun...*

CHAPTER 10
THE LETTER *J*

JACK	VB/N: device for raising heavy weights *...needed to use the jack because he couldn't lift it alone...*
JOCK	SLANG: athlete *...loved being a jock...*
JACKAL	N: small animal N: person who performs menial tasks for another *...acted as a jackal for his brother...*
JEKYLL	N: split personality *...was a Jekyll and Hyde...*
JAM	VB: press into a tight place *...tried to jam everything into the tiny room...* VB: render unable to perform *...paper tended to jam in the printer...* N: jellylike preserves N: crowded mass that impedes or blocks traffic *...resultant traffic jam was a nightmare...* EXPRESSION *in a jam* = in trouble
JAM SESSION	N: impromptu performance by a group especially of jazz musicians that is characterized by improvisation
JAMB	N: side post of a doorway or window frame *...sprained her toe on the door jamb...*
JAMS	ACRONYM: Judicial Arbitration and Mediation Services, "rent-a-judge"
JEALOUS	ADJ: envious of something someone else has or is *...jealous of her fame...*
ZEALOUS	ADJ: enthusiastic *...zealous in his pursuit of knowledge...*

JEWEL	N: gem, something valued
	...was a jewel to work with...
JOULE	N: unit of work
	...measure that in joules...

JEWELRY	N: personal adornment
	...wedding ring was the only jewelry she wore...
JEWRY	N: Jewish people
JURY	N: group chosen to decide guilt or innocence
	...sat on the jury of a murder trial...

JINKS	N: pranks
	...part of the jinks played on his parents...
JINX	VB: bring bad luck
	...constant tardiness is going to jinx her success...

JOIST	N: supporting beam
	...problem with the joist that caused the wall to fall...
JOUST	VB: combat via horseback
	...participated in a joust...

JUDICIAL	ADJ: relating to the courts
	...under judicial review...
JUDICIOUS	ADJ: wise
	...judicious use of his time...

JUKE	VB: fake, deceive
	...will try to juke his parents into thinking he is in school...
JUTE	N: loosely woven fiber
	...stored in bags made of jute...

CHAPTER 11
THE LETTER *K*

KEY

VB: damage a surface by using a key
...tried to key his car...
N: means of gaining entrance
...used his hidden key to get in...
N: list of answers
...need a key to check my work...
ADJ: crucial, important
...is a key witness for the defense...

QUAY

Pronounced /key/ (rhymes with *see*)
N: wharf
...sat on the quay to fish...

CAY

Pronounced /key/ or /kay/
N: coral reef
...did the dive near the cay...

KIBBUTZ

N: communal living community in Israel
...lived on a kibbutz as a kid...

KIBITZ

VB: chat
...time to kibitz as we played cards...

KIND

ADJ: nice, sympathetic
...needed to be kind to his neighbors...

KINE

Pronounced /kine/ (rhymes with *mine*)
N: cattle

KNAVE	N: rogue
	...known to be a knave with women...
NAVE	N: main part of a church
	...nave was filled to capacity...
NAIVE	ADJ: deficient in worldly wisdom or informed judgment
	...so naive that she believed every word he said...
KNEAD	VB: mix by pressing and squeezing
	...have to knead the dough for ten minutes...
NEED	VB: require, have to, must
	...need to get a flu shot...
	N: necessity
	...felt the need to reveal what he knew...
KNEE(D)	VB: strike with the knee, as in the groin
	...kneed in the groin during the soccer match...
KNEE	N: middle of the leg
	...injury to his knee...
NÉE	Pronounced /nay/ (rhymes with *say*)
	French: *born as*
	...Jane Simpson, née Miller...
KNELL	N: sounding of a bell
	...was a death knell to the project...
KNOLL	N: hill
	...sat on the grassy knoll in Dallas...
KNEW	Past tense of *to know*
NEW	ADJ: having been in existence only a short time (opposite of *old*)
	...new to the neighborhood...
GNU	N: animal

KNIGHT	N: noble and brave soldier of the British feudal period
	N: person exhibiting these qualities
	...viewed him as her knight in shining armor...
NIGHT	N: period of darkness between sunset and sunrise
	...bad dreams always came at night...
KNIGHTLY	ADJ: noble, courageous
	...knightly actions after the accident...
NIGHTLY	ADV: each and every night
	...getting the kids to bed was a nightly struggle...
KNIT	VB: bind together
	...knit his brows as he considered the problem...
	...was a closely knit family...
NIT	N: small bug
	...picked the nits from the sweater...
NITWIT	N: someone of small intelligence
	...always thought of him as a nitwit...
NITPICK	N: find fault with needlessly
	...always did nitpick everything I did...
KNOB	N: rounded protuberance
	...needs a knob on it to turn the mechanism...
NOB	N: one in a superior position
	...lives on Nob Hill in San Francisco...
	EXPRESSION
	hobnob with the brass = associate familiarly with superiors

KNOT	N: fastening made by tying together pieces of rope or cord
	...*tied it into a knot*...
	N: tight constriction
	...*stomach was in knots*...
	N: lump or swelling
	...*has a knot in the muscle*...
	N: measure of speed at sea (greater than one mile per hour)
	...*speed at an average of 30 knots*...
	EXPRESSION
	tie the knot = get married
NOT	ADV: negative
NAUGHT	N: nothing
	...*all her efforts came to naught*...
KNOTTY	ADJ: having knots
	...*made of knotty pine*...
	ADJ: tangled up, complicated
	...*has a knotty problem*...
NAUGHTY	ADJ: guilty of disobedience or misbehavior
KNOW	VB: have information about
NO	ADV: negative
KNOW(S)	Third person singular, present tense of *to know*
	VB: be aware of
	...*knows that there are problems with the plan*...
NOSE	N: part of the face that bears the nostrils
NO'S	Plural of *no* (one of two forms)
	...*answer with yes's and no's*...
NOES	Plural of *no* (one of two forms)
	...*answer with yeses and noes*...

CHAPTER 12
THE LETTER *L*

LABORATORY N: location where experiments take place
...works in a laboratory for cancer research...

LAVATORY N: bathroom, washroom
...spent time in the lavatory with a stomach problem...

LACHES N: delay in asserting a legal right

LATCH(ES) VB/N: lock, close
...latches the gate to keep the dog in...

LACK(S) Third person singular, present tense of *to lack*
VB: is deficient in, is without
...lacks a clear direction...

LAC(S) N: resinous substance used chiefly in the form of shellac

LAX ADJ: loose, slack, not strict
...rules were rather lax...

LACUNA N: missing part
...lacuna in the explanation...

LAGUNA SPANISH: *pool, lagoon*

LAGOON N: body of water separated from the ocean by sand dunes
...stagnant water in the lagoon...

LADDER N: structure for climbing up and down
...placed the ladder against the house...

LATTER N: second of two persons or things mentioned
...John and Joe, the latter of whom...

LATER ADV: at a future time
ADV: at or toward the end
...later in life...

LADE	VB: load
	...will lade the ship later this evening...
LADING	Present participle of *to lade*
	...received a bill of lading...
LAID	[See *lay/lie/lie*]
	Past tense and past participle of *to lay*
	No such word as *layed*
	VB: place, put
	...laid it on the shelf...
LAYED	This word does not exist!
LAIN	[See *lay/lie/lie*]
	Past participle of *to lie*
	VB: rest, recline
	...have lain here too long...
LANE	N: path
	...down a narrow lane...
LAIR	N: shelter for a wild animal
	...stumbled onto a bear's lair as we hiked...
LAYER	VB/N: sheet, cover, stratum
	...several layers of intrigue...
LIAR	N: one who does not tell the truth
	...accused of being a liar...
LAM	N: sudden flight
	EXPRESSION
	on the lam = on the run
	...has been on the lam more than three weeks...
LAMB	N: young sheep
	...tended to the lamb...

LANGUAGE   N: body of words used by a people
...does not speak the English language natively...

LANGUISH   VB: pine away, be feeble or weak
...tough to watch him languish with the illness...

LAST   VB: continue in time, go on, endure
...won't last much longer...
VB: be enough for the needs of
...supplies will last no more than a week...
N: form which is shaped like the human foot and over which a shoe is shaped or repaired
N: at the end of a period of time, finally
...at last you have come home...
N/ADJ: farthest from a specified quality, attitude, or likelihood
...would be the last to fall for that...
ADJ: following all the rest
...the last one out of the building...
ADJ: only one remaining
...down to your last dollar...
ADJ: final stage
...his last hours on earth...
ADJ: most recent
...last week that we are going to do that...
ADJ: conclusive
...there is no last answer...
ADV: after all others, at the end, most recently
...saw him last in New York...
ADV: in conclusion
...last, I would like to...

LATEST   ADJ: most recent or currently fashionable style or development
...latest in diving techniques...
EXPRESSION
    at the latest = last acceptable time

LATH	N: thin, narrow strips of wood *...lath and plaster...*
LATHE	N: machine in which things are rotated on a horizontal axis *...used a lathe to form the lamp base...*
LATTICE	N: interlaced structure *...flowers growing on the lattice in front of the porch...*
LETTUCE	N: leafy vegetable
LAUD	VB: praise, extol *...laud his efforts on behalf of the food pantry...*
LOUD	ADJ: noisy, not quiet *...defended his client in loud tones...*
LAUNCH	VB/N: initiate, instigate *...waiting for the launch of the new product...*
LUNCH	N: meal in the middle of the day
LAY	VB: put, place The principal parts of the verb are *...lay the book down today...* *...laid the book down yesterday...* *...have laid the book down each evening this week...*
LIE	VB: rest, recline The principal parts of the verb are *...lie in bed today...* *...lay in bed yesterday...* *...have lain in bed all day...* VB: tell a falsehood The principal parts of the verb are *...lie today...* *...lied yesterday...* *...have always lied about that...*

LAY(S)	[See *lay/lie/lie*] VB: put or place *...lays the keys on the table...*
LEI(S)	N: Hawaiian necklace of flowers *...came home with three leis around her neck...*
LAZE	VB: pass time in idleness or relaxation *...decided to laze around the house...*
LEACH	VB: percolate, pull out of *...salt from the lake will leach into the surrounding soil...*
LEECH	N: blood-sucking worm N: person who takes from others *...is a leech on the whole family...*
LEAD	Pronounced /leed/ (rhymes with *seed*) VB/N: conduct, guide, direct *...chosen to lead the discussion...* Pronounced /led/ (rhymes with *said*) N: heavy metallic element *...too much lead in the water...*
LED	Past tense and past participle of *to lead* VB: guide, be foremost *...led the tour of the plant...* *...led in the polls...*
LEDE	N: opening sentence of a news article, summarizing the main points *...lede caught my attention...* *...lede was insubstantial...*
LEADER	N: person who guides
LITER	N: measurement *...needs to drink two liters of water per day...*
LEAF	VB: page through a book *...will leaf through the book to find it...* N: part of a plant N: page of a book
LIEF	ADV: soon, gladly, rather *...as lief go with him...*

LEAK	VB: enter or escape through an opening *...did leak into the water system...* N: crack, hole to let something escape *...leak the details of the crime...*
LEEK	N: vegetable
LEAN	VB: rest at an angle on something *...needed to lean in to hear every word...* VB: depend or rely upon *...needed to lean on my brother during that tough time...* ADJ: with little or no fat *...bought very lean hamburger...*
LIEN	N: legal claim on the property of another for the payment of a debt *...placed a lien on the property...*
LEASE(D)	Past tense and past participle of *to lease* VB: rent property for a specified period of time *...leased it for a year...*
LEAST	N: smallest amount, degree *...the least I could do for him...* ADJ: smallest in degree or size *...least desirable property...* ADJ: lowest in position or importance *...least important worker in the department...*
LEST	CONJ: for fear that *...leaving it with him lest I lose it...*
LECTOR	N: person who speaks publicly *...was a lector for the church on Sundays...*
LECTURE	VB/N: speech, reprimand *...had to lecture him about his behavior on the job...*
LECTERN	N: stand for notes of a speaker *...stood at the lectern...*

LEGION	N: very large number, military force *...had a legion of medical problems that had to be addressed...*
LESION	N: change in the structure of tissue *...had a massive lesion just under his eye...*
LEGISLATOR	N: lawmaker or elected member of a lawmaking body *...spoke with the legislator from my district...*
LEGISLATURE	N: lawmaking body *...going to speak in front of the state legislature...*
LEND(S)	Third person singular, present tense of *to lend* VB: make a loan *...lends him money on a regular basis...* VB: give for temporary use or condition *...lends him her watch for the race...*
LENS	N: piece of glass used in eyeglasses N: part of the eye *...had to replace the lens...*
LESSEN	VB: make less, decrease *...need to lessen my workload...*
LESSON	N: something learned or studied, instructive experience *...learned a valuable lesson...*
LESSER	ADJ: smaller or less important, to a reduced degree *...pled guilty to a lesser offense...*
LESSOR	N: one who lets or leases *...finally met the lessor of the apartment...*
LET(S)	Third person singular, present tense of *to let* VB: allow *...lets her do whatever she wants...*
LET'S	CONTRACTION: *let us* *...let's ask him to do it...*

LEVEE	N: embankment for preventing water from spilling over *...flood was from a break in the levee...*
LEVY	VB/N: impose or collect a tax or fine, fine *...will levy a 5 percent increase in taxes...* *...levy will be imposed...*
LIABLE	ADJ: responsible, legally obligated *...is liable for the attorney fees...* ADJ: likely to occur (when the outcome is expected to be negative) *...liable to fail if you try that...*
LIKELY	ADJ: likely to occur (when the outcome is expected to be positive) *...likely to succeed if you try that...*
LIBEL	N: written or printed statement that injures a person's reputation *...accused of libel by the newspaper...*
APT	(Incorrectly used to mean *likely* or *liable*) ADJ: having an ability to do something *...is apt in the arts...*
LICHEN	N: ground cover *...hills covered with lichen in the spring...*
LIKEN	VB: compare *...always try to liken her to her sister...*
LIE	[See *lay/lie/lie*] VB: recline, rest *...intended to lie on the beach...* VB/N: untruth *...recognized that he would lie about the whole incident...* EXPRESSION *lie low* = bide one's time but remain ready for action
LYE	N: strong caustic alkaline solution used in making soap *...lye burned through the rug...*

LIFELONG	ADJ: continuing through life
LIVELONG	ADJ: whole, entire
	..."*I've been working on the railroad all the livelong day*"...
LIGHTENING	Present participle of *to lighten*
	VB: make lighter or brighter, reduce the load
	...*needs to be lightening his workload*...
LIGHTNING	N: discharge or flash of electricity in the sky
	...*heavy lightning and thunder*...
LIGHTING	Present participle of *to light*
	VB: illuminate, ignite
	...*was lighting a candle*...
	N: illumination
	...*very dim lighting*...
LITERAL	ADJ: obvious, not figurative
	...*received a literal translation of the passage*...
LITTORAL	ADJ: growing near the shore
	...*littoral plants in the area*...
LOAD	VB: place on or in something
	...*load the packages on the truck*...
	N: burden
	...*bearing a heavy load*...
	N: shipping unit
	...*load of tomatoes bound for market*...
LODE	N: major vein of metallic ore
	...*looking to find the lode*...
	EXPRESSION
	hit the mother lode = find the major source or supply (can be capped)
	...*hit the mother lode when she met him*...
LOW(ED)	Past tense and past participle of *to low*
	VB: sound a cow makes
	...*cattle lowed in the field*...

LOAN	(Very correct English says this form should not be used as a verb) N: something lent *...received a loan from the bank...*
LONE	ADJ: standing by itself, solitary *...lone person left on the stage...*
LEND	VB: give for temporary use on the condition it will be returned *...lend him my car for the evening...*
LOANER	N: car that one has borrowed *...driving a loaner while my car is in the shop...*
LONER	N: one who stays by himself *...is a loner with few friends...*
LOATH	ADJ: reluctant, unwilling to do something contrary to one's way of thinking (usually used after a form of the verb *to be*) *...am loath of get involved in that problem...* *...was loath to be a part of that...*
LOATHE	VB: dislike greatly and often with disgust or intolerance *...loathe his inappropriate behavior...* VB: detest, abhor, hate *...loathe being in that situation...*
LOCAL	ADJ: having to do with a certain place *...was a local hangout...* *...took the local train and stopped at every street...*
LOCALE	N: place where something specific occurred or will occur, locality *...never had that kind of food in that locale...*
LOCH(S)	SCOTTISH: *lakes*
LOCK(S)	Third person singular, present tense of *to lock* VB/N: fasten, bar *...always locks the door whether he is in the house or out...*
LOX	N: smoked salmon

LOCUS N: place, location
...within the locus of the town...

LOCUST N: type of grasshopper
...plagued by locusts...

LOOP VB/N: circle around
...made three loops of the block before we stopped...

LOUPE N: jeweler's magnifying glass
...studied it through the loupe...

LOOSE ADJ: not tight, not bound together or fastened down
...tooth was loose...
...suitcase was lying loose in the cargo hold...
ADJ: careless about morals or conduct
...accused her of having loose morals...

LOSE VB: mislay or be deprived of
...do not want to lose this game...

LOSS N: harm or privation resulting from loss or separation
...felt the loss acutely...
N: person or thing or an amount that is lost, as in killed, captured, or wounded soldiers
...huge loss of life in the most recent battle...
N: failure to gain, win, obtain, or utilize
...loss was particularly heartfelt...
N: decrease in the amount, magnitude, or degree
...loss of power after the election...
N: amount of an insured's financial detriment by death or damage that the insurer becomes liable for
...loss is in the millions...

LOST Past tense and past participle of *to lose*
VB: no longer have control of, did not win
...won the battle but lost the war...
ADJ: not tracking, gone, vanished
...felt lost after just one day in class...

LOOSER   ADJ: less tight
...looser now that she has lost more weight...

LOSER   N: one who does not win
...college is a chronic loser in football...

LORE   N: knowledge, learning

LOWER   VB: make low
...going to have to lower his standards...
ADJ: more low than the other
...have a lower opinion of her now...

LUMBAR   ADJ: pertaining to the low back
...always has had trouble with the lumbar area...

LUMBER   VB: plod along, move with a heavy step
...had to lumber along through the heavy mud...
N: wood

LUNG   N: organ that oxygenates the blood
...cancer in the lower lobe of the left lung...

LUNGE   VB: suddenly thrust, attack
...saw him lunge at the small child...

CHAPTER 13
THE LETTER *M*

MACH

N: measurement of an object's speed in relation to the speed of sound
...traveling at Mach 1...

MOCK

VB: make fun of
...always used to mock his younger brother...

MACRO-

Prefix meaning "large" as in *macrobiotics* and *macroeconomics*

MICRO-

Prefix meaning "small" as in *micromanage* and *microscope*

MAD

ADJ: angry
...always mad at something...

MADD

ACRONYM: Mothers Against Drunk Driving
...joined MADD after the accident...

MADDENING

Present participle of *to madden*
VB: anger, enrage
...maddening not to be able to find anything...

MADDING

ADJ: frenzied
...far from the madding crowd...

MADDER

ADJ: more angry
...madder than I have ever been...

MATTER

VB: make a difference
...doesn't matter to me at all...
N: substance
...pure vegetable matter...
...some type of foreign matter on his shoes...

MADE	Past tense and past participle of *to make*
	VB: form, prepare
	...made from cardboard...
	VB: complete, finish
	...made it just in time...
	VB: force
	...made me stay late almost every night...
	VB: construct
	...made from a material I do not recognize...
MAID	N: girl or young, unmarried woman
	N: female servant
MAGNATE	N: important or influential person in any field of activity
	...oil magnate from Saudi Arabia...
MAGNET	N: person or thing that attracts
	...used a magnet to pick up the nails...
	...was a magnet for girls...
MAIL	VB: send by the postal system
	...will mail it tonight...
	N: correspondence transported by the postal system
	N: armor worn by a knight
	...coat of mail...
MALE	N/ADJ: masculine sex
MAIN	N: large pipe
	...break in the water main...
	ADJ: chief in importance
	...main reason for going...
MAINE	N: Northeastern state in the United States
MANE	N: long hair on the neck of a horse or lion
	N: woman's hair, particularly long and thick hair
	...thick red mane...

MALL	N: shaded or enclosed walk or promenade, often for shopping
	...spent the evening at the mall...
MAUL	VB: handle roughly, mangle
	...fear that the lion will maul the trainer...
	N: type of hammer
MOLL	N: prostitute, doll, gangster's girlfriend
	...his gun moll was with him...
MULL	VB: grind or mix thoroughly, pulverize
	VB: consider at length, ponder (usually used with *over*)
	...need to mull this over for a while...
	VB: heat, sweeten, and flavor with spices
	...will mull the wine tonight...
MAMMARY	N: milk-secreting gland
MEMORY	N: remembrance
	...no memory of the details of the accident...
MANNER	N: way of acting or of doing something
	...used any manner necessary...
MANOR	N: mansion, landed estate
	...lived in the grand manor...
MANTEL	N: shelf above a fireplace
	...family pictures sat on the mantel...
MANTLE	VB: cloak, cover, become covered with a coating
	N: something that envelops and covers literally or figuratively, cloak
	...mantle of responsibility...
	...under the mantle of darkness...
	N: netting of a lantern that glows when lit
	N: part of the interior of a planet that lies beneath the lithosphere
	...deep within the earth's mantle...

MANUFACTURE(S)	VB: produce goods
	...will manufacture it on his own...
	N: something made by machine or hand from raw materials, goods
	...manufacture of that company...
MANUFACTURER(S)	N: one who produces goods
	...several manufacturers represented at the show...
MARCH	VB/N: walk in step with a group
	...made us march 20 minutes every day...
	EXPRESSION
	march to your own drummer = do things your own way
	march someone in/into = make someone go
	...teacher marched him into the principal's office...
MARCH	N: third month of the calendar year
MARSH	N: swamp
	...bug-infested marsh...
MARE	N: female horse
	...riding the mare in the race...
MAYOR	N: city's chief executive
	...spoke with the mayor before the press conference...
MARRY	VB: wed, combine into one
	...will marry my idea with his...
MARY	N: proper name
MERRY	ADJ: happy
	...having a merry time...

MARSHAL	(Spelled with just one *l*)
	VB: arrange in order, gather
	...*need to marshal our forces...*
	N: law officer
	...*marshal arrived to restore order...*
MARSHALL	N: proper name
MARSHALL PLAN	N: plan for aid to Europe after World War II
MARTIAL	ADJ: pertaining to or suitable for war or the military
	...*imposed martial law for a time...*
	...*facing court martial...*
MARTIAN	N/ADJ: pertaining to Mars
MARITAL	ADJ: pertaining to marriage
	...*having marital difficulties...*
MASK(ED)	Past tense and past participle of *to mask*
	VB/ADJ: covered up, hidden
	...*"Who was that masked man?"...*
MASS(ED)	Past tense and past participle of *to mass*
	VB/ADJ: assembled
	...*massed on the borders of the small country...*
MAST	N: part of the rigging of a ship
	...*broken mast...*

(Slightly out of alphabetical order to make it fit on the page!)

MASK	VB: cover up or disguise
	...*tended to mask the symptoms*...
	N: something that conceals from view
	N: protective covering for the face
	...*wore a gas mask*...
MASQUE	Short for *masquerade*
MASS	VB: form or collect into a group
	...*troops began to mass on the borders*...
	N/ADJ: expanse, bulk
	...*bought that in mass quantities*...
	N: principal part or main body
	...*great mass of the continent*...
	N: large body of persons in a compact group
	...*in fear of the mass of people that had gathered*...
	N: body of people as contrasted with the elite (often used in the plural)
	...*said to be good for the masses*...
	...*will offend the masses*...
	ADJ: average, commonplace
	...*affected mass man*...
	ADJ: participated in by or affecting a large number of individuals
	...*held mass demonstrations*...
	...*left behind mass destruction*...
MASS	N: church service
MOSQUE	N: temple
	...*met in the mosque*...

MAT	VB: form into a tangled mass *...sleep will mat her hair...* VB: pack down to form a dense mass *...fibers will mat into a tight wad...* N: rug for wiping shoes N: large thick pad used in wrestling, tumbling, and gymnastics *...took him to the mat in the match...* N: border going around a picture inside the frame *...had a mat of a slightly darker color...*
MATTE	ADJ: having a smooth even surface free from shine or highlights *...one of the matte metals...* N: crude mixture of sulfides formed in smelting sulfide ores of metals
MATERIAL	N: element or substance of which something is composed or can be made *...material to make explosives...* N: data to be used to compose something *...material for his next novel...* ADJ: relating to the physical or worldly nature *...all the trappings of material wealth...* ADJ: having real importance or consequences *...facts material to the case...*
MATERIEL	N: equipment, apparatus, and supplies used by an organization *...in charge of the materiel for the project...* N: in the military, that which is not weaponry or ammunition
MAY BE	VB: verb form expressing possibility *...may be that he is a suspect...*
MAYBE	ADV: perhaps

ME	PRO: first person singular, objective case
MI	N: third note in the musical scale
MEAN	VB: have in mind, intend, indicate
	...didn't mean to offend him...
	VB: serve as, intend to convey, have importance
	...threatening skies mean rain...
	...servant spirit does mean a great deal to her...
	N/ADJ: middle point between two extremes
	...mean was around 60...
	...mean temperature in the winter...
	ADJ: bad tempered, vicious
	...had a mean temper...
	ADJ: penurious, stingy, characterized by petty selfishness or malice
	...was really mean to her...
	ADJ: excellent, effective
	...plays a mean piano...
MEANS	N: resources available for disposal
	...live within your means...
MIEN	N: way of carrying and conducting oneself, manner
	...pleasant mien when she is working...
MESNE	Pronounced /meen/ (rhymes with *seen*)
	ADJ: intermediate, intervening (used in law)
MEAT	N: flesh of an animal
	N: central part
	...get to the meat of the matter...
MEET	VB: come together with
	...will meet with them again tomorrow...
	N: competition
	...competed at the track meet...
METE	VB: allot (used with *out*)
	...had to mete out the meager provisions...
METES AND BOUNDS	N: legal term having to do with boundary lines on property

MEATIER	ADJ: having more substance *...may be a meatier problem than he had anticipated...*
METEOR	N: small celestial body *...enjoyed the early-morning meteor shower...*
METER	N: unit of measure *...meter is a little more than a yard...*
MEDAL	N: token intended to honor/preserve the memory of a person or event *...received the medal as a tribute to his efforts...*
MEDDLE	VB: put oneself into other people's affairs without being asked or needed *...continued to meddle in everything I did...*
METAL	N: substance such as iron, lead, gold, or silver *...considered a heavy metal...*
METTLE	N: spirit, courage *...has the mettle to attempt this feat...*
MUDDLE	VB/N: confuse *...in a muddle with all of the details...*
MEDIAN	N/ADJ: middle position *...careened onto the median strip...*
MEDIUM	N/ADJ/ADV: intermediate in amount or quantity or degree *...likes his steak medium rare...* *...collected a medium number of signatures for the day...* N: psychic *...hoped the medium could give me the answers...*
MELD	VB: combine, merge *...tried to meld the two divergent personalities...*
MELT	VB: become liquid, soften *...need to melt his heart...*

MIDST	N: middle
	...right in the midst of the controversy...
MISS(ED)	Past tense and past participle of *to miss*
	VB: fail to hit, reach, or contact
	...missed the target by plenty...
MIST	N: fog or vapor
MIGHT	VB: auxiliary (helping) verb indicating possibility
	...might be able to help...
	N: power
	...had the might of the corporation behind him...
MITE	N: tiny bug
	...had to deal with dust mites...
	N: small amount
	...will have a mite more...
MIME	VB/N: mimic, act with gestures and actions, usually without words
	...tried to mime what his sister did...
	...tried to make a living as a mime...
MINE	VB: extract ore, search for
	...intended to mine the area for clues...
	N: quarry, excavation pit
	...worked too many years in the mine...
	PRO: first person singular, possessive
	...looked for mine in among the purses...
MINCE	VB/N: cut into small bits
	...does not like mince pie...
	EXPRESSION
	does not mince words = says exactly what one means
MINT(S)	VB: makes coins
	...mints enough each day to cover the need...
	Plural of *mint*
	N: candies

MIND	VB: give heed to ...*do not mind his intrusion*... VB: take care of ...*needs to mind the children*... VB: behave ...*does not mind well*... N: opinion ...*of like mind with her*... N: intellect ...*has a keen mind for figures*...
MINE(D)	Past tense and past participle of *to mine* VB: dig ore and coal from earth ...*several valuable ores were mined from that region*...
MINER	N: one who works in a mine, digging coal and ore ...*severe lung diseases of miners*...
MINOR	N: person under the legal age of responsibility ...*accused of serving drinks to a minor*... ADJ: smaller, less important ...*was a minor accident*...
MISSAL	N: prayer book ...*came from the Episcopal missal*...
MISSILE	N: object or weapon with a projectile ...*fired the missile*...
MISSIVE	N: written communication (usually negative in nature) ...*received a vituperative missive from the boss*...
MISTLETOE	N: Christmas greenery ...*steal a kiss under the mistletoe*...

MISS(ES)	Third person singular, present tense of *to miss*
	VB: fail to hit
	...misses his goals by plenty...
	VB: fail to attend
	...misses the meeting most of the time...
	VB: fail to comprehend
	...misses the point of the lecture...
	VB: escape
	...just miss the accident...
	N: young women
MISSUS	N: wife (used with *the* and without a name after it)
	...went to the meeting with the missus...
MRS.	N: title for a married woman
MNEMONIC	N/ADJ: memory device
	...used a mnemonic to remember the names...
PNEUMONIC	ADJ: pulmonary
	...had pneumonic symptoms...
MOAN	VB/N: groan, lament
	...heard him moan...
MOWN	Alternate form of the past participle of *to mow*
	VB: cut, as in grass or hay
	...new-mown hay...
MOAT	N: wide trench filled with water
MOTE	VB: may, might (archaic)
	...so mote it be...
	N: small particle, speck
	...mote of dust reflected in the light...
MOT	FRENCH: *word*
	Pronounced /mo/ (rhymes with *toe*)
	N: pithy or witty saying
	...bon mot...

MODAL	ADJ: relating to structure as opposed to substance *...modal auxiliary in grammar...*
MODEM	N: device that converts signals from one form to a form compatible with another kind of equipment *...used a modem for transmitting the data...*
MODEL(ED)	VB: serve as a pattern, display *...will model the behavior he is looking for...* N: person who serves as an example *...is a model citizen...*
MOTTLE(D)	VB: mark with spots or blotches *...mottle the surface of the cement...*

MUDDLE(D)	VB: confuse, jumble
	...tried to muddle through the problem...
	EXPRESSION
	    muddleheaded = inept, bungling
	      ...has always been a muddleheaded kid...

MOTLEY	ADJ: variegated in color *...motley display of flowers...* ADJ: composed of diverse often incongruous elements, ragtag *...motley crowd in attendance...* *...gathered together a motley crew for the job...*
MODE	N: prevailing style, fashion, or custom *...mode similar to her sister's...*

MOW(ED)	Past tense of *to mow*; alternate past participle form with *mown*
	VB: cut, as in grass or hay
	EXPRESSION
	    mowed down = hit by a car; killed
	      ...mowed down by a drunk driver...

MOOD	N: state of mind or feeling *...not in a good mood...*
MOO(ED)	Past tense of *to moo* VB: make the sound of a cow, low

MOISTER	ADJ: more moist
	...felt moister than it had before...
MOISTURE	N: wetness, dampness
	...moisture had accumulated under the ledge...
MOOR(S)	VB: tie up a boat
	...going to moor the boat at Friday Harbor...
	N: vast expanse of grassland
	...on the moors of Spain...
MOOR(S)	N: one of the mixed Arab and Berber conquerors of Spain
MORES	Pronounced /mo-<u>rayz</u>/
	N: customs, moral attitudes
	...part of the mores of society...
MORAY	N: type of eel
MOIRE	N: fabric
MOOSE	N: large animal
MOUSE	N: small animal
MOUSSE	N: dessert
	...chocolate mousse is her favorite...
	N: hair product
	...needed a lot of mousse to hold the style...
MOOT	ADJ: debatable
	...that is a moot point...
	ADJ: academic
	...students participated in moot court...
MUTE	ADJ: absence of sound or speech
	...pushed the mute button on the remote...

MORAL	Pronounced /<u>mor</u>-uhl/
	N: lesson or inner meaning of a story, fable, or event
	...tried to get her to understand the moral of the story...
	ADJ: good or virtuous in character or conduct
	...lived by a strict moral code...
	ADJ: according to civilized standards of right and wrong
	...had a moral decision facing her...
	ADJ: dealing with the difference between right and wrong
MORALE	Pronounced /mo-<u>ral</u>/
	N: mental or emotional condition of courage, confidence, enthusiasm
	...tough to keep up the morale with so much stress...
MORTAL	N/ADJ: capable of dying
	...was a mere mortal...
MORALITY	N: moral discourse, statement, or lesson
	...strange sense of morality he espoused...
MORTALITY	N: quality or state of being mortal
	...come face to face with his own mortality...
MORNING	N: early part of the day, ending at noon
MOURNING	VB/ADJ: showing of sorrow by observing certain rituals
	...has been mourning for months...
	N: sorrow for a person's death
MOTIF	N: theme in art
	...had a lacy motif...
MOTIVE	N: reason for action
	...had to find the motive for what he did...

MUCH	PRO/ADJ/ADV: large quantity
MULCH	VB/N: organic matter used to spread on a garden or flowers
	...had to put mulch on the garden...
MUSH	N: soft and spongy substance
	...all the ice turned to mush...
	N: drivel
	...words just sounded like mush...
	N: porridge
MUCOUS	ADJ: secreting mucus
	...problem in the mucous membranes...
MUCUS	N: viscous secretion
	...accumulation of mucus...
MUSCLE	VB: move or force by or as if by great effort
	...tried to muscle him out the door...
	VB: make one's way by brute strength or by force
	...decided to muscle his way in...
	N: bundle of special tissues that function to move a part of the body
	N: muscular strength, brawn
	...no muscle behind the decision...
	N: effective strength, power
	...has political muscle because of his dad...
MUSSEL	N: edible, clamlike animal
	...don't like the taste of mussel...
MUZZLE	VB/N: quiet, silence
	...need to muzzle him...
	...put a muzzle on it...
	N: snout of a dog
	N: discharging end of a weapon
	...took hold of the muzzle end of the barrel...

MUSE	VB: ponder, think about
	...muse about her future...
MUSE	N: any of the nine sister goddesses in Greek mythology
MEW(S)	VB/N: utter sound a kitten, bird, or small animal makes
	...mews each evening at feeding time...
	N: enclosure for trained hawks
	N: stables usually with living quarters built around a court
	...lived in the mews for a number of years...
	N: back street; alley
MUSE(D)	Past tense and past participle of *to muse*
	VB: ponder, think about
	...mused on the possibility that she could win...
MUSS(ED)	Past tense and past participle of *to muss*
	VB: make untidy
	...mussed her hair in the wind...
MUST	VB: auxiliary (helping) verb meaning *have to*
	...must go with him...
	N: something which has to be accomplished
	...is a must for all lovers of music...
MUSTARD	N: plant, yellow powder or paste used for seasoning food
	EXPRESSION
	cut the mustard = suffice, be enough, measure up
MUSTER(ED)	Past tense and past participle of *to muster*
	VB: gather together, assemble, convene
	...mustered his resources for the fight...
	VB: formally enroll (usually used with *in* or *out*)
	...mustered out of the Army last month...
MUSTER	N: formal military inspection
	...did not pass muster...

CHAPTER 14
THE LETTER N

NAP
N: short rest
N: raised hairs on a surface
...saw clearly the direction of the nap...

NAPE
N: back part of the neck
...deep gash right at the nape of the neck...

NARCOTIC
N/ADJ: drug that dulls the senses
...under the influence of a narcotic...

NECROTIC
ADJ: localized death of living tissue
...discovered necrotic tissue around the site of the wound...

NAUSEA
N: stomach distress with distaste for food and an urge to vomit
...nausea came in waves as the ship rocked...

NAUSEATE
VB: become affected with nausea
VB: feel disgust
...his foul language and nasty disposition nauseate me...

NAUSEATE(D)
Past tense and past participle of *to nauseate*
(something that happens to a person)
ADJ: felt disgusted
...details of the murder nauseated me...

NAUSEOUS
ADJ: be affected with nausea, feeling nausea
(something that happens within a person)
...became nauseous after she ate...

NOXIOUS
ADJ: physically harmful or destructive to living beings
...noxious fumes filled the room...

NAVAL
ADJ: relating to the Navy
...involved in naval maneuvers...

NAVEL
N: small depression in the abdomen
...decided to have her navel pierced...
N: type of orange

NAY	ADV: negative reply ...*counted his as a nay vote*...
NÉE	Pronounced /nay/ (rhymes with *say*) FRENCH: originally or formerly called, used to identify a woman by her maiden or family name ...*Sarah Jane Martin, née Miller*...
NEIGH	VB: make the prolonged cry of a horse ...*began to neigh as the pain increased*...
NIGH	ADV: approach, near ...*time is drawing nigh*...
NEITHER	PRO/ADJ: not either ...*neither the boys nor the men*...
NETHER	ADJ: situated below or beneath the earth's surface ...*located on the nether side*...
NICHE	N: recess in the wall ...*stuck it into the niche above the light switch*...
NICK	VB/N: small groove or notch ...*wound was just a nick*...
NICK(S)	Third person singular, present tense of *to nick* VB/N: small grooves or notches ...*nicks the edge of my car every time he pulls up next to it*...
NIX	VB/N: reject, nothing ...*going to nix the project he is proposing*...
NONE	PRO/ADJ: not any
NUN	N: woman belonging to a religious order
NOUGAT	N: candy ...*rich chocolate nougat*...
NUGGET	N: small bit ...*has just a nugget of information on this*...

CHAPTER 15
THE LETTER *O*

O   INTERJ: variant of *oh*
              Used in the Latin vocative
              ...O Lord...

O'   CONTRACTION: *of the*
              ...7:00 o'clock...

OH   INTERJ: exclaims
              ...oh, I am not sure...

OWE   VB: be in debt, obligated
              ...owe him my life...

EAU   FRENCH: *water*
              ...eau de cologne...

OAR   N: pole used to row a boat
              ...tried to do it with just one oar...

O'ER   CONTRACTION: *over*
              PREP: poetic form
              ...sailed o'er the waves...

OR   CONJ: denotes an alternative
              ...chocolate or vanilla...

ORE   N: mineral containing a metal
              ...mined the ore on a regular basis...

OCCIDENT(AL) N/ADJ: relating to the West
                 ...grew up with Occidental values...

ACCIDENT(AL) N/ADJ: unplanned, by chance
                 ...during an accidental meeting with her...

ODDER   ADJ: more strange
              ...seems odder this time around...

OTTER   N: large mammal

ODE	N: lyric poem *...ode to his mother...*
OWE(D)	Past tense and past participle of *to owe* VB: obligated, was in debt *...owed her for all she had done...* *...owed more than the house was worth...*
ODOR	N: smell, aroma *...strong odor coming from the closet...*
ORDER	VB/N: command, request (especially food or drink) *...gave an order to proceed...* *...tried to order alcohol...*
ODIOUS	ADJ: hateful, nasty *...made odious remarks on the record about him...*
ODOROUS	ADJ: having a strong, distinctive smell *...odorous cheese was tightly wrapped...*
OFFICIAL	ADJ: authentic, authorized *...official decision to withdraw troops...*
OFFICIOUS	ADJ: meddlesome, impertinent *...officious remarks about my decision...* *...his officious behavior was a source of conflict...*
OLEO	N: margarine *...used oleo as a substitute for butter...*
OLIO	N: hodgepodge *...had an olio of ideas that were presented...*

ONE	PRO: number
	...needed more than one computer...
	PRO: first in a series
	...one in a number of ideas...
	PRO/ADJ: sole, single unit
	...only one that he could procure...
WON	Past tense and past participle of *to win*
	VB: gain, come out on top
	...won the first prize in the contest...
ONE(S)	N: single units
	...had only ones in my wallet...
ONCE	ADV: formerly
	...was once a valet for an entrepreneur...
	ADV: one time only
	...was in New York City just once...
ORAL	ADJ: spoken
	...recorded an oral history of the event...
AURAL	ADJ: relating to the ear or to the sense of hearing
	...went in for aural testing...
ORDINANCE	N: law, rule, regulation
	...ordinance against smoking...
ORDNANCE	N: military weaponry and ammunition
	...in charge of the ordnance depot...
OUR	PRO: belonging to, made by, or done by us
HOUR	N: 60 minutes
	N: specified time
	...at the hour of his death...

OVERDO	VB: do too much, overwork, exhaust
	...tends to overdo...
OVERDUE	ADJ: expected or due some time ago but not yet arrived
	...package overdue to arrive...
	ADJ: not yet paid
	...bill is ten days overdue...
OVERSEAS	N/ADJ: across the water
	...shipped it overseas...
OVERSEE(S)	Third person singular, present tense of *to oversee*
	VB: supervise
	...oversees the entire operation...

CHAPTER 16
THE LETTER *P*

PACE(D)
Past tense and past participle of *to pace*
VB: walk with a slow and measured step
...began to pace the floor as he awaited the news...
N: rhythm of progress
...go at a good pace for me...
EXPRESSION
    set the pace = set an example, establish a standard
    ...set the pace for the rest of the program...
    pace off = measure by stepping
    ...had to pace off the distance...

PASTE
VB: adhere one thing to another
...going to paste this onto the original...
N: adhesive
...had to use a high-grade paste to make it stick...
N: brilliant glass of high lead content used for artificial gems
...though it looked like a real diamond, it was just paste...

PACIFIC
ADJ: calm, serene
...boating in pacific waters...

PACIFIC
N: ocean on the western side of the U.S.
...fished in the Pacific off the coast of California...

SPECIFIC
ADJ: precise, definite
...was not given specific instructions...

PACK(ED)

Past tense and past participle of *to pack*
VB: make into a compact bundle
...packed them close together to make them fit...
VB: fill completely or to crowd together
...room was packed with people...
VB: gather into tight formation
...wolves usually packed together...
EXPRESSIONS
    pack it in = quit, bring to an end
    ...decided to pack it in for the night...
    packing = wearing a weapon
    ...was told everyone at the funeral was packing...
    pack a jury = select members to bring about a desired result
    ...tried to pack the jury for his perjury trial...
    pack someone off = send a person somewhere
    (usually under difficult circumstances)
    ...parents packed him off to school...

PACT

N: agreement
...made a pact to begin the project in September...

PACKET

N: small package
...two packets of pain relievers...

POCKET

N: pouch in clothing
...pocket full of miracles...

PADDED/PADDING

Past tense and past participle/present participle of *to pad*
VB/N: cushion
...padded his answer with fluff...
...chairs need more padding to be comfortable...

PATTED/PATTING

Past tense and past participle/present participle of *to pat*
VB/N: stroke gently
...patted my shoulder to reassure me...
...was patting her hand during the service...

PADDY	N: rice field
	...worked in a paddy 12 hours a day...
PATTY	N: small cake of chopped meat
	...enjoyed the patty without the bun...
PAIL	N: bucket
PALE	VB: lose color
	...began to pale as the news sank in...
	N: one of the stakes of a palisade, picket
	ADJ: without much color, whitish
	...turned pale upon hearing the news...
	EXPRESSION
	beyond the pale = beyond the limit, go too far
	...raunchy conduct was beyond the pale...
PAIN	VB/N: cause suffering; ache, sting, tenderness
	...will pain me if that turns out to be true...
	...pain in the left lower quadrant...
PANE	N: sheet of glass
	...broken pane in the middle of the window...
PAIR	VB: form in twos
	...pair him with his brother for the task...
	N: two of a kind
	...make a great pair...
PARE	VB: trim, reduce
	...need to pare expenses by 10 percent...
	N: trim the peel off the outer part
	...pare the apple for the baby to eat...
PEAR	N: fruit

PAIRED/PAIRING Past tense and past participle/present participle of *to pair*
...paired with her best friend for the event...
...will be pairing them to work on the project...
N: coupling
...liked the pairing for the final match...

PARED/PARING Past tense and past participle/present participle of *to pare*
...pared the budget to bare bones...
...paring expenses to meet the criteria...
N/ADJ: pealing
...used a small paring knife...

PAL N: friend
...hung around with a pal for the day...

PALL VB/N: fade, diminish, wither, enshroud with gloom
...pall over the crowd with the news of the crash...
N: cloth for the coffin
...folded the pall after we removed it from the coffin...

PALATE VB: withstand
...unable to palate the changes...
N: roof of the mouth
...burned the palate when biting into the pizza...
N: sense of taste
...wide palate of tastes in music...

PALLET N: small, temporary bed
...made a pallet on the floor for the kids...
N: portable platform for handling, storing, or moving materials
...job was to move the pallets around in the warehouse...

PALETTE N: board on which a painter mixes paint
...used a brand-new palette for his paints...
N: particular range, quality, or use of color
...used the whole palette of colors...

PALLID	ADJ: pale *...pallid complexion...*
PELLET	N: small rounded or spherical body as of food, medicine, debris, or snow *...left out pellets for the birds to eat...*
PULLET	N: young hen
PALPATE (-TION)	VB/N: examine by touch *...could not palpate the liver...* *...examined her by palpation...*
PALPITATE (-TION)	VB/N: throb *...his heart began to palpitate as he neared the church...* *...palpitations overwhelmed her...*
PALTRY	ADJ: trivial, inferior, small *...paltry sum for such a quality purchase...*
POULTRY	N: domestic fowl
PARA-	Prefix meaning "beside" as in *paramedic* and *parasite*
PER-	Prefix meaning "through" as in *permeate* and *pervade*
PERI-	Prefix meaning "around" as in *perimeter* and *pericarditis*
PARCEL	VB: divide into parts, distribute *...parcel out to those in attendance...* N: tract or plot of land N: company, collection, or group of persons, animals, or things *...whole story was a parcel of lies...* N: wrapped bundle
PARTIAL	ADJ: relating to a part rather than the whole *...offered only a partial solution to the problem...* ADJ: inclined to favor one party more than the other, biased *...partial to her oldest child...* ADJ: markedly fond of someone or something (used with <u>to</u>) *...partial to pepperoni and anchovy pizza...*

PARCH	VB: go without water *...sun and dryness will parch us all...*
PERCH	VB/N: rest on something elevated *...perch on the edge of the cliff...*
PARISH	N: ecclesiastical unit, area committed to one pastor *...belong to an Episcopal parish in Westchester...* N: civil division corresponding loosely to a county *...part of the Natchitoches Parish in Louisiana...*
PERISH	VB: cease to exist, become destroyed or ruined *...discovered that several did perish in the fire...*
PARITY	N: equality, equivalence *...looking for parity in the pay of men and women...*
PARODY	N: travesty, caricature *...did a parody of the situation with his boss...*
PARLAY	VB/N: convert into something larger *...thinks he will parlay his $100 into $10,000 in just a few days...*
PARLEY	VB/N: discuss terms with an enemy *...will parley to decide how to settle the dispute...*
PAROL	ADJ: given by word of mouth *...listened to parol evidence...*
PAROLE	VB/N: release a prisoner early and with certain restrictions *...will parole him six months early...* *...will be on parole for two years...*
PAYROLL	N: list of wages of a group of workers *...weekly payroll of over $50,000...*
PARSON	N: clergyperson
PERSON	N: human being *...known to be a moral person...*

PARTITION	VB: divide or separate into parts
	...intended to partition the room to keep the boys apart...
	N: something that separates or divides
	...set up a partition in the middle...
PERDITION	N: eternal damnation, hell
	...condemned to perdition...
PETITION	VB: make a formal request to another
	...decided to petition to dissolve the marriage...
	N: formal request for a privilege, right, or benefit
	...filed a petition the day he was released...
PASSOVER	N: Jewish holiday beginning on the 14th of Nisan and commemorating the Hebrews' liberation from slavery in Egypt
	...celebrate Passover with my family...
PASS OVER	VB: overlook
	...going to pass over the whole group for this opportunity...
PASS TIME	VB: spend time
	...pass time in the waiting room, looking through magazines...
PASTIME	N: hobby, recreation
	...reading is my favorite pastime...

(Slightly out of alphabetical order to make it fit on the page!)

PASSED	Past tense and past participle of *to pass*
(This form is ALWAYS part of the verb)
VB: go by
...*passed all but one car in the race*...
VB: distribute
...*was passed from one table to the next*...
VB: succeed, do well
...*passed the exam with flying colors*...
EXPRESSIONS
  pass on something = decline
  ...*passed on going with us*...
  pass over = omit, ignore
  ...*passed over for promotion*...

PAST	(This form is NEVER part of the verb)
N: earlier time, time before now
...*is all in the past now*...
...*past keeps coming back to haunt her*...
ADJ: preceding, gone by, earlier point in time
...*because of her past experience*...
...*within the past week*...
ADJ: one time
...*past president of the organization*...
...*one of her past loves*...
ADV: later than a particular time
...*her time was past*...
ADV: by
...*walked past several times*...
...*drove past later*...
PREP: on the far side of
...*just past midnight*...
...*past the fence*...
PREP: beyond
...*am past understanding*...

PASTOR
N: clergyperson in charge of a church or congregation
...spoke to the pastor about the donation...

PASTURE
N: grazing field for animals
...pasture filled with Guernsey cows...

PASTEUR
N: French scientist Louis Pasteur, who devised the process of pasteurization

PASTRY
N: baked sweet treat
...served a delectable pastry with breakfast...

PASTY
ADJ: pale
...looked pasty when he returned to work after the illness...

PATIENCE
N: willingness to wait or endure
...his patience was wearing thin...
EXPRESSION
    has the patience of Job = endless patience

PATIENT(S)
Plural of *patient*
N: person being treated by a doctor or dentist
...patients were seen immediately...

PAUPER
N: very poor person
...had been a pauper most of his life...

POPPER
N: someone or something that pops
...used a popcorn popper rather than the pan he usually used...
N: alcoholic beverage: tequila and 7UP
...immediately ordered a popper...
N: amyl nitrate, broken under the nose for a "high"
EXPRESSION
    pill popper = someone who takes an excess of medication
    ...was clear she was a pill popper when I saw her stash...

PAUSE	N: temporary stop or hesitation, interruption *...was a long pause before he could get the words out...*
PAWS	Third person singular, present tense of *to paw* VB: use the paw to reach out and touch *...would paw the door when he wanted out...* Plural of *paw* N: feet of a four-footed animal with claws *...cat would sit with its paws out in front of him...*
PEA(S)	Plural of *pea* N: vegetable
PEE(S)	Third person singular, present tense of *to pee* VB/N: urinate
PEACE	N: calm, absence of fighting *...sought peace in an ashram in India...*

PIECE	N: part of something, section
	...added a piece to the puzzle of where she was hiding...
	EXPRESSION
	    piece together = figure out to reach a conclusion
	    ...tried to piece together the details from the clues he had...

PEAL	VB/N: loud, long sound *...bells will peal at noon...* *...peal of the bells woke me...*

PEEL	VB: strip the skin from
	...trying to peel the banana as he drove...
	VB: remove by stripping
	...peel the paint from the bathroom...
	N: skin of a fruit
	...doesn't like the peel of an apple...
	EXPRESSION
	    peel out = accelerate quickly and leave rubber on the pavement
	    ...intended to peel out to show his anger...

(Slightly out of alphabetical order to make it fit on the page!)

PEAK VB: reach the highest point
...doesn't want to peak too soon before the Olympics this summer...
N: top or highest point
...reached the peak of the mountain first...

PEAKED Pronounced /<u>peek</u>-ed/
ADJ: looking pale or wan
...looked peaked after a week with the flu...

PEEK VB: look quickly and furtively
...tried to peek into the closed room...

PEKE N: Pekingese dog

PIQUE Pronounced /peek/ (rhymes with *seek*)
VB: arouse emotion or interest
...trailer for the movie really did pique my interest...
EXPRESSION
   in a pique = feeling resentment
      ...in a pique about being fired...

PIQUÉ Pronounced /pee-<u>kay</u>/
N: durable ribbed clothing fabric of cotton, rayon, or silk
...dress of soft pink piqué...

PEKOE Pronounced /<u>pee</u>-ko/
N: tea made from the two youngest leaves and the end bud of the shoot

PICO SPANISH: proper name (major street in Los Angeles)

PEARL N: concretion used in jewelry
...gave her a pearl necklace...
N: something very choice or good
...dropped a pearl of wisdom on them...

PURL VB/N: knitting stitch
...knit one, purl two...

PEC(S)	Short for *pectoral(s)* N: muscles in the chest *...worked to build up his pecs...*
PECK(S)	Third person singular, present tense of *to peck* VB: strike or pierce *...continued to peck away at the wall...* VB: carp, nag *...they always peck at her about her chores...* N: quick kiss *...gave her a peck on the cheek...*
PEDAL	VB: move by a foot action *...decided to pedal his bike back and forth to work...* N: lever operated by the foot *...bike had a broken pedal...*
PEDDLE	VB: go from place to place with merchandise to sell *...will peddle his wares at the swap meet...* EXPRESSION *peddle her wares* = said of a woman who is a prostitute
PETAL	N: one of the leaves of a flower *...rose petals strewn along the aisle...*
PADDLE	VB/N: move through the water *...decided to try to paddle the boat for the two miles...* VB/N: spank *...did not believe in using a paddle on children...*
PEDANT	N: learned person *...came across in the discussion as a pedant...*
PENDANT	N: something suspended *...wore a pendant around her neck...*
PENDENT	ADJ: hanging, supported from above *...pendent lamp...*
PENNANT	ADJ: banner, flag, emblem *...Dodgers won the pennant...*

PEEN	N: wedge at the head of a hammer
	...used a ball-peen hammer...
PEON	N: low, working class
	...lived among the peons...
PEN	VB/N: write; writing instrument
	...decided to pen his memoir...
	N: enclosure, corral
	...built a pen for the horses...
	SLANG: prison (short for *penitentiary*)
	...just got out of the pen...
PIN	VB/N: attach
	...pin my hopes for a win on the play of the quarterback...
PENANCE	N: expression of atonement or apology
	...paying his penance for his transgressions...
PENNANT(S)	N: flag or banner
	...have won several pennants in the league...
PENETRATE	VB: pierce, infiltrate, go into
	...tried to penetrate the inner circle...
PERMEATE	VB: pervade, saturate, flood
	...water will permeate through the carpet...
PEER(S)	Third person singular, present tense of *to peer*
	VB: look at closely
	...decided to peer into the window that evening...
	N: person of the same rank, ability, or status
	...take his chances with a jury of his peers...
PIER(S)	Plural of *pier*
	N: structure built out over water and supported by pillars, dock
	...small pier gave way and spilled people into the water...
PIERCE	VB: penetrate
	...will pierce the membrane surrounding the organ...

PER	ADV: each *...will be $250 per person...* PREP: according to *...carried out per your instructions...*
PURR	N: sound a cat makes N: smooth sound of an engine *...engine seemed to purr when I got it back from the mechanic...*
PERPETRATE (-TION)	VB/N: bring about or carry out as a crime *...perpetrate this on the unsuspecting customer...* *...was arrested for the perpetration of the crime...*
PERPETUATE (-TION)	VB/N: cause to last indefinitely *...will perpetuate this tradition long after his father is gone...* *...involved in the perpetuation of the problem...*
PERPETUAL	ADJ: continuing forever; everlasting, valid for all time *...perpetual care at the cemetery...*
PERQUISITE	Often shortened to *perk* N: something earned in addition to salary *...car was a perquisite of the job...*
PREREQUISITE	N: precedent requirement *...basic math was the prerequisite for this class...*
PERSECUTE (-TION)	VB: plague, oppress, hunt down *...felt his peers would persecute him for his stance...* VB/N: bring undeserved suffering or unhappiness upon someone *...persecute him for his religious beliefs...* *...could not endure the persecution...*
PROSECUTE (-TION)	VB/N: bring before a court of law *...enough evidence to prosecute him...* *...served as a witness for the prosecution...*

PERSECUTOR	N: person who persecutes
PROSECUTOR	N: person who prosecutes
	...met with the prosecutor before my testimony...
PERSONAL	ADJ: done in person directly by oneself
	...paid a personal visit to his brother...
	ADJ: pertaining to the body or bodily appearance
	...declared it is a personal problem...
PERSONNEL	N: persons employed in any work, business, or service
	...new directive sent to all personnel...
PERSPECTIVE	N: art of drawing objects as they appear to the eye with respect to relative depth and distance
	...did not seem to be in perspective...
	N: point of view or opinion based on certain factors
	...is not fair, from my perspective...
PROSPECTIVE	ADJ: looking to the future, expected, likely
	...prospective client for my business...
PERSPICACITY	N: keenness of mind, perceptiveness, discernment
	...exhibited perspicacity in understanding the problem...
PERSPICUITY	N: clarity, lucidity
	...explained it with perspicuity so that we all understood...
PERSUASIVE	ADJ: able to sway or convince
	...used a persuasive argument to convince them...
PERVASIVE	ADJ: omnipresent, enveloping, all inclusive
	...odor was pervasive...

PETIT   Pronounced: /<u>pet</u>-ee/ or /puh-<u>teet</u>/
ADJ: small, minor (used as the opposite of *gran* or *grand*)
...had a petit mal seizure...
...served on a petit jury...

PETITE   Pronounced /puh-<u>teet</u>/
N: clothing size for small women
ADJ: small, dainty
...was petite but very strong...

PETTY   Pronounced /<u>pet</u>-ee/
ADJ: having secondary rank or importance, minor, subordinate
...was a chief petty officer in the Navy...
ADJ: having little or no importance or significance
...paid it out of petty cash...
...filed a petty grievance against her co-worker...
ADJ: marked by narrow interests and sympathies, small minded
...always made petty remarks about his sister...

PHYSIC   N: medicinal purgative
...had to take a physic before the colonoscopy...

PHYSICS   N: study of motion
...decided to major in physics...

PHYSIQUE   N: bodily makeup
...worked on his physique because of the upcoming role...

PI   N: 16th letter of the Greek alphabet
N: mathematical formula 3.14159265

PIE   N: dessert

PICTURE   N: image or likeness of something produced by painting, drawing, or photography
...is the picture of health...

PITCHER   N: container with a handle and lip for holding and pouring liquids
...used a pitcher for the water instead of a bottle...
N: player who throws the ball to the batters (baseball)
...Koufax was one of the greatest pitchers of all time...

PIETY	N: reverence for God
	...tried to demonstrate piety in all his dealings...
PITHY	ADJ: terse, condensed, concise
	...did not appreciate his pithy comments...
PITY	VB/N: show compassion or mercy for
	...hard not to pity them in their misfortune...
PINCHER	N: one who pinches (not a common word -- if it is a word at all!)
PINSCHER	N: breed of dog
	...owned a Doberman pinscher...
PINCERS	Pronounced /<u>pin</u>-cherz/
	N: jaw-gripping tool
	...used pincers to loosen the bolt...
PISTOL	N: gun
	...carried a pistol on her hip...
PISTIL	N: ovule-bearing organ of a seed plant
PLAIN	N: flat stretch of land
	...attempted to cross the plains in a covered wagon...
	ADJ: undecorated
	...very plain looks...
	ADJ: easy to understand
	...make it plain that I am not going to be involved...
GREAT PLAINS	N: regions in the central part of the United States
PLANE	Short for *airplane*
	...refused to fly in a small plane...
	VB: make level or smooth
	...needed to plane the surface to make it perfectly smooth...
	N: carpenter's tool for smoothing surfaces
	...used a plane to make it smooth...
	N: flat surface (used in geometry)
	...studied plane geometry...

PLAINTIFF	N: one who brings a suit into a court of law ...*was a plaintiff in the action*...
PLAINTIVE	ADJ: sad, melancholy ...*heard her plaintive cry*...
PLAIT	VB: interweave the strands or locks of, braid ...*decided to plait her hair for the event*... N: braid, pigtail ...*wore her hair in a thick plait*...
PLATE	N: dish N: very thin layer of metal ...*covered with a layer of gold plate*... N: part of a denture that is fitted to the mouth ...*wore a bite plate at night to keep from grinding his teeth*... N: any of the huge movable segments into which the earth's crust is divided and which are held to float on and travel over the mantle ...*concept of plate tectonics has revolutionized the study of earthquakes*...
PLAT	N: small piece of ground, plot N: plan, map, or chart of a piece of land with actual or proposed features as lots ...*studied the plat to see where the house is located*... ...*made a plat of the new development*...
PLATTE	N: river in the central part of the United States
PLANTAR	ADJ: pertaining to the sole of the foot ...*had plantar fasciitis*...
PLANTER	N: farmer ...*meeting of the planters before the harvesting*...

PLEA(S)	Plural of *plea*
	N: statement in defense or justification, excuse
	...made a plea about her circumstances...
	N: urgent request or appeal
	...pleas for help went unheard...
	EXPRESSION
	cop a plea = bargain for a lesser offense
PLEASE	VB: give pleasure to, satisfy
	...futilely tried to please her mother...
	ADV: term of politeness
	...give me the information, please...
	...please bring it in from the car...
PLEAT(ED)	Past tense and past participle of *to pleat*
	VB/N: fold
	...just one pleat on the side of the skirt...
	...pleated the fabric for the curtains...
PLEAD(ED)	Past tense and past participle of *to plead*
	VB: argue a case or cause in a court of law
	...will plead not guilty...
	...pleaded his case in front of the judge...
	VB: beg
	...pleaded for his life with the intruder...
PLEURAL	ADJ: referring to the lining of the lungs
	...infection in the pleural lining...
PLURAL	N/ADJ: more than one
	...plural form of the noun...

PLUM	N: fruit
	N/ADJ: something superior or very desired
	...this job was the plum of them all...
PLUMB	VB: drop a vertical line
	...plumb the line so that the drainage is improved...
	N: lead weight attached to a line and used to indicate a vertical direction
	...used a plumb to make sure it was straight up and down...
	ADJ: straight down or up, vertical
	...dropped a plumb line...
	ADV: thoroughly, completely
	...am plumb out of energy...
PLUME	N: feather of a bird
	N: elongated and usually open and mobile column or band
	...saw a small plume of smoke...
	...plume of snow blowing across the road...
APLOMB	N: complete and confident composure or self-assurance, poise
	...seems to be able to do everything with aplomb...
POLE	N: long, slender piece of wood
	...ran directly into the power pole...
	N: either end of the earth's axis
	...flew over the North Pole...
	N: either of two parts where opposite forces are strongest
	...part of the magnetic pole...
POLE	N: person from Poland
POLL	VB: take a vote or survey
	...poll the electorate on their views...
	N: place where votes are cast
	...electorate will go to the polls in November...
	N: survey of public opinion about a particular subject
	...winning by a slim margin, per the latest poll...

POPLAR	N: type of tree
POPULAR	ADJ: liked by many or most people
	...popular remedy for insomnia...
	ADJ: accepted among people in general, common
	...supported by popular opinion...
POPULACE	N: all the people in a country or region
	...listened to the populace in the region...
POPULOUS	ADJ: full of people, crowded
	...in a populous area...
POPULIST	N/ADJ: believer in the rights, wisdom, or virtues of the common people
	...believed in the populist ideals...
POPULIST	N: member of a U.S. political party formed in 1891 primarily to represent agrarian interests and to advocate the free coinage of silver and government control of monopolies
PORE	VB: study intently (usually used with *over*)
	...need to pore over my books to find the error...
	N: opening in the skin
	...resulted from a clogged pore...
POUR	VB: cause to flow in a steady stream
	...people began to pour out of the building...
	VB: rain heavily
	...began to pour just as we got out of the car...
POOR	N: people with no money
	...referred to as the "working poor"...
	ADJ: lacking material possessions
	ADJ: pitied
	...sympathize with the poor neglected child...
PORTABLE	ADJ: capable of being carried
	...small enough to be portable...
POTABLE	ADJ: suitable for drinking
	...clear that the water was not potable...

PORTION	VB/N: part of anything *...intended to portion out the pieces...* *...shared a portion of the estate...*
POTION	N: drink, especially of medicine or poison *...mixed up an old family potion...*
POST-	Prefix meaning "after" as in *postoperative* and *postprandial*
PRE-	Prefix meaning "before" as in *precede* and *predetermine*
PRO-	Prefix meaning "forward" as in *promote* and *procreate*
PRACTICABLE	ADJ: workable, possible, theoretically capable of being put into practice *...does not feel like a practicable solution -- just wouldn't work...*
PRACTICAL	ADJ: useful, having to do with action or practice rather than theory *...did not have a practical bone in her body...*
PRAISE	VB: express a favorable judgment of *...would praise her without reason...* VB: glorify by the attribution of perfection *...praise God...* N: expression of approval *...received nothing but praise for her performance...*
PRAY(S)	Third person singular, present tense of *to pray* VB: speak to God in worship *...prays daily for relief...* VB: ask for by prayer *...pray for healing...*
PREY(S)	Third person singular, present tense of *to prey* VB: seize upon something as a victim *...preys upon his neighbors...* N: animal hunted by another animal *...fell prey to the hunter...* N: victim *...seemed to be prey for every scam out there...*

PRECEDE	VB: be or go before in importance, position, or time
	...*speech will precede the nomination of the candidate*...
PROCEED	VB: go forward, carry on after having been stopped
	...*will proceed with the original plan*...
PROCEEDS	N: money received from the sale of merchandise
	...*will share the proceeds with the food pantry*...
PROCEDURES	N: particular way of accomplishing something or of acting
	...*said they were just following the normal procedure*...
PROCEEDINGS	N: official record of things said or done
	...*proceedings were halted after the outburst*...
PRECEDENT	Pronounced /<u>pres</u>-uh-dent/
	N: case or instance that may serve as an example or reason for a later case
	...*no precedent for this decision*...
	Pronounced /pree-<u>seed</u>-ent/
	ADJ: going before
	...*precedent to the actual surgery*...
PRESIDENT	N: elected head of a nation, firm, association
	...*made a run for the office of president*...
PREDOMINATE	Pronounced /... -ait/
	VB: exert controlling power or influence
	...*expects to predominate in this argument*...
PREDOMINANT	(Often mispronounced -- without the final *n*)
	ADJ: having superior strength or authority
	...*predominant trait of his personality*...
PREDOMINANTLY	(No such word as *predominately*)
	ADV: for the most part, mainly
	...*group was predominantly male*...
	...*predominantly middle class neighborhood*...

PREMIER

N: Prime Minister
...lived in a country where he was the Premier...
ADJ: first in position, rank, or importance
...premier book on this topic...
ADV: first in time, earliest
...premier voyage of the shuttle program...

PREMIERE

VB: give a first public performance
...will premiere the play here in his hometown...
VB: have a first public performance
VB: appear for the first time as a star performer
...premiere the role as Evita...
N: first performance or exhibition
...attended the premiere of a play...
N: chief actor in a theatrical cast

PREMISE

N: prior statement or assertion that serves as the basis for an argument
...problem is that she used a faulty premise for her opinion...

PREMISES

N: piece of real estate
N: house or building and its land
...body was found on the premises of his company...

PROMISE

VB: vow or pledge, assure
...will promise her that I will participate...
N: guarantee or agreement
...on the promise that he would attend...

PREPOSITION

N: part of speech that shows a relationship between two words
...can sometimes use but *as a preposition...*

PROPOSITION

N: proposal
...proposition that she could not refuse...
SLANG: make an offer for sex
...propositioned her in the bar...

PRESCRIBE	Pronounced /pruh-<u>scribe</u>/
	VB: order as a remedy
	...will prescribe a rather infrequently used drug...
	VB: set down as a rule
	...prescribe the steps he needs to follow to gain admittance...
PROSCRIBE	Pronounced /pro-<u>scribe</u>/
	VB: forbid or prohibit
	...will proscribe smoking in the entire hotel...
PRESENCE	N: condition of being present in a place
	...his presence was requested...
	N: commanding appearance
	...is a real presence in the group...
PRESENT(S)	Pronounced /pre-<u>sents</u>/
	Third person singular, present tense of *to present*
	VB: offer, give to
	...presents gifts to the family when she visits her native India...
	Pronounced /<u>prez</u>-unts/
	Plural of *present*
	N: gifts
	...received lavish presents for his graduation...
	N: people in attendance
	...know by all these presents that we are...
PRETEST	N: test given before, preliminary
	...took the pretest to see what I could do...
PRETEXT	N: excuse, action that cloaks
	...entered on the pretext of inspecting the house...
PRETENSE	N: professed rather than real intention or purpose
	...pretense of needing medical attention was easy to see through....
PREFACE	VB: precede, herald
	...will preface my remarks with this caveat...
	N: introductory remarks of a speaker or author
	...mentioned her husband in the preface...

PREVENTATIVE	Substandard form (should not have the *-ta-* in the middle)
PREVENTIVE	ADJ: serving to hinder or retard
	...tried several preventive measures...
PREVIEW	VB/N: look at ahead of time
	...intended to preview it before recommending it...
	...wanted to read the preview of the book...
PURVIEW	N: scope, range
	...not in my purview...
PRICE	N: cost of something
	...believe the price is too high...
PRIZE	VB: value highly
	...really prize his friendship...
	N: something won in a game or contest, reward
PRIES	Third person singular, present tense of *to pry*
	VB: look closely at or inquisitively into; peer, snoop
	...always pries into my business...
	VB: raise, move, or pull apart with a lever
	...pries open the latch to gain entrance...
PRIDE	N: self-esteem
	...said that "Pride goes before a fall"...
	N: group of lions
	...filmed the pride of lions...
PRIED	Past tense and past participle of *to pry*
	VB: look at closely and inquisitively
	...pried into everyone else's business...
	VB: wedge open
	...pried the jammed door open...

PRIER	N: person who pries
PRIOR	ADJ: before, formerly
	...left over from a prior relationship...
	N: superior ranking next to the abbot of a monastery
	...served as prior in his later years...
PRINCE	N: son of a king
	..."Someday my prince will come," says the young girl...
PRINT(S)	Third person singular, present tense of *to print*
	VB: duplicate, copy, reproduce
	Plural of *print*
	N: copies
	...overheard at the drugstore: "Someday my prints will come"...
PRINCIPAL	(Match the *a* in *main* and the *a* in *principal)*
	N: main, chief
	N: main school administrator
	...spoke with the teachers and the principal...
	N: significant participant
	...names of the principals in the land deal...
	...principal in the lawsuit...
	N: original amount invested
	...interest payment is higher than the principal...
	N: owner of a firm/company/corporation
	...spoke with the principal in the company...
	...five principals of the law firm...
	ADJ: primary, main, chief
	...principal reason for the lawsuit...
	...principal motivation for leaving...
PRINCIPLE	(Match the *-le* of *rule* with the *-le* of *principle)*
	(Alone, *principle* cannot ever be an adjective)
	N: rule, standard, belief
	...against my principles to engage in this...
	...stand on principle...

PRINCIPALED	(No such word!)
PRINCIPLED	ADJ: having values and beliefs
	...known him to be a very principled person...
	...find his despicable behavior to be unprincipled...
PRISM	N: instrument that disperses light
	...colors coming from a prism...
PRISON	N: jail, location to hold those who have broken the law
	...have to spend some time in prison...
PRODIGY	N: person with exceptional abilities, usually a child
	...child prodigy on the piano...
PROGENY	N: offspring
	...did not leave a cent to his progeny...
PROFIT	N: financial gain from a business transaction
	...established as a for-profit company...
PROPHET	N: person who speaks of inspired religious truths
	...words spoken by the prophet Isaiah...
	N: person who foretells the future
	...regarded as a stock market prophet...
PROPHECY	Pronounced /... -see/
	N: prediction, foretelling of future events
	...fulfilled the prophecy for his success...
PROPHESY	Pronounced /... -sigh/
	VB: predict, foretell the future
	...did prophesy the breakdown of the relationship...

PROPOSE

VB: suggest
...propose we discuss it further before taking action...
VB: make plans, intend
VB: offer marriage
...will propose while they are at the Dodger game...

PURPOSE

N: aim, intention
...not my purpose to upset her...
...has no purpose in this context...

PRO(S)

Plural of *pro*
N: those in favor of
...several pro votes...
Short for *professional*
...plays as a pro with the Yankees...

PROSE

N: writing that is not poetry
...cannot really follow his prose...

PROSTATE

N: male gland at the neck of the bladder
...had prostate cancer...

PROSTRATE

VB/ADJ: prone, stretched out face down
...lying prostrate from the pain...
...fell prostrate when the bullet hit...

PROVIDENCE

N: divine guidance or care
...relied on divine providence to guide him...
...attributed his success to providence...

PROVINCE

N: administrative division or district of a country
...one of the provinces in Canada...
...lived in a nearby province...

PSYCH	Pronounced /sike/ (rhymes with *bike*)
	VB: analyze, figure out
	...psych it out by himself...
	EXPRESSIONS
	psych out = undermine someone's confidence
	...tried to psych out his opponent...
	psych up = build up confidence to perform a task
	...psych himself up for the race...
PSYCHE	Pronounced /<u>sigh</u>-key/
	N: soul, self, mind
	...hard on his psyche to hear the criticism...
PSYCHE	N: princess loved by Cupid
PSYCHIC	N: person who sees the future
	...went to a psychic to ask her about my future...
	ADJ: of soul, mind
	...witnessed the psychic phenomenon...
PUBIC	ADJ: lower part of the abdomen
	...scar in the pubic area...
PUBLIC	N/ADJ: out in the open
	...suffered public humiliation...
PUS	N: exudate, infection
PUSS	N: cat
	SLANG: face
	...have to love that little puss on that kid...
PUT	VB: place, locate to a specific location
	...have to put her into a hospice facility...
PUTT	VB/N: strike a golf ball so that it rolls along the ground
	...missed a very short putt...

CHAPTER 17
THE LETTER *Q*

QUALIFY

VB: modify
...have to qualify my answer to include this...
VB: exhibit ability to join, perform
...will qualify for the Olympics...

QUANTIFY

VB: determine, express, or measure the amount of
...need to quantify the amount needed...

QUALITATIVE

ADJ: relating to quality or kind
...do a qualitative analysis to determine efficiency...

QUANTITATIVE

ADJ: relating to or expressible in terms of quantity
...do a quantitative analysis to determine numbers...

QUALITY

N: peculiar and essential character, trait
...has an ethereal quality about her...
N: value, worth
...first in quality...
ADJ: degree of excellence
...does very high-quality work...
...quality performance...

QUANTITY

N: amount
...reduce the quantity to save money...

QUARRY

VB: delve into
N: prey
...became the quarry of the predator...
N: excavation site
...found at the quarry...

QUERY

VB/N: question
...his query went unanswered...

QUARTS	Plural of *quart* N: measurement equal to two pints *...consumed several quarts of milk...*
QUARTZ	N: mineral
QUASH	VB: nullify, make void *...motion to quash the evidence...*
SQUASH	VB: crush, mash *...will be squashed between them...*
QUIET	VB: become silent or peaceful, put to rest *...need to quiet her nerves before she speaks...* ADJ: marked by little or no motion or activity, calm *...quiet seas the day we set sail...* ADJ: gentle, easygoing ADJ: enjoyed in peace and relaxation *...had a quiet cup of tea...* ADJ: secluded *...found a quiet nook to meditate...* ADJ: make secure by freeing from dispute or question *...attempt to quiet title to the property...*
QUITE	ADV: to an extreme, positively *...need to be quite sure about it...* ADV: to a considerable extent, rather *...quite near where I live...*
QUIT	VB: set free, relieve, release *...going to quit bugging her...* VB: relinquish, abandon, give over, forsake VB: give up an action, activity, or employment; leave *...decided to quit his long-time job...* VB: admit defeat *...going to quit trying as he is never going to succeed...* ADJ: release from obligation, charge, or penalty, free *...has a quitclaim deed to the property...*

CHAPTER 18
THE LETTER *R*

(Check the section at the end of this letter *R* for words that have *re-*, meaning "again," as a prefix.)

RABBET	N: channel, groove, or recess cut out of the edge or face of any body, especially one intended to receive another member as a panel *...cut a rabbet in order to attach the adjoining piece of wood...*
RABBIT	N: animal
WELSH RABBIT	N: cheesy mixture served on toast (second spelling: *Welsh rarebit*)
RABID	ADJ: extremely violent, furious *...has a rabid temper when he drinks...* ADJ: going to extreme lengths in expressing a feeling, interest, or opinion *...had a rabid interest in football...* ADJ: affected with rabies *...bitten by a rabid dog...*
RABBLE	N: disorderly mob *...sustained an injury in the midst of the rabble...*
RUBBLE	N: waste, loose stone *...found the body in the rubble of the burned-out house...*

RACE	VB/N: move quickly ...*will race along the beach*... VB/N: movement in competition against others ...*ran a 10K race*...
RAISE	Principal parts: *raise, raised, raised* VB: lift up something (transitive verb) ...*will raise the flag at dawn*... N: elevation in pay ...*got a long-expected raise the first of the year*...
RISE	Principal parts: *rise, rose, risen* VB: get up (intransitive verb) ...*will rise at dawn and begin the day*... VB: go higher, grow ...*bread dough will rise in time to bake it for dinner*... N: elevation ...*sun is coming up just over the rise*...
RAZE	VB: tear down and destroy completely ...*old building was razed to erect a new high rise*...
RAY(S)	Plural of *ray* N: fish ...*caught several rays in the Gulf*... N: beam of light or radiant energy ...*rays of sunlight beaming into the room*...
RE	N: musical syllable ..."*re, a drop of golden sun*"... PREP: in regard to (with *in*) ...*sending this in re my physical exam*...
REY	SPANISH: *king* ...*live in Playa del Rey or Marina del Rey*...
RACER	N: person or vehicle involved in a race ...*top racer was injured*...
RAZOR	N: instrument used to shave ...*blade in the razor was dull*...

RACK	VB: cause to suffer torture, pain, or anguish; stretch or strain violently ...*would rack his brain to come up with a solution*... VB/N: place pool balls in a triangular frame ...*his turn to rack the balls for the new game*... N: wind-driven mass of high, often broken clouds N: instrument of torture on which a body is stretched ...*placed on a rack and tortured*... N: framework, stand, or grating on which articles are placed ...*clothes hanging on the rack*... N: type of automobile steering mechanism ...*had a rack and pinion gear system*... N: pair of antlers N: neck and spine of a forequarter of veal, pork, or esp. mutton ...*ordered rack of lamb*... SLANG: woman's breasts ...*has a nice rack*...
WRACK	VB: utterly ruin, wreck ...*wrack the town and surrounding area*... N: wreckage, ruin destruction ...*go to wrack and ruin*...
RACKET	N: implement with a handle used in various games N: confused, clattering noise, clamor ...*racket coming from the house next door*... N: fraudulent scheme, enterprise, or activity ...*running a racket on his unsuspecting neighbors*... N: illegitimate enterprise made workable by bribery or intimidation N: easy and lucrative means of livelihood ...*job with his dad is a real racket*... SLANG: business or occupation ...*what's your racket?*...
RACQUETBALL	N: game played in a walled court (only time that this spelling is used)
RATCHET	N: mechanism that allows effective motion in one direction only ...*used a ratchet wrench to loosen the bolt on the underneath side*...

RAIL	VB: bitterly criticize
	...rail at the injustices in the system...
	N: track
	...careful not to touch the third rail...
	N: support bar
	...hit his side on the rail between the aisles...
RALE	Pronounced /rall/ (rhymes with *ball*)
	N: abnormal sound from the lungs, common with pneumonia
	...intense rales on the left side...
RAIN	VB/N: water falling in drops from the clouds
	...California always needs more rain...
	EXPRESSION
	rain on my parade = turn out badly
	...refuse to let this rain on my parade...
	when it rains, it pours = sometimes it is bad and just gets worse
REIGN	VB: rule, be prevalent
	...hamburger will reign supreme in our culture...
	N: period during which a ruler holds power
	...long reign of Elizabeth II...
REIN	N: part of an animal's bridle
	N: restraining influence
	...put the rein on his eating...
	EXPRESSION
	free rein = opportunity for unhampered activity or use
	...given free rein to run the company...
	rein in = check or stop by pulling in
	...needs to rein in his temper...
RANCOR	N: bitter, deep-seated ill will, enmity
	...seems to do everything with rancor and hatred...
RANKER	ADJ: offensively gross or coarse, foul (comparison form)

RANKLE	VB: irritate, cause resentment
	...attitude always seemed to rankle her...
WRANGLE	VB: dispute
	...wrangle over every detail of the plan...
	VB: herd cattle
WANGLE	VB: obtain by scheming
	...tried to wangle the money from her...
RAP	VB: knock sharply
	...rap at the door...
	VB: smack
	...sharp rap on the knuckles...
	VB/N: arrest, hold, or sentence on a criminal charge
	...tried to beat the rap...
	VB/N: perform a style of popular music
	...always trying to rap like the pros...
	...enjoys rap more than any other kind of music...
	N: sharp rebuke or criticism
	...rap against his behavior...
	N: talk, conversation
	EXPRESSIONS
	take the rap = take responsibility for something
	beat the rap = get off without a conviction
	bad rap = unfair accusation
	rap sheet = list of problems with the law
WRAP	VB/N: cover by folding something around
	...find something to wrap the gift in...
	N: material used for wrapping
	...sealed it with plastic wrap...
	EXPRESSION
	that's a wrap = something has been finished (usually a movie take)

RAPPEL	VB: descend via a rope *...rappel into the deep cave...*
REPEL	VB: drive back *...intended to repel his advances...*
RAP(-PED)	Past tense and past participle of *to rap* *...salesman rapped at the door...*
WRAP(-PED)	Past tense and past participle of *to wrap* *...wrapped all the gifts...*
RAPT	ADJ: spellbound, engrossed *...listened with rapt attention...*
RAPPER	N: person who performs rap music *...well-known rapper Eminem...*
WRAPPER	VB: covering, loose gown *...wearing nothing but a wrapper...*
RAPPORT	Pronounced /ra-<u>poor</u>/ N: accord, mutual understanding *...lacked a good rapport among the staff...*
REPORT	VB/N: statement of something, accounting *...details of the heinous crime in the news report...* N: explosive sound *...heard the report miles away...*
RETORT	VB/N: sharp reply *...tends to retort before he thinks...*
RAPTOR	N: bird of prey
RAPTURE	N: ecstasy *...in a state of rapture after the proposal...*
RUPTURE	VB/N: tear or break *...went to the ER with a rupture of his appendix...*

RATIONAL	ADJ: sensible
	...acted in a rational manner in the time of crisis...
RATIONALE	N: reasoning, basis for doing something
	...faulty rationale led to the demise of the project...

RAUCOUS	ADJ: loudly disorderly
	...led to a raucous debate to no avail...
RUCKUS	N: fracas, commotion
	...ruckus that left four people with minor injuries...

READ	Pronounced /reed/ (rhymes with *seed*)
	VB: understand something written or printed
	...want to read the latest on the scandal...
	Pronounced /red/ (rhymes with *said*)
	Past tense and past participle of *to read*
	...have not read the details about it...
REED	N: kind of tall grass
	...piercing wound from a dried-out reed...
	N: part of a wind instrument
	...played in the reed section...
RED	N: color
	SLANG: Communist
	EXPRESSIONS
	see red = be angry
	in the red = show a financial loss

READMISSION	N: return, as to a hospital
	...readmission just four days later...
REMISSION	N: period in which something has abated
	...finally in remission after months of treatment...

REAL	ADJ: existing as a fact, true, genuine, not made up *...prefer real butter to margarine...*

REEL	VB: move in a swaying or staggering manner
	...began to reel as she heard the devastating news...
	N: spool
	...took rod and reel to the pond to fish...
	N: roller for film or the film itself
	...was done reel to reel...
	EXPRESSION
	    reel in = cause someone to believe, bring someone to a point of
	    view
	    ...tried to reel me in with his sweet talk...

REALITY	N: state of being real *...does not deal well with reality...*
REALTY	N: real estate *...worked in realty for several years...*
REALTOR	Pronounced /<u>real</u>-tor/, not /<u>re</u>-la-tor/ N: real estate agent, salesman (Dictionary shows this word capped)
REBAIT	VB: bait again *...had to rebait the hook several times...*
REBATE	VB: reduce the force or activity of, diminish VB/N: return part of a payment *...will rebate part of his down payment...* *...received a rebate on the purchase...*

RECANT	VB: retract, withdraw
	...immediately began to recant his story...
RECOUNT	VB/N: explain, tell
	...witness did not recount the story accurately...
RE-COUNT	VB: count again
	...demanded a re-count after the close vote...
RECEDE	VB: move back or away, withdraw
	...hairline began to recede...
	...flood waters are slow to recede...
	VB: slant backward
	VB: grow less or smaller, diminish, decrease
	...image began to recede in the distance...
RESEED	VB: plant again
	...need to reseed the law...
RECEIPT	N: writing acknowledging the receiving of goods or money
	...did not get a receipt for the purchase...
RESEAT	VB: seat again
	...will reseat the guests because of the mix-up...
RECIPE	N: instructions for making something from various ingredients
	...did not usually follow the recipe...
	...this is a recipe for disaster...
RECENT	Pronounced /<u>ree</u>-sunt/
	ADJ: done or made not long ago, modern
	...is a recent change...
RESENT	Pronounced /ree-<u>zent</u>/
	VB: feel insulted, indignant
	...would resent her interference...
RE-SENT	VB: sent again

REC	Short for *recreation*
	N/ADJ: leisure time
	...participated at the rec center...
RECK	N: worry, care
	(Used mainly in *reckless*, as in "not to have a care about")
	...is reckless with his money...
WRECK	VB: crash, cause to be ruined
	...tried not to wreck his new car the first time out...
	N: broken remains of something wrecked or otherwise ruined
	...hard to call the wreck he drives a real car...
	N: something disabled or in a state of ruin or dilapidation
	...house was a wreck after having five kids there for the weekend...
	N: person or animal of broken constitution, health, or spirits
	...was a total wreck while he waited for the test results...
REEF	N: ridge under the water of the ocean
	...diving near the coral reef...
WREATH	N: circle of flowers and/or leaves
	...time to put up the Christmas wreath...
	...decoration in the shape of a wreath...
REEK	VB: have a strong, unpleasant smell
	...would always reek of alcohol when he came home...
	...began to reek as the body decayed...
	N: odor
	...certain reek that came from that place on the ground...
WREAK	VB: inflict vengeance or punishment
	...will wreak vengeance on his enemies...
	VB: bring about, cause
	...their dog wreaked havoc in the neighborhood...

REFLECT(S)	Third person singular, present tense of *to reflect* VB: give back or exhibit as an image, likeness, or outline, mirror *...lake reflects the clouds...* VB: bring or cast as a result *...attitude reflects his upbringing...* VB: think quietly and calmly *...reflects on the years she spent with him...* VB: tend to bring reproach or discredit *...accusation reflects on all in the office...* VB: bring about a specified appearance or characterization *...success reflects well on his leadership...*
REFLEX	N/ADJ: automatic, inborn response to a stimulus *...was an automatic reflex to her comment...* *...tested his reflex time...*
REFRACT (ION)	VB/N: bending of a ray *...refraction of the light as it came through the window...*
RETRACT (ION)	VB/N: withdrawal of a statement or opinion *...issued a retraction almost immediately...*
RELAID	VB: laid again *...relayed the carpet after the flood...*
RELAY(ED)	VB: pass along by stages as a message *...message was relayed to me by my assistant...*
RELEVANT	ADJ: pertinent, related *...did not seem relevant to the facts of the case...*
REVERENT	ADJ: worshipful *...reverent in the presence of the Pope...*
RENDER	VB: cause to be *...render her speechless...*
RENTER	N: person who pays to live somewhere *...does not allow one to be a renter in the complex...*

REPRIEVE	VB/N: official pardon, delay *...got a reprieve on the timing of the deadline...*
RETRIEVE	VB: regain, rescue, take back *...went to retrieve his possessions from her apartment...*
RESIDENCE	N: place where one lives *...residence for those with disabilities...*
RESIDENT(S)	Plural of *resident* N: people who live in a given place *...several residents had to be evacuated...*
RESONATE	VB: reverberate with sound *...sound will resonate throughout the area...* VB: strike a chord *...does not resonate with me...*
RESONANT	ADJ: continuing to sound, echoing *...resonant sound throughout the hallway...*
RESPECTABLY	ADV: in a decent or acceptable fashion *...respectably attired for the occasion...*
RESPECTFULLY	ADV: in a manner showing respect or honor *...respectfully submitted my resignation...*
RESPECTIVELY	ADV: number of items taken as individual units in the order named *...John, Jezzi, and Kahlua, respectively...*
REST	VB: relax, pause *...ordered to rest between activities...* N: remainder *...rest will be in my office...*
WREST	VB: tear away by violent twisting *...had to wrest the gun from the defendant...* VB: gain with difficulty *...wrest control of the company from my partner...*

RESUME	VB: continue after a break
	...came back after surgery to resume his position...
RÉSUMÉ	N: listing of one's education and work record
	...sent a résumé to several firms...
RETCH	VB: vomit
	...started to retch as soon as he came out of the surgery...
WRETCH	N: miserable or despicable person, one who is profoundly unhappy
	...was always a wretch because he drank too much...
REVEILLE	N: signal to get up in the morning
	N: bugle call at sunrise in the military
	...reveille at 5:00 most days...
REVELRY	N: party, noisy partying or merrymaking
	...revelry continued into the night...
REVERIE	N: dream, dreamlike state
	...lost in reverie most of the afternoon...
REVIEW	VB: examine or study
	...need to review before the final exam...
	VB/N: critical evaluation, as of a book or play
	...decided to review his most recent work...
	...got a good review...
	N: formal military inspection
	...troops passed the stand in review...
	N: general survey
	...did a review of the procedure...
	N: judicial examination (of proceedings of a lower tribunal by a higher)
	...review of the trial testimony by the court...
REVUE	N: theatrical production consisting typically of brief, loosely connected, often satirical skits, songs, and dances
	...enjoyed the vaudeville revue...

RIDER	N: one that rides *...rider was thrown from the horse...* N: addition to a document often attached on a separate piece of paper *...attached a rider to the policy to cover her jewelry...* N: clause appended to a legislative bill to secure a distinct object *...rider was attached at the last minute...*
RIGHTER	N: one who sets things right -- Superman! *...is a righter of wrongs...*
RYDER	N: vehicle-rental business
WRITER	N: one who writes *...did not appreciate him as a writer...*
RIDGED	ADJ: ribbed, grooved, wavy *...had a ridged surface that caused problems...*
RIGID	ADJ: stiff, unyielding *...rigid in his views on abortion...*
RIFE	ADJ: extensive, prevalent *...rife with suspicion about his role in the scheme...*
RIPE	ADJ: prepared, ready to eat *...fruit was not yet ripe enough to eat...*
RIGGER	N: one that rigs *...worked as a rigger on the ship...* N: long slender, pointed sable paintbrush
RIGOR	N: harsh inflexibility in opinion, temper, or judgment; severity (usually used in the plural) *...deal with the rigors of the harsh climate...* N: tremor caused by a chill; condition that makes life difficult, challenging, or uncomfortable, especially extremity of cold N: rigidness or torpor of organs or tissue that prevents response to stimuli *...rigor mortis had set in...*

RIGHT(S)	Third person singular, present tense of *to right*
	VB: make correct or just
	...trying to right the wrongs of the situation...
	N: opposite of *left*
	...sat to his right...
	N: politically conservative
	...to the right of Barry Goldwater...
	...conservative right...
	N: just claim, privilege
	...in violation of his civil rights...
	ADJ: correct
	...large number of his answers were right...
DOWNRIGHT	ADJ: totally, thoroughly
	...downright mean...
	...that is downright wrong...
COPYRIGHT	N: exclusive legal right to reproduce, publish, and sell the matter and form of a literary, musical, or artistic work
	...owns the copyright on the book...
	...filed for a copyright on the book...
RITE(S)	N: solemn ceremony performed in accordance with prescribed rules
	...given last rites...
WRITE(S)	VB: compose
WRIGHT(S)	N: one who constructs or repairs something
	...spent time during the war as a shipwright...
WRIT(S)	Pronounced /rit/ (rhymes with *sit*)
	N: formal written document
	...issued a writ of mandate...

RING	VB: give forth a clear sound *...bell will ring later in the day...* N: circle of metal or other material generally worn on the finger *...gave her a diamond ring...* N: exclusive group of persons working together for selfish or illegal purposes *...theft ring was finally caught...*

WRING	VB: twist with force
	...took hours to wring out all the water...
	EXPRESSION
	    wrung out = exhausted
	    ...was wrung out after the long race...

RINGER	N: imposter
	...substituted a ringer for the man supposedly in charge...
	EXPRESSION
	    dead ringer = exact lookalike
	    ...dead ringer for his dad...

WRINGER	N: mechanism to get water out of clothes
	...hand got caught in the wringer...
	EXPRESSION
	    put him through the wringer = make it very difficult
	    ...put him through the wringer because of his disastrous mistake...

RISKY	ADJ: hazardous *...doctor said the surgery would be risky...*
RISQUÉ	ADJ: verging on impropriety or indecency, off-color *...did not appreciate his risqué remarks...*
RIVAL	VB/N: compete against *...will rival his brother's achievement...*
RIFLE	VB: throw hard *...rifle the ball to his receiver...* N: weapon

ROAD	N: street, thoroughfare for vehicles
	...happened on the road to the capital...
RODE	Past tense of *to ride*
	VB: be carried on
	...rode on the back of his motorcycle...
ROW(ED)	Past tense and past participle of *to row*
	VB: move through the water by means of oars
	...rowed all the way to the far end of the lake...
ROE(S)	N: fish eggs
	...when I learned that "shad roe" is caviar...
	N: small deer noted for nimbleness and grace
ROSE	Past tense and past participle of *to rise*
	VB: ascend, awake
	...always rose early to read the paper leisurely over coffee...
	N: flower
	N/ADJ: color
	...dress was a deep rose...
ROW(S)	Third person singular, present tense of *to row*
	VB: propel as with oars
	...rows several miles a day for exercise...
	N: objects arranged in a straight line
	...rows and rows of tomato plants...
ROLE	N: actor's part in a play
	...thought it was the role of a lifetime...
	N: part played in real life
	...parent role is tough...
ROLL	VB: move along by turning over and over
	...need to roll it up the hill...
	N: list of names
	...called the roll every day...
	N: small loaf of bread

ROOD	N: cross symbolizing the cross on which Jesus Christ died
RUDE	ADJ: lacking refinement or delicacy
	...was rude to his companions on the trip...
RUE(D)	Past tense and past participle of *to rue*
	VB: regret
	...rued the day he met her...
ROOMER	N: person who rents one or more rooms to live in, lodger
	...needed one new roomer to make ends meet...
RUMOR	N: unconfirmed report, gossip, hearsay
	...rumor had already started before he even came in...
ROOT	VB: furnish with or enable to develop roots
	VB: remove altogether, find and get rid of (usually used with *out*)
	...root out dissenters in the group...
	VB: dig in the earth with the snout, grub (usually used with *around*)
	...pigs would root around for food...
	VB: turn over, dig up, or discover and bring to light
	...root out the cause of the problem...
	VB: noisily applaud or encourage a contestant or team, cheer
	...root for the home team...
	N: underground part of a seed plant
	N: part of an organ or physical structure that is attached to the body
	...abscess in the root of the tooth...
	N: something that is the origin or source
	...alcoholism is the root of all his problems...
ROUTE	Correctly pronounced /root/ (rhymes with *boot*)
	VB: send by way of a certain road or direction
	...had to route the traffic around the construction...
	N: road, course, path, direction
EN ROUTE	Pronunciation may vary; spelling does not
	PREP PHRASE: be on the way
	...police were en route within minutes...

ROUT	Pronounced /rout/ (rhymes with *shout*)
	VB: disperse in disorderly defeat, defeat completely
	...rout that team by 40 points every time they play...
	VB: cause to emerge, especially from bed
	...had to rout him out of bed every morning...
	N: disastrous defeat, debacle
	...game was a rout after the team scored 12 runs in the first inning...
	N: state of wild confusion or disorderly retreat
	...in a complete rout of the troops...
ROTE	N: fixed, mechanical way of doing something
	...just seemed to be doing it by rote...
	N: by memory alone, without thought or understanding
	...recited the words by rote...
WROTE	Past tense of the verb *to write*
	VB: compose
	...always wrote it down...
ROT	VB: decay
WROUGHT	VB: excite (usually with word *up*)
	...wrought up over nothing...
	ADJ: manufactured, hammered
	...made of wrought iron...
ROUX	Pronounced /roo/ (rhymes with *boo*)
	N: thickening agent for sauces
	...prepared the roux from the drippings...
RUE(S)	Third person singular, present tense of *to rue*
	VB: regret, be sorrowful
	...rues every day that he is stuck in the facility...
	N: strong-scented perennial woody herb used in medicine
RUSE	N: wily subterfuge
	...used a ruse to get him into the shop...

RUMBLE   VB/N: make a heavy continuous sound
...heard the rumble of the thunder...

RUMPLE   VB: mess up, tousle
...rumple the bed after it was made

RUNG   Past participle of *to ring*
                  VB: make a sound with a bell
                  ...had rung the bell at exactly 8:00...
                  N: step on a ladder
                  ...fell from the fourth rung...
                  ...standing on the second rung when it broke...

WRUNG   Past tense and past participle of *to wring*
                  VB: twist
                  ...wrung the water out of the clothes by hand...
                  VB: squeeze, force out
                  ...wrung every penny from her he could...

THE PREFIX RE-

One of the meanings of the prefix *re-* is "again" as in *reread* and *redo*. Generally, this prefix is added to the front of a word and made a solid word. When there is already a word that begins with "re-" that has its own meaning, the prefix *re-* meaning "again" has to be hyphenated to the word rather than making it a solid word.

The words here are a sample of such words but are by no means a complete list of these pairs.

RECOIL	VB: fall back under pressure
	VB: shrink back physically or emotionally
	...recoil at the sight of the decomposing body...
RE-COIL	VB: coil again, rewind
	...need to re-coil the hose...
RECOUNT	VB: tell about
	...had to recount the events that surrounded the incident...
RE-COUNT	VB: count again
	...had to re-count the ballots because the election was so close...
RECOVER	VB: bring back to normal
	...misspoke but did recover from the gaffe...
	VB: get well
	...need to recover quickly from the surgery...
	VB: restore, regain
	...will recover all we lost...
RE-COVER	VB: cover again
	...needed to re-cover the baby several times in the night...
RECREATE	VB: give new life or freshness to, refresh
	...spent time to recreate my life...
RE-CREATE	VB: create again
	...tried to re-create the scene that I observed...

REDRESS	VB/N: compensate, remedy
	...need to redress the grievances...
RE-DRESS	VB: dress again
	...spilled coffee on myself and had to re-dress for work...
REFORM	VB/N: revise, improve
	...instituted necessary reform within the organization...
RE-FORM	VB: form again
	...ice will re-form on the lake because of the cold temperatures...
	...had to re-form the corporation after the changes...
REFUND	VB/N: give back money
	...had to refund her money for the defective product...
RE-FUND	VB: fund again
	...had to re-fund the loan for another year after it expired...
RELAY	VB: send, transmit, spread
	...had to relay the message to her...
RE-LAY	VB: lay again
	...had to re-lay the carpet after the construction...
REMARK	VB/N: comment
	...felt the need to remark on her appearance...
RE-MARK	VB: mark again
	...had to re-mark the exhibit in the second proceeding...
RESENT	VB: feel envy toward
	...resent that she got all the attention...
RE-SENT	VB: sent again
	...re-sent the package after the first one was lost...

RESIGN	VB: quit, leave a job
	...had to resign because of the scandal...
RE-SIGN	VB: sign again
	...had to re-sign the papers at the bank...
RESORT	VB: have recourse
	...had to resort to underhanded tactics...
	N: vacation spot
	...spent time at a golf resort in the desert...
RE-SORT	VB: sort again
	...had to re-sort the coins after the kids got into them...
RESTRAIN	VB: hold back, keep from doing
	...had to restrain him from rushing into the burning building...
RE-STRAIN	VB: strain again
	...take care not to re-strain the muscle when he resumes activity...

CHAPTER 19
THE LETTER *S*

SAC(S)
Plural of *sac*
N: small internal pocket in an animal or person
...small sac filled with pus...

SACK(S)
Third person singular, present tense of *to sack*
VB/N: get to the quarterback before he gets rid of the ball
...tried to sack the quarterback on every play...
N: bag
...had her lunch in a sack...

SAX
Short for *saxophone*
N: reed instrument
...plays a mean sax...

SADDEST
ADJ: most unhappy
...the saddest I have ever seen him...

SADIST
N: person who takes delight in cruelty
...was a sadist in regard to his treatment of women...

SAIL
VB: travel by water
...always wanted to sail around the world...
N: cloth spread to the winds to make a ship move
...ripped the sail in half...

SALE
N: exchange of goods for money
...sale will be completed in 30 days...
N: offering of something at lower prices than usual
...on sale for 30 percent off...

SALLOW	ADJ: pale yellow color that implies sickness *...sallow complexion after weeks in the hospital...*
SHALLOW	ADJ: not deep *...went wading in shallow water...* ADJ: small minded, petty *...seems shallow and lacking in concern for others...*
SALON	N: living room; stylish place to have nails/hair done *...spent a couple of hours at the hair salon...*
SALOON	N: bar, tavern, place to drink *...shoot-out at the saloon after a night of drinking...*
SALVAGE	VB: recover property from wreckage *...tried to salvage what we could from the burned-out building...* VB: restore property damaged by fire or some other disaster VB/N: something extracted (as from rubbish) as valuable or useful *...salvage from the fire was stored in the warehouse...* N/ADJ: act of saving or rescuing a ship or its cargo or property in danger *...salvage operation was in full swing when he arrived...* N: property saved from destruction in a calamity *...had no place to store the salvage that was collected...*
SAVAGE	N: primitive person ADJ: particularly brutal *...endured a savage beating...*
SELVAGE	N: woven edge that prevents cloth or fabric from raveling *...cut along the selvage of the material...*
SAND(S)	Plural of *sand* N: small rock material *...trekked through the sands of the desert...*
SANS	FRENCH: *without* *...she was there sans husband...*

SANE	ADJ: free from hurt or disease, mentally sound
	...was declared sane and competent to stand trial...
	ADJ: wise, reasonable
	...count on him for sane advice...
SEINE	N: large fish net
Seine	N: river that runs through Paris
SAVER	N: person who saves
	...has always been a saver and now has enough for a down payment...
SAVOR	VB: delight in, enjoy
	...savor the time that he was home...
SAVIOR	N: one that saves from danger or destruction
	...has been my savior on more than one occasion...
Savior	N: in the Christian tradition, Christ
SAW(ED)	Past tense and past participle of *to saw*
	VB: cut
	...sawed through the heavy door...
SOD	VB/N: grass, turf
	...intend to sod the yard...
	...got the sod from a local gardener...
SCAM	VB/N: ruse, fraudulent plan
	...worked a scam on the senior citizens...
SCAN	VB/N: make a copy of
	...had to scan the documents into the record...
	VB/N: look through
	...scan for any signs of the wreckage...

SCENE	N: place where an event occurs
	...jurors visited the scene of the crime...
	N: division in a play
	...each scene seemed to be quite long...
	N: view of people or places
	...came upon the scene as I rounded the corner...
	N: display of strong emotion before others
	...count on him to always cause a scene and embarrass her...
SEEN	Past participle of *to see*
	VB: perceived by the eye
	...have not seen him since the accident...
SCEPTER	N: staff that is a symbol of authority
	...carried the scepter for the king...
SPECTER	N: ghost
	...appearance of a specter had her frightened...
SCRAP	N: small piece
	...only a scrap of the paper remained...
SCRAPE	VB: remove the surface of
	...had to scrape against the edge of the wall...
	N: altercation
	...got into a scrape with the other kids...
SCRIP	N: paper money issued for temporary emergency use
	...scrip they were paid was good only in the company store...
SCRIPT	N: something written or prescribed
	...just following the script that was set out for me...
	N: written text of a stage play, screenplay, or broadcast
	...had to make changes in the script...
	SLANG: prescription
	N: directions for medication
	...got a script from the doctor...

SCULL	VB: propel a boat *...would scull through the calm waters...* N: long narrow rowing boat propelled by oars *...using a scull to get across the lake...* N: long oar mounted over the stern of a boat and moved from side to side
SCULLERY	N: room for cleaning and storing dishes and cooking utensils and for doing messy kitchen work
SCULLERY MAID	N: poor creature doing the messy kitchen work!
SKULL	N: skeleton of the head *...remains of a badly decomposed skull...*
SCULPTOR	N: person who produces a sculpture *...wanted to be a sculptor...*
SCULPTURE	N: art object that is three dimensional *...sculpture had no identifiable form...*
SEA	N: ocean *...went to sea with the Navy...*
SEE	VB: look at
SÍ	SPANISH: *yes*
SEA(S)	N: large body of salt water *...sailed the seas for most of his life...*
SEE(S)	VB: perceive with the eyes *...sees what she wants to see...*
SEIZE	VB: take hold of suddenly or violently *...seize at least twice a day because of epilepsy...* VB: take possession by force *...agents will seize the drugs...*

SEAM	N: line formed by sewing together two pieces of material *...small tear along the seam of the skirt...* N: any line marking the joining of edges *...seam in the walls showed through the paint...*
SEEM	VB: appear to be *...did not seem to last long...* VB: be apparently true *...did seem that they are happy...*
SEAMY	ADJ: unpleasant, degraded, sordid *...represents the seamy side of life...*
SEEMLY	ADJ: good looking, handsome, attractive *...quite a seemly young woman...* ADV: decorous; fit for the occasion, purpose, or person *...what he wore was seemly for the occasion...*
SEEMINGLY	ADV: having a deceptive or delusive appearance *...seemingly good relationship...* *...seemingly bad advice that he followed...*
SIMI (VALLEY)	N: location in Los Angeles area
SEAR	VB: char, scorch, or burn the surface of *...tried not to sear an imprint of the iron on the silk blouse...* VB: cause to dry and wither *...sear the edges of the meat to lock in the juices...* N: catch in a gunlock that keeps the hammer half cocked or fully cocked
SERE	ADJ: withered, dry *...walked through the sere leaves...*
SEER	N: one that sees, clairvoyant, psychic *...accused of being a seer...*

SEAT(ED)	Past tense and past participle of *to seat* VB: set in place *...was seated next to my brother...* *...tire was seated on the rim...*
SEED(ED)	Past tense and past participle of *to seed* VB: plant, sow *...seeded the lawn in the spring...*
CEDE(D)	Past tense and past participle of *to cede* VB: formally give over *...ceded the property to the State...*
SECRET	N/ADJ: something that is not public; private, not to be shared *...met in secret to make the decision...* *...had a secret she could not reveal...*
SECRETE	VB: release a substance *...secrete a sticky substance...*
SECT(S)	N: dissenting religious body *...member of a small sect on the fringe of Catholicism...* N: divisions, sections, segments
SEX	N: sexual act N: either of two divisions as in male and female *...did not care about the sex of the baby...*
SEIZE	VB: grasp, take forcibly, capture *...tried to seize the opportunity to get ahead...*
SIEGE	N: long period of being powerless *...siege of the area lasted more than one month...*
SEPTIC	ADJ: infected, harmful *...had to empty the septic tank...*
SKEPTIC	N: doubter, one who does not believe *...remains a skeptic about the validity of the opinion...*

SERF	N: member of a servile feudal class
	...reduced to the status of a serf...
SURF	VB: ride the waves in the ocean
	...surf in the high waves...
	N: swell of the sea that breaks upon the shore
	...played in the surf but did not go far out into the water...
	EXPRESSION
	surf the web = search on the internet
SERGE	N: kind of cloth with slanting lines on its surface
	...blue serge suit was the symbol of success...
SURGE	VB: rise and fall violently
	...crowd tried to surge toward the stage...
	VB: rush forward in a great wave
	...had to get a surge protector for the computer...
	N: course, pitch, increase
	...debating the effect of the surge in Iraq...
	...storm surge along the beach left homes flooded...
SERIES	N: sequence, succession, chain
	...best book of the whole series...
	...series of events that led to the slaying...
SERIOUS	ADJ: grave, solemn, somber
	...serious discussion about her drinking...
SEROUS	ADJ: relating to serum; thin, watery exudate
	...serous exudate from the wound...
CIRRUS	N: wispy white cloud

SEW	VB: fasten with needle and thread
SO	ADV: very
	CONJ: in this manner or in order that
	...*went to the bank so I could cash my check*...
	CONJ: therefore
	...*lost my job; so I filed for unemployment*...
SOW	VB: scatter seed on the ground
	...*will sow the corn for late-summer harvest*...
	VB: introduce into a selected environment, implant
	VB: set in motion, foment
	...*sow the seeds of suspicion about him*...
	VB: spread abroad, disperse
	EXPRESSION
	reap what you sow = what happens is a result of your own actions
	sow wild oats = do wild and foolish things in one's youth
SEWED, SEWING	Past tense and past participle/present participle of *to sew*
	...*sewed the rip in time for her to wear the dress*...
	...*took sewing lessons as a young child*...
SOWED, SOWING	Past tense and past participle/present participle of *to sow*
	...*sowed the field with wildflowers*...
SEWER	Pronounced /so-er/ (rhymes with *lower*)
	N: one who sews
	Pronounced /soo-er/ (rhymes with *brewer*)
	N: artificial usually subterranean conduit to carry off sewage and sometimes surface water as from rainfall
	...*trapped in the sewer for hours*...
SOWER	N: one who sows
SOUR	VB: go bad, turn rancid
	...*milk will sour in the heat*...
	ADJ: acid, tart, disagreeable, unpleasant
	...*had a sour disposition*...

SHAKE	VB: move irregularly to and fro
	...began to shake as the medication took effect...
	VB: vibrate, shudder, tremble
	...earthquakes shake the Southern California area...
	N/ADJ: long shingle split directly from a log
	...burned because of the shake roof...
SHEIKH	Correctly pronounced /sheek/ (rhymes with *cheek*)
	N: Arab nobleman
CHIC	ADJ: stylish, currently fashionable
	...always looked chic and stylish...
SHAM	VB: act intentionally, as to give a false impression
	N: something that is not genuine, that is false
	...carried out the sham on the senior citizen couple...
	N: decorative piece of cloth
	...had pillow shams that matched...
SHAME	VB: cause to feel guilty
	...tried to shame him into action...
	N: painful emotion caused by guilt, shortcoming, or impropriety
	...felt the shame of his reprehensible actions...
CHAMOIS	Pronounced /sham-ee/
	N: soft pliant leather prepared from the skin of the chamois or from sheepskin
	...used a chamois to dry the car...
SHEAF	N: collection of papers bound together
	...overwhelmed by the sheaf of papers to review...
SHEATH	N: tight-fitting cover or case
	...wrapped in a sheath for protection...
SHEATHE	Pronounced /sheethe/ (rhymes with *seethe*)
	VB: cover or wrap around
	...needs to sheathe his sword...
SHEAVE	VB: gather, collect, bind
	...attempted to sheave the collection of exhibits...

SHEAR VB: cut with scissors

    WIND SHEAR N: change in wind direction and speed between slightly different altitudes, especially a sudden downdraft
...plane crash was attributed to wind shear...

SHEER ADJ: very thin, almost transparent
...fabric so sheer that you could see her underwear...
ADJ: not mixed with anything else, absolute
...reacted with sheer delight...
ADJ: straight up or down
...hiking and came to a sheer drop-off...

SHOE N: foot covering
...scuffed his shoe on the rocks...
EXPRESSION
    shoe-in = a sure thing
    ...was a shoe-in to win the Senate seat...

SHOO VB: scare away
...had to shoo the flies away...

SHONE Past tense and past participle of *to shine*
VB: emit rays of light
...full moon shone brightly through the window...
...light shone into my eyes...

    SHINE Principal parts for the transitive verb: *shine, shined, shined*
VB: flash a light at somebody
...shined the light into the darkened room...
VB: polish something
...has shined his shoes for the occasion...
Principal parts for the intransitive verb: *shine, shone, shone*
VB: emit rays of light
...lamp did shine brightly...

SHOWN Past tense and past participle of *to show*
VB: displayed, exhibited
...exhibits were shown to the jurors...

SHUDDER	VB: tremble convulsively, shiver, quiver *...shudder at the thought of his murder...*
SHUTTER	N: movable cover or screen for a window or door *...used a shutter to close off the room...*
SHUFFLE	VB/N: drag one's feet *...gait had turned to a shuffle...* VB: jumble, mix up *...need to shuffle the cards well...*
SHUTTLE	VB: move from one place to another *...shuttle the students back and forth between classes...* N/ADJ: vehicle to move things from place to place *...took the shuttle to the hotel...* *...involved in the space shuttle program...*
SIC	Used inside of brackets in written texts to indicate that there is an error and that the editor knows it is an error. Means "as in the original." *...happened on June 31 [sic]...* VB: set upon, attack *...sic the dogs on the intruders...* VB: urge or incite to hostile action *...tried to sic him on the editor of the paper...*
SICCED	Past tense and past participle *to sic*
SICK	ADJ: affected with disease or ill health *...was sick the whole nine months of the pregnancy...* ADJ: spiritually or morally corrupt *...criminal act of a sick mind...* ADJ: sickened by strong emotion *...made me sick to think of the horror of the molestation...*
SIGH(S)	VB: take in and let out a deep breath *...sighs heavily every time I open my mouth to speak...*
SIZE	N/ADJ: extent, magnitude, amount *...awed by the size of the project...*

SIGH(ED) Past tense and past participle of *to sigh*
VB: take in and let out a deep breath
...sighed heavily when she heard the news...

SIDE VB: agree with, support
...always did side with his brother against me...
N: lateral part of something
...set it to the side...

SILVER N: luscious gray metal
...necklace of pure silver...

SLIVER N: small slice or section
...just a small sliver more of that pie...

SING VB: utter words in musical tones
...tried to sing the song...
EXPRESSION
    sing = tell all one knows about a criminal activity
        ...threatened with life in prison, he began to sing...

SINGE VB: slightly burn
...did not singe anything but her eyebrows...

SINK VB: go to the bottom, submerge
...economy could sink to a new low...
N: pool or pit for the deposit of waste or sewage
N: basin in the kitchen or bath
...sink was overflowing when we came in...

SYNC Short for *synchronize*
VB/N: occur or operate in unison
...always out of sync with everyone else...

ZINC N: bluish white crystalline metallic element

SIT(S)	Third person singular, present tense of *to sit*
	VB: take weight off your feet, be seated
	...sits at the computer too long each day...
SITZ	N: therapeutic bath where much of the body is immersed
	...recommended a sitz bath for her problem...
SLACK	VB: not do something one should do (usually used with *off*)
	...know he will slack off on getting this done...
	N: part that is hanging free or loose
	...take up the slack in the rope...
	ADJ: negligent, slovenly, weak
	...slack muscles...
	...slack mouth as a result of the stroke...
SLAKE	VB: ease thirst
	...only water can slake this thirst...
SLAY	VB: kill
	...always trying to slay the dragon...
	SLANG: overwhelm with laughter
	...his corny jokes just slay me...
SLEIGH	N: carriage mounted on runners for use on ice or snow, sled
	...in a one-horse open sleigh...
SLEEK	ADJ: shiny, smooth
	...sleek-looking car...
	...tall and sleek since she lost the weight...
SLICK	ADJ: slippery, shrewd
	...slipped on the slick surface...
	...really a slick operator who fooled us all...

SLEIGHT	N: dexterity, skill
	EXPRESSION
	sleight of hand = deceptiveness, cunning
	...practiced his sleight of hand on his parents...
SLIGHT	VB: treat discourteously or indifferently
	...acted to slight her in front of everyone...
	ADJ: small, thin, meager
	...could perceive only a very slight difference...
	...very slight build...
SLEW	Past tense and past participle of *to slay*
	VB: kill
	...slew the dragon...
	VB: rotate, turn on an axis
	...will slew around the center...
	VB: cause to skid, veer
	...ice caused the car to slew...
	VB: turn, twist, or swing about, pivot; skid (also spelled *slue*)
	...braked too hard and began to slew around the corner...
	N: large number
	...whole slew of things to do today...
SLOUGH	Pronounced /sloo/ (rhymes with *glue*)
	N: place of deep mud or mire; swamp or marsh
	...lived very near a slough and marsh lands...
	Pronounced /sluff/ (rhymes with *bluff*)
	VB: cast off skin (as of a snake)
	...slough the skin each year...
	VB: act lazy (usually used with *off*)
	...always slough off on the job...
	VB: get rid of or discard as irksome, objectionable, or disadvantageous
	...try to slough off her bad moods...

SLEUTH	VB: act as a detective, to track or follow *...will sleuth around to try to determine the culprit...* N: detective *...playing sleuth in looking for the cause of the leak...*
SLOTH	ADJ: disinclination to action or labor, indolence *...sloth-like behavior when there were chores to do...* N: any of several slow-moving arboreal edentate mammals
SLICE	N: portion of *...offered a generous slice of the profits...*
SLUICE	VB: flood or drench with a flow of released water *...sluice the low-lying lands...* VB: send (logs) down a waterway N: manmade channel for conducting water with a valve or gate to regulate the flow (also a *sluiceway*) *...caught in the sluice...*
SLOE	N: plum tree or shrub and the dark plumlike fruit of these plants *...always enjoyed a sloe gin fizz...*
SLOE-EYED	ADJ: having slanted, dark eyes
SLOW	VB: cause to reduce speed *...traffic always began to slow in the same places...* ADJ: not fast, not smart *...was slow in school...*
SLOG	VB: plod through, walk with a plodding step *...had to slog through the mud to get to the step...*
SLUG	VB: hit hard *...so frustrated with his brother that he just wanted to slug it out...*

SMOOTHER	ADJ: more even, more equable, more steady *...expect a smoother flight with no bumps on the return...* *...smoother transition because we did it just a year ago...*
SMOTHER	VB: deprive of oxygen *...tried to smother her with a pillow...* VB: overwhelm with attention *...smother her so that she feels she cannot do anything on her own...*
SOAR	VB: fly at a great height, fly upward *...wanted to soar above the clouds...*
SORE	N: localized source of pain, break in the skin *...diabetes caused a sore that just would not heal...* ADJ: painful, aching *...sore shoulder prevented her from playing...*
SOAR(ED)	Past tense and past participle of *to soar* VB: fly upward *...balloons soared above the buildings...*
SWORD	N: weapon with a long blade for cutting or thrusting
SOLDER	Pronounced /<u>sod</u>-er/ VB: join metals together *...need to solder the loose ends...*

SOLDIER	N: person serving in the military or for a cause
	...soldier in Iraq...
	EXPRESSION
	    soldier on = continue under difficult circumstances
	    ...need to soldier on to finish the task...

SOLD	Past tense and past participle of *to sell* VB: give over to someone else in exchange for payment *...sold to the highest bidder...*
SOLE(D)	Past tense and past participle of *to sole* ADJ: having soles

SOLE	N: bottom of a shoe or foot
	...hole in the sole of the shoe...
	ADJ: one and only
	...listed as a sole proprietor...
SOUL	N: inner spirit
	...did it with a lot of soul...
	...need to do some soul searching...
	N: totality
	...is the heart and soul of the company...
SOLITAIRE	N: card game
	N: gem set by itself
	...gave her a diamond solitaire...
SOLITARY	ADJ: alone
	...spent time in solitary confinement...
SOME	PRO/ADJ: unspecified number, quantity
	...have some that I can exchange...
	...bring some expertise to the company...
SUM	N: total amount
	...for the grand sum of a dollar...
	...total sum of the parts...
SON	N: male offspring
	...son she was proud of...
SUN	N: celestial body that the earth and planets revolve around
	...early-morning sun was blinding me as I drove east...

SOOT	N: ashes, dirt *...cleaned the soot from the fireplace...*
SUIT	VB: meet the requirements of, be acceptable *...house does not suit me...* N: set of matching outer garments *...wore a three-piece suit to the meeting...* N: costume or clothes for a special activity *...had a diving suit that he wanted to use...* N: four kinds of cards in a deck *...collecting a different suit...* N: court procedure to recover a right or claim *...will file suit in court on Monday...*
SUITE	N: set of matching furniture *...felt a need to have a new living room suite...* N: series of connected rooms used as a living unit *...had to get a suite at the hotel to accommodate everyone...* N: instrumental composition *...composed a suite for the conductor...*
SWEET	ADJ: not sour *...too sweet for my taste...* ADJ: extremely advantageous *...sweet deal for him...*
SUET	N: hard fatty tissues around the kidneys of cattle and sheep used in cooking and for making tallow *...used the suet to flavor the gravy...*
SPACIOUS	ADJ: roomy, having a lot of space *...spacious office with room for everything...*
SPECIOUS	ADJ: false but appearing true *...his specious argument convinced several people...*

SPADE	VB: dig up with a shovel
	...spade the dirt off the driveway...
	N: shovel
	N: suit of cards
	...jack of spades...
SPAY(ED)	Past tense and past participle of *to spay*
	VB: remove the reproductive organs of a female animal
	...had the dogs spayed early on...
SPEC(S)	Short for *specifications*
	N: details of a plan
	...working on the specs for the project...
SPECK	N: small spot, mote
	...didn't see a speck of dust...
SPRAIN	VB/N: wrenching or tearing of a joint
	...sustained a severe ankle sprain playing basketball...
STRAIN	VB/N: injury from excessive use or effort
	...showing the strain of working long hours...
STAFF	VB: supply with workers
	...need to staff the event on Friday...
	N: long walking stick
	...carried a staff to help with his balance...
	N: horizontal lines with spaces on which music is written
	N: workers
	...had a problem with a man on the kitchen staff...
STAPH	Short for *staphylococcus*
	N/ADJ: bacteria-causing infection
	...diagnosed with a staph infection...

STAID	ADJ: sedate, settled, steady, solemn
	...found her to be staid and rather unfriendly...
STAY(ED)	Past tense and past participle of *to stay*
	VB: remain or dwell
	...stayed with his parents during college...
	VB: granted a postponement
	...judge stayed the sentencing...
STAY	N: certain period of time
	...happened during her stay in the islands...
	N: suspension or postponement of a legal action or an execution
	...granted a stay of his execution...
STAIR(S)	N: step
	...fell on the third stair...
STARE(S)	VB: look long or directly at something with eyes wide open
	...will stare for hours at the TV without really seeing it...

STAMP	VB: strike in a downward motion with the foot
	...*stamped the bug into oblivion*...
	VB/N: put a mark on
	...*used a Bates stamp on the exhibit*...
	EXPRESSION
	    stamp out = eradicate
	      ...*hope to stamp out cancer in our lifetime*...

STOMP	VB: tread heavily ...*stomp out of the room in anger*...
STANCH	VB: stop the flow of ...*tried to stanch the flow of blood from the wound*...
STAUNCH	ADJ: strong and firm in commitment ...*staunch supporter of gay rights*...
STATIONARY	ADJ: not moving, standing still, unchanging ...*seemed to be stationary rather than movable*...
STATIONERY	N: writing materials (paper, cards, envelopes, et cetera) (Think of the *e* in *paper* and the *e* in *stationery*) ...*loved to use nice stationery and write old-fashioned notes*...
STATUE	N: three-dimensional representation of a person, animal, or mythical being that is produced by sculpturing, modeling, or casting ...*statue of the town hero*...
STATURE	N: natural height (as of a person) in an upright position N: quality or status gained by growth, development, or achievement ...*gained stature in the community with his stand on women's rights*...
STATUTE	N: law enacted by the legislative branch of a government ...*new statute in regard to GMO's*...

STEAL	VB: rob
	...tried to steal my identity...
	VB: move secretly (used with *away*)
	...steal away in the middle of the night...
	EXPRESSION
	real steal = bargain
	...house in that neighborhood was a real steal for under a
	million...
STEEL	VB: fill with resolution or determination
	...will steel himself against her argument...
	N/ADJ: metal made from iron
	...worked at the steel mill all his life...
STEP	VB: move from one level to another
	...decided to step up and speak on what he believed...
	N: rest for the foot in ascending or descending a stair
	...carpet on the fourth step was ripped...
	N: degree, rank, or grade in a scale
	...moved to the next step on the pay scale...
	EXPRESSION
	step on someone's toes = offend, intrude on someone's territory
	...stepped on her toes when he volunteered to take over...
	...don't want to step on the boss's toes on this matter...
	step on it = speed up
	...going to have to step on it to make it on time...
STEPPE	N: vast area that is flat and treeless (usually plural)
	...traveled across the steppes...
STILE	N: step or set of steps for passing over a fence or wall
	...noticed a stile that was partially hidden by weeds...
TURNSTILE	N: gate used for controlling the entrance
	...over a million people passed through the turnstile...
STYLE	N: way in which something is said or done
	...did everything with style...

STRAIGHT	ADJ: direct, not curved
	...has very straight hair...
	...stared straight ahead...
	ADJ: candid, frank
	...gave me a straight answer...
	ADJ: coming directly from a trustworthy source
	...straight tip on the horses...
	ADJ: consecutive
	...intense pain for 20 straight days...
	ADJ: plumb, vertical
	...picture isn't quite straight...
	ADJ: exhibiting honesty and fairness
	...always count on him for straight dealing...
	ADJ: properly ordered or arranged
	...get the facts straight...
	ADJ: free from extraneous matter
	...was drinking straight gin...
	ADJ: no exceptions or deviations in support of a principle or party
	...votes a straight Democratic ticket...
	ADJ: not using or under the influence of drugs or alcohol
	...it's time to get straight...
	ADJ: heterosexual
STRAIT	N: narrow body of water
	...sailed through the Bering Straits...
	N: position of difficulty or distress
	...found himself in dire straits...
	ADJ: confined, fitting tightly
	...put him into a straitjacket...
STRAP	VB/N: strip of something that holds things in place
	...always strap the child into the carseat...
	...used a strap to secure the packages in the vehicle...
STROP	VB/N: strip of leather or a machine on which to sharpen a razor
	...had to use the strop daily on his razor...

STRIP	VB: remove clothing or covering from *...tried to strip her of the title to the property...* VB: dismantle *...decided to strip the bed and wash everything...* N: long narrow piece of uniform width *...always enjoyed that comic strip...* *...landed on a small airstrip...* *...drove up onto the median strip on the highway...*
STRIPE	VB/N: mark with bands of color or texture *...must stripe the road after resurfacing it...* *...needs a stripe of color...*
STRIPED, STRIPING	Past tense and past participle/present participle of *to stripe* *...was wearing a striped top with jeans...* *...striping on the road was slightly crooked...*
STRIPPED, STRIPPING	Past tense and past participle/present participle of *to strip* *...stripped the floor down to the bare wood...* *...put new weather stripping around all the windows...*
SUB-	Prefix meaning "below" as in *subterranean* and *subconscious*
SUPER-	Prefix meaning "above" as in *superstructure* and *superimpose*
SUPRA-	Prefix meaning "above" as in *suprarenals* and *suprapubic*
SUBORDINATE (-TION)	Pronounced /su-<u>bord</u>-nait/ (ends in a long vowel *a*) VB: reduce to an inferior position or rank *...subordinate her will to his...* Pronounced /su-<u>bord</u>-nat/ (ends in a schwa sound) N: person in an inferior position *...did not treat his subordinate in a professional manner...* ADJ: inferior, lower in rank *...reduced to a subordinate position in the company...*
SUBORN (-ATION)	VB: secretly induce someone to do something illegal *...was revealed that he tried to suborn a witness...*

SUEDE	N: leather with a napped surface *...grease spot on his favorite suede jacket...*
SWAY(ED)	Past tense and past participle of *to sway* VB: swung slowly back and forth *...swayed in time with the music...* VB: convince *...swayed her to vote for their candidate in exchange for future favors...*
SUMMARY	N: synopsis, digest, review *...turned in a summary of my expenses...* *...accurate summary of the details of the case...* ADJ: covering the main points succinctly *...turned in a summary review...*
SUMMERY	ADJ: resembling or fit for summer *...unusual summery day in the middle of February...*
SUMMON	VB: call, order to appear *...summon the family members together for the discussion...*
SUMMONS	VB/N: call by means of a formal order or command *...summons him to appear on the charge...* *...received an unexpected summons...*
SURELY	ADV: in a sure manner without danger or risk of injury or loss *...will surely call me about the results of the test...*
SURLY	ADJ: upset all the time, cranky, arrogant, imperious *...did not appreciate his surly attitude toward his mother...* ADJ: irritably sullen and churlish in mood or manner *...always surly and unpleasant to be around...* ADJ: menacing or threatening in appearance *...frightened of his surly face...*

SWATCH	N: sample piece
	...got several swatches to match the color...
SWATH	N: long, broad strip or belt
	N: devastated area
	...tornado left a swath of destruction...
SWATHE	VB: envelop, wrap in
	...fog will swathe the coastline...
SYSTEMATIC	ADJ: in a deliberate and organized manner
	...systematic search of the premises...
SYSTEMIC	ADJ: affecting the entire organism or body
	...apathy is a systemic problem in our democracy...

TACH	Short for *tachometer*
	N: device for measuring the speed of rotation
TACK	VB: fasten or affix with pins
	...*will tack it up on his bulletin board*...
	VB: add as a supplement
	...*decided to tack on the extra charge*...
	...*has to tack this to the present bill*...
	VB: change the direction of as in sailing, follow a zigzag course
	...*boat will tack out of the harbor*...
	N: modify one's policy or attitude abruptly
	...*took a different tack to try to convince her*...
	...*came to a new tack after her talk with her boss*...
	N: short nail or pin with sharp point and a large flat head
	...*colored tack for different categories*...
	N: rope to hold in place a sail
	N: sticky or adhesive quality or condition
	...*felt the tack on the surface*...
	N: stable gear
	...*get out all the tack to prepare to ride*...
	...*bring the horse over to put the tack on it*...
TACK(ED)	Past tense and past participle of *to tack*
	...*tacked it to the board*...
TACT	N: diplomacy
	...*tried to do it with as much tact as possible*...
INTACT	ADJ: in one piece
	(Always one word)
	...*remained intact despite the high winds*...
	...*stayed intact through the storm*...

TACK(S)	Third person singular, present tense of *to tack*
	VB: fasten, affix
	...tacks everything to the wall...
	Plural of *tack*
	N: nail, pin
	...use tacks to affix it...
TAX	VB/N/ADJ: mandatory fee
	...levy the tax equally...
TAXI	VB: go at low speed along the surface of the ground or water
	...will taxi along the shoreline...
	VB: operate an aircraft on the ground under its own power
	...plane needed to taxi a long way to get to the gate...
	Short for *taxicab*
	N: vehicle used to ferry people from one place to another
	...took a water taxi to the resort...
TAIL	VB: follow closely, track
	...decided to tail the suspect...
	N: hind part
	...wound was near the horse's tail...
TALE	N: story
	...tale of the two sisters...
	N: lie
	...is telling a tale about her...
TAMPER	VB: meddle with, alter
	...tried to tamper with the locks...
TEMPER	VB: soften, moderate
	...have to temper your attitude with compassion...
	VB: make stronger through hardship
	...temper the troops in battle...
	N: disposition, passion
	...no effort to control his vile temper...

TANKARD	N: large vessel for drinking
	...had more than one tankard of beer...
TANKER	N: vehicle that carries bulk shipments of liquid
	...collision with the tanker spilled millions of gallons of oil...
	...tanker had a slow leak...
TAP	VB: draw off as from a bottle of liquid
	...tried to tap it for the last few drops...
	VB/N: strike lightly, sound of a light striking
	...will tap against it to see whether there is anything in there...
	...heard an intermittent tap that came from the attic...
	N/ADJ: spigot for water
	...content to drink tap water...
TAPE	VB: fasten, tie, bind, cover, or support with tape
	...will tape it to the wall...
	VB: record on magnetic tape
	...set to tape later in the day...
	N: long, narrow, often sticky strip of cloth
	...not enough tape to close the package...
	...used a special tape on the package...
	N: magnetic tape
	...have it on tape...
	...played the tape for the jury...
TAPED/TAPING	Past tense and past participle/present participle of *to tape*
	...show was taped in front of a live audience...
	...will be taping the box on all sides...
TAPPED/TAPPING	Past tense and past participle/present participle of *to tap*
	...tapped out the message to her in Morse code...
	...felt him tapping me on the shoulder...

TAPER	VB: narrow down
	...will taper down at the smaller end...
	VB: gradually stop (used with *off*)
	...taper off the medication...
	N: candle
	...one lighted taper...
TAPIR	N: swinelike animal
TARE	N: weed of grain fields
	...separate the tare from the wheat...
	N: deduction from the gross weight of a container made as an allowance for weight of the container
	...tare is a little over 500 pounds...
TEAR	Pronounced /tair/ (rhymes with *hair*)
	VB/N: rip, rend, split, cleave
	...had to tear it into tiny pieces...
	...had a tear along the edge...
	Pronounced /teer/ (rhymes with *here*)
	VB: produce moisture from the eyes
	...began to tear up during the speech...
	N: drop of clear saline fluid
	...had a tear in the corner of her eye...
TIER	N: row, layer
	...sat in the second tier...
	...played on a third-tier team...
TARO	N: tropical plant
TAROT	N: fortune-telling cards
	...prediction from the tarot cards...
TARRY	VB: delay, lay back
	...should not tarry if you expect to get in on this...
TERRY	N: cotton fabric
	...terry cloth was not enough to keep her warm...

TART	N: small pie
	...made an apple tart for each person...
	N: prostitute
	ADJ: filled with acrimony
	...did not appreciate her tart remark...
	ADJ: tangy
	...bit into the very tart apple...
TORT	N/ADJ: wrongful act
	...brought a tort action against us...
TORTE	N: rich cake
TAUGHT	Past tense and past participle of *to teach*
	VB: train or impart knowledge to
	...has taught children of all ages...
TAUT	ADJ: tight, not slack
	...nerves were taut from anxiety over the upcoming test...
TOT	N: small child, little kid
TOUT	VB: praise or publicize loudly or extravagantly
	...came to tout his choice for President...
TAUNT	VB/N: sarcastic challenge or insult
	...made it a habit to taunt the other children on the playground...
	...taunt was ringing in his ears...
TEA(S)	N: drink prepared from leaves
TEE(S)	N: starting place for each hole of golf
	...accident happened on the second tee...
	N: small peg from which the ball is driven
	EXPRESSION
	tee off on somebody = deride someone, criticize someone
	...teed off on her when he found out about the accident...
	be teed off = be really angry
	...was teed off about his firing...
TEASE	VB/N: make fun of, especially playfully or unpleasantly; laugh at
	...would tend to tease her unmercifully...

TEAM	N/VB: persons joined in some action or contest *...will team up to get the job done...*
TEEM	VB: be overflowing, full of something alive *...room that will teem with reporters in a few hours...*
TEAMED/TEAMING	Past tense and past participle/present participle of *to team* *...teamed up for the show...* *...will be teaming with his sister...*
TEEMED/TEEMING	Past tense and past participle/present participle of *to teem* *...room teemed with flying gnats...* *...teeming with a variety of unsavory characters...*
TEMBLOR	N: earthquake *...felt the temblor over a large area...*
TREMBLER	N: one who trembles
TREMOR	N: small earthquake N: shaking or trembling *...had a series of small tremors on his right side...*
TENANT	N: person who pays rent to occupy or use property *...looking for a new tenant for the house...*
TENET	N: principle, doctrine, or belief held as truth *...is a tenet of my faith...*
TENEMENT	N: shabby apartment house in the poorer, crowded part of the city *...tenement was condemned because of the rodent infestation...*
TENDER	ADJ: gentle *...treated her with tender care during her illness...*

TENTER	N: framework for drying cloth
	EXPRESSION
	    on tenterhooks = state of uneasiness or discomfort
	      ...waited on tenterhooks for the test results...

TINDER	N: highly flammable brush *...hillsides covered with tinder after a dry summer...*

TENDON	N: band of cord connecting muscle to another part
	...tends to stretch the tendons too far...
TENON	N: projection on the end of a piece of wood
	...part of the mortise and tenon construction...
TEND(S)	VB: be inclined to, have a tendency
	...tend to drink too much...
	VB: watch out for
	...has to tend her brothers and sisters while her mom is at work...
TENT(S)	VB: cover something, often in a loose fashion
	...have to tent the house for termites...
	N: portable shelter of canvas with poles
	...decided to stay in tents for the duration of the trip...
TENSE	ADJ: showing mental or emotional strain
	[Natural state for a court reporting student!!]
	...tense as she prepared for the test...
	ADJ: stretched tight
	...was tense with excitement...
INTENSE	ADJ: existing in an extreme degree
	...was in intense pain after the surgery...
	ADJ: marked by great zeal, energy, determination, or concentration
	...was intense as he planned his strategy...
	ADJ: exhibiting strong feeling or earnestness of purpose
	...is an intense athlete...
IN TENTS	N: on the inside of portable shelters of canvas with poles
	...camped in tents at the beach...
TINT(S)	Third person singular, present tense of *to tint*
	VB/N: impart or apply a different color to, color
	...going to tint the picture with a blue hue...
	...had a light tint put on her hair...
	N: coloration, hue
	...heavy gold tint in the picture...
	N: dye for the hair
	...has a blond tint on her hair...

TENOR   N: highest male voice
...voice was too low to be a tenor...

TENURE   N: holding or possessing something
...during his tenure on the bench...
N: job security in the academic world
...achieved tenure after five years...

TENSER   ADJ: more anxious, more nervous, more stressed
...becoming tenser the closer he gets to the test...

TENSOR   N: muscle that tightens a part of the body
...strain in the tensor in his lower leg...

TENSILE   ADJ: capable of being stretched
...had no tensile strength...

TINSEL   N: metallic decoration for a Christmas tree
...had away too much tinsel on the tree...

TERN   N: sea bird

TURN   VB: switch directions
...decided to turn at the corner...
VB/N: change in direction
...winds usually turn to the north at that location...
N: place in a rotation
...take his turn at the wheel...
...his turn to pay for dinner...
EXPRESSION
    turn into = become
    ...turns into a monster when he drinks...
    ...turns into a tyrant at the job...
    [So if one <u>turns in to</u> the driveway or roadway, *in to* is two words.]
    ...turn in to the roadway at the intersection...

TEST	VB/N: exam
	...will be put to the test...
TEXT	VB/N: send a typed/written message via cell phone
	...I believe that texting is going to kill this beautiful language!!...
	N: wording of a written document
	...tricky provision was buried in the text of the document...
TESTED/TESTING	Past tense and past and present participle of *test*
	...tested the brakes before going down the hill...
	...testing my nerves with his constant chatter...
TEXTED/TEXTING	Past tense and past and present participle of *text*
	...texted her the phone number...
	...seems to be texting every time I look up at her...
THAN	CONJ: used to indicate a comparison
	...taller than his brother...
THEN	ADV: next, soon afterward, at that time
	...went to the bank, then to the store...
	...waited for them to then show up...
	CONJ: next, at that time
	...paid the bill; then we made the call...
THEIR	ADJ: possessive form for third person plural
	...has their best interest at heart...
THERE	ADV: in that location, in that place
	...put it there for the time being...
	STRUCTURE WORD: placeholder with no meaning
	...there were 25 vehicles involved in the accident...
	...there comes a time...
	...there has to be an answer...
THEY'RE	CONTRACTION: *they are*
	...I know they're coming soon...

THEIRS	PRO: possessive form for third person plural
	...have theirs in my garage...
THERE'S	CONTRACTION: *there is*
	...there's no reason to...

THEREFOR	ADV: for or in return for that
	(Most often this word is seen at the end of a sentence or unit)
	...gave him $900 therefor...
	...received just compensation therefor...
THEREFORE	ADV: because of that, to that end
	...was therefore unable to perform his duties...
	CONJ: consequently, for that reason
	...had to have surgery; therefore, he could not participate...

THREW	Past tense of *to throw*
	VB: toss or hurl, propel from something
	...threw the case out of court...
THROUGH	(Substandard use as an adjective meaning *done, finished*)
	...he is through with it...
	PREP: in one side and out the other
	...bullet went through his arm...
	PREP: various places in
	...went through the book...
	PREP: by means of
	...entered through the door...
THOROUGH	ADJ: complete, very exact and painstaking
	...thorough interrogation...
	...thorough examination of his eyes...
THOUGH	ADV: even if, nonetheless, still
	...haven't seen him, though...
	CONJ: in spite of the fact that
	...was there, though I did not see him...

THROES	N: any violent convulsion or struggle
	...in the throes of death...
	...in the throes of passion...
THROW(S)	Third person singular, present tense of *to throw*
	VB: toss or hurl, propel from something
	...her abrupt demeanor always throws him into a tizzy...
	EXPRESSION
	throw the game = deliberately lose
	...seemed as if they were trying to throw the game...
THRONE	N: chair on which a king or queen sits on formal occasions
THROWN	Past participle of *to throw*
	VB: toss or hurl, propel from something
	...thrown against the wall in the fight...
THYME	N: garden herb
	...put in a pinch of thyme...
TIME	VB: mark the tempo or speed
	...tried to time the race to finish in the top ten...
	N: point when something occurs
	...at the time that he left...
	N: amount of time one has to work
	...done on company time...
	N: occasion
	...time that he was in the house...

TIC	N: spasmodic, involuntary muscular contraction, particularly of the face *...tic in his eye made it hard for him to focus...*

TICK	VB: make a light rhythmic, audible tap or beat
	...began to tick loudly...
	VB: operate as a functioning mechanism, run
	...is what makes him tick...
	VB: mark, count, or announce by ticking beats
	...tick off prices...
	VB/N: mark with a written check
	...tick off the things I have to do...
	N: type of insect
	...tick was embedded under the skin...
	N: sound a clock makes
	EXPRESSION
	    ticked off = angry, upset
	      ...really ticked off about her attitude...

TICKING	Present participle of *to tick*
	VB: tap
	N: strong linen or cotton fabric used in upholstering and as a covering for a mattress or pillow
	...blue-striped pillow ticking...
	EXPRESSION
	    clock is ticking = time is running out
	      ...clock is ticking on her ability to have children...

TIDAL	ADJ: relating to the tides *...was a tidal variation in the water level...* *...there were tidal surges over a one-week period...*
TITLE	N: legal right to ownership *...passed title to his son...* *...will take title in his own name...*

TIDE	N: daily rise and fall of a body of water
	...happened during high tide...
	N: change from one condition to the other
	...have to ride out the changing tides...
	EXPRESSION
	tide someone over = help someone through a tough time
	...money to tide me over until the end of the month...
	turn the tide = change the course of things
	...looks as if this job will turn the tide for her...
TIED	Past tense and past participle of *to tie*
	VB: fasten, join
	...forever tied to the legacy of his father...
TIGHTER	ADJ: more limited, more restricted
	...space was tighter than I thought...
TITER	N: strength of a solution
TIMBER	N: lumber, wood
	...had loose timber stacked up next to the house...
TIMBRE	Pronounced /<u>tam</u>-ber/
	N: distinctive tone or character
	...distinctive timbre to his voice...
TINNY	ADJ: lacking depth or substance, light, cheap
	...really tinny sound quality on the TV...
TINY	ADJ: extremely small
	...tiny tear in the aorta...
TO	PREP: toward
TOO	ADV: also
TWO	N: second number

TOAD	N: amphibian N: one exhibiting callous behavior *...acting like a toad about her sister's illness...*
TOE(D)	ADJ: having toes *...saw a three-toed sloth...*
TOW(ED)	Past tense and past participle of *to tow* VB: pull along *...towed a car behind the RV...*

TOE	N: digit of the foot
	EXPRESSIONS
	    toe the line = behave, follow the rules
	    ...had to toe the line in his presence...
	    toe the mark = do what is expected
	    ...toe the mark, and everything will be fine...

TOW	VB: pull along
	...had to tow the boat to the shore after the engine died...
	N: short or broken fiber as of flax, hemp, or synthetic
	EXPRESSION
	    towhead = very blond child (resembling flax in color)
	    ...real towhead as a kid...

TOLL	VB: sound a bell by pulling a rope
	..."Ask not for whom the bell tolls; it tolls for thee"...
	VB: collect a tax or fee
	...toll the business owners for an additional 3 percent...
	VB: entice game or fish to approach
	EXPRESSIONS
	    took a toll = great cost, heavy burden
	    ...his lengthy illness took a toll on him...
	    toll the statute = legal term regarding the statute of limitations

TOLE	N: sheet metal and tinplate for use in domestic and ornamental wares in which it is painted and elaborately decorated *...beautiful tole tray in shades of blue...*

TOLD	Past tense and past participle of *to tell*
	VB: say, aver, state
	...everything I told him...
	EXPRESSION
	    all told = everything taken together
	    ...all told, there were more than 20...

TOLL(ED)	Past tense and past participle of *to toll* *...bell tolled 12 times at noon...*
TORTIOUS	ADJ: having to do with a wrongful act *...was a tortious act...*
TORTUOUS	ADJ: winding; crooked, tricky *...tortuous route through the mountains...*
TORTUROUS	ADJ: unpleasant, painful *...torturous decision to have to make...*
TRACK	N: mark left by something or someone *...following the tracks in the snow...* *...needle tracks on her arm...* N: parallel rails of a train

TRACT	N/ADJ: area of land
	...bought a tract of land near the water...
	N: pamphlet or leaflet
	...distributed the religious tract...
	EXPRESSION
	    tract house = houses built together that look similar
	    ...lived in a small tract house...

TRACK(ED)	Past tense and past participle of *to track* VB/N: leave marks *...tracked mud into the house...* VB: follow or hunt someone or something *...tracked the suspect to his hometown...*
TREK	VB/N: make a journey or the journey itself *...it was a real trek up the hill to his property...*

TRADER	N: person who sells or swaps goods or merchandise
	...*trader of fine wines*...
TRAITOR	N: person who betrays another, a cause, or any trust
TRANSVERSE	ADJ: lying across
	...*transverse section of piping*...
TRAVERSE	VB: pass or move over
	...*have to traverse the maze of sections*...
TRAY	N: flat receptacle for carrying or holding
TREY	N: 3 of any suit in cards
TRÈS	FRENCH: *very*
	...*is regarded as tres chic*...
TREATY(-IES)	N: formal agreement between nations
	...*intended to sign a treaty regarding trade*...
	...*violated several treaties*...
TREATISE	N: systematic essay or book on some subject
	...*wrote the treatise on quantum physics*...
TRICKLE	VB/N: small flow
	...*information began to trickle out*...
TRUCKLE	VB: submit tamely, act subservient
	...*began to truckle in order to gain favor with the boss*...
TROOP	VB: move in large numbers
	...*ten boys troop through the house daily*...
	N: one soldier (usually used in the plural)
	...*troops were moved under the mantle of darkness*...
	N: group of scouts
	N: great number
	...*whole troop of them*...
TROUPE	N: group of performers
	...*acting troupe came to town to perform*...

TROOPER	N: member of the military or police force *...state trooper spotted the car off the road...*
TROUPER	N: person who persists through hardship *...was a real trouper during the crisis...*
TRUSS(ED)	Past tense and past participle of *to truss* VB: support or bind *...cargo was trussed to the sides of the hold...*
TRUSS	N: pad held in place by a belt for support, such as for a hernia *...had to wear a truss for several weeks...*
TRUST	VB: rely, believe *...trust you will be with us on this...* N: legal document about the disposition of one's estate *...did not mention his oldest son in his trust...*
TRUSTEE	N: person who holds something in trust *...was the trustee of my business...* *...sent it to the trustees to make the decision...*
TRUSTY	Pronounced /trus-<u>tee</u>/ N: convict considered trustworthy and allowed special privileges *...was the trusty in charge of the laundry in the prison...* Pronounced /<u>trust</u>-ee/ ADJ: trustworthy, dependable *...found him to be trusty in business dealings...* *...trusty friend that I really needed at the time...*
TRUSTEES	Plural of *trustee* N: one who is entrusted with something *...board of trustees met to vote on the matter...*
TRUSTIES	Plural of *trusty* N: prisoner who has special responsibilities *...rely on the trusties to help...*

TURBAN	N: headdress made of a cap around which is wound a long cloth
	...wore a turban during the ceremony...
	N: woman's close-fitting hat without a brim
	N: rolled, stuffed fillet of fish
	...ordered turban of sole...
TURBINE	N: rotary engine
	...propelled by a turbine...
TURBID	ADJ: thick or opaque with or as if with roiled sediment
	...looked into the turbid waters...
	ADJ: heavy with smoke or mist
	...turbid air in the burned-out factory...
	ADJ: deficient in clarity or purity; foul, muddy
	...turbid depths of degradation and misery...
	ADJ: characterized by or producing obscurity, as of mind or emotions
	...seemed to be an emotionally turbid response...
TURBINATE	N: one of the thin plicated membranes on the walls of the nasal chamber
	ADJ: shaped like the top of an inverted cone
	...turbinate capsule on the seed...
TUCK(S)	Third person singular, present tense of *to tuck*
	VB: pull up into a fold
	...tucks in the covers every night...
	VB: put into a snug, often concealing or isolating place
	...intends to tuck the cottage deep into the woods...
	VB: eat heartily (used with *away*)
	...really tucks away the food...
	N: folds or pleats
	...take tucks along the edge of the fabric...
	N: body position that is bent at the waist
	...do the dive in a tuck position...
TUX	Short for *tuxedo*
	N: formal suit
	...wore a tux to the wedding...

CHAPTER 21
THE LETTER *U*

UNALIGNED ADJ: not lined up, not on the same side
...unaligned vertebrae causing the problem...

UNLINED ADJ: without lines
...face was unlined, giving her a young look...

UNALIKE ADJ: not the same
...as unalike as twins can be...

UNLIKE PREP: not similar to
...unlike what her sister would do...

UNCHARTED ADJ: not being found on a map
...came upon an uncharted island...

UNCHARTERED ADJ: without regulation, lawless
...takes us into unchartered waters...

UNCOOKED ADJ: raw
...prefer uncooked veggies...

UNDERCOOKED ADJ: not thoroughly cooked
...undercooked meat was the culprit with the food poisoning...

UNCOVER VB: find something being searched for
...tried to uncover the facts behind the scandal...

UNDERCOVER ADJ: secret
...was working vice undercover...

UNDERDEVELOPED ADJ: not built up or enlarged to the full potential
...pictures were washed out and underdeveloped...

UNDEVELOPED ADJ: not built up or enlarged
...bought an undeveloped piece of land...

UNDERDONE   ADJ: not cooked all the way through
...chicken was underdone and had to be sent back...

UNDONE   ADJ: not completed, unfastened
...hooks were undone to reveal bare skin...

UNDERFUNDED   ADJ: not fully financed
...program for teachers is underfunded...

UNFUNDED   ADJ: having no money
...program remains unfunded and will not go forward...

UNDERPAID   ADJ: not compensated enough
...workers at the hotels are underpaid...

UNPAID   ADJ: not compensated at all
...bill remains unpaid after two months...

UNDO   VB: unfasten, loosen, disengage
...has to undo the damage he has done...
VB: destroy
...her death will undo him...

UNDUE   ADJ: not fitting, not proper
...exerted undue influence...
ADJ: too great, too much, unwarranted
...undue publicity for the inappropriate prank...

UNIT   N: single quantity, entity, piece
...acted as a unit in approaching him...
N: amount of work in education
...taking a three-unit class...

UNITE   VB: join, fix, bond, connect
...will unite behind the workers...

UNREAL	ADJ: lacking reality *...unreal devastation from the tornado...*
UNREEL	ADJ: unwind
UNSEAT(ED)	Past participle of *to unseat* VB: remove from office, not having a seat *...unseated the incumbent in the last election...*
UNSEEDED	ADJ: not having seeds planted *...left the lawn unseeded...* VB: having no ranking in a tournament *...was beaten by an unseeded player...*
UPEND	VB: radically change, tip over, overthrow *...scandal will upend his plans to run for office...*
APPEND	VB: add as a supplement *...need to append that to the document...*
UPPERMOST	ADV: in the highest position or place *...has been uppermost in my mind...*
UTMOST	N: most possible *...do my utmost to help...* ADJ: extreme, farthest *...utmost effort to accomplish that...*
URBAN	ADJ: relating to the city *...case of urban blight...*
URBANE	ADJ: suave, polished *...his urbane manner impressed us...*
UVEA	N: middle layer of the eye
UVULA	N: small suspended skin at the back of the palate *...had the uvula reduced in size to lessen his snoring...*

CHAPTER 22
THE LETTER V

VACATION   VB/N: time spent away from work

VOCATION   N: profession
...has enjoyed success in his vocation...
N: call to religious life

VAIL   VB: lower one's hat or banner, often as a sign of respect or submission

VAIL   N: mountain town in Colorado

VALE   N: valley
...cried a vale of tears...

VEIL   VB: cover, obscure, or conceal
...veil his intentions to infiltrate the company...
N: cloth worn as a covering for the head
...wore a lacy bridal veil...
N: concealing curtain or cover of cloth
N: something that hides or obscures
...under the veil of darkness...

VAIN   N: no use, without success (used after the word *in*)
...tried in vain to reach her...
ADJ: having too much pride
...too vain to let her hair go natural...

VANE   N: indicator of wind direction
...used a weather vane...

VEIN   N: blood vessel
...problem with the veins in his left leg...
N: large deposit of ore
...vein of gold...
N: general tone running through something
...talked in the same vein as his father...

VALANCE	Pronounced /<u>val</u>-uhns/ (rhymes with *pal*)
	N: short curtain
	...hung a valance of a contrasting color...
	...left the window with curtains but no valance...
VALENCE	Pronounced /<u>vail</u>-uhns/ (rhymes with *pail*)
	N: capacity of an atom to combine
	...has a valence of two...
VALUABLE	ADJ: of great worth
	...valuable only to her...
VOLUBLE	ADJ: glib, talkative
	...very voluble once she got started...
VANISH	VB: disappear
	...seemed to vanish without a trace...
BANISH	VB: send away
	...tried to banish them from the small country...
VANQUISH	VB: conquer
	...tried to vanquish his demons through intense therapy...
VARY	VB: change, alter, modify
	...weight did not vary over the year...
	...temperatures vary as much as 20 degrees from one day to the next...
VERY	ADJ: mere, bare
	...very thought of it...
	ADJ: being just what is needed or suitable
	...very one I was looking for...
	ADV: to a great extent, extremely
	...was very happy about the appointment to the council...

VAULT	VB: leap over, jump
	...vault over the railing to reach her...
	N: tomb, crypt
	...in the vault at the mausoleum...
	N: secure place to store things
	...put her jewels into the vault in the room...
VAUNT	VB: boast, brag
	...continued to vaunt his cooking skills...
VENAL	ADJ: open to corrupt influence, especially bribery
	...had a venal relationship with the local police...
VENIAL	ADJ: forgivable, as a sin
	...dismissed it as a venial sin...
VENERABLE	ADJ: highly respected because of longevity
	...was a venerable actor of 60 years...
VULNERABLE	ADJ: able to be hurt or wounded or injured
	...feeling vulnerable after her father's death...
	...vulnerable to the elements as they camped in the mountains...
VERACIOUS	ADJ: truthful
	...seemed to be a veracious statement...
VORACIOUS	ADJ: having a huge appetite
	...had always been a voracious eater...
	ADJ: insatiable
	...voracious reader even as a teenager...
VERACITY	N: truth
	...question the veracity of his statement...
VORACITY	N: huge appetite
	...her voracity for historical novels...

VERSE(S)

Plural of *verse*
N: poetry
...poem had only two verses...

VERSUS

PREP: against
...Adam versus his sister in this action...

VERTEX

N: highest point of something, summit
...collided at the vertex of the hill...

VORTEX

N: whirlpool
...caught in the vortex of the pool...

VIAL

N: small container for liquids
...small vial of liquid in her purse...

VILE

ADJ: foul, disgusting, offensive
...vile behavior when he drank...
...vile comment...

VIOL

N: stringed instrument
...changed his life when he began to play the viol...

VICE

N/ADJ: evil conduct, corruption
...has no vice...
...works in the vice squad...

VISE

N: tool used for holding an object firmly while it is being worked upon
...old vise did not hold well...
N: holding something in a tight grip
...caught in the vise the police put in place...

VICIOUS

ADJ: brutal, violent
...vicious attack by the young cub...

VISCOUS

ADJ: thick, sticky
...viscous fluid draining from the wound...

VIRAL ADJ: spreading rapidly
...video went viral overnight...
ADJ: coming from a virus
...trying to overcome the viral infection around his heart...

VIRILE ADJ: manly, forceful
...particularly virile strain of the flu...

CHAPTER 23
THE LETTER *W*

WADE

VB: step into water
...decided to wade into the very cold ocean water...
VB: move through with difficulty
...tried to wade through the volumes of exhibits...
VB: begin, commence (usually used with *into*)
...need to wade into this project...

WEIGH(ED)

Past tense and past participle of the verb *weigh*
VB: consider
...need to weigh my options...
VB: assess poundage
...weighed the suitcase to determine the charge...
EXPRESSION
> *weigh in on* = express an opinion
> *...weighed in on the gun controversy...*

WADER(S)

N: pants worn for fishing
...wore waders while fishing in the river...

WAITER(S)

(Politically correct term is *waitperson*)
N: person who serves food at a restaurant
...best waiter I have ever encountered...

WAFER

N: cracker
...could not keep down even a small wafer...

WAIVER

N: relinquishment of a right
...got a waiver for the ticket...
EXPRESSION
> *on waivers* = remove a player from the roster and put him up for
> another team to pick up (sports)

WAVER

VB/N: be hesitant, indecisive
...always seemed to waver on important decisions...

WAIF	N: child who is homeless and friendless
	...took the small waif into his house...
WAIVE	VB: give up a right or claim to something
	...waive his right to a jury trial...
WAVE	V: move the hand back and forth
	...wave good-bye...
	N: moving swell of water or any movement like it
	...unusually high wave every once in a while...
	...wave of nausea...
WAIL(S)	VB/N: moan or cry as in grief
	...began to wail when she heard the sad news...
WALES	N: country that is part of Great Britain
	...tennis player is from Wales...
WALE(S)	N: width of corduroy between the ribs
	...made with wide-wale fabric...
GUNWALE	Pronounced /<u>gun</u>-uhl/ (rhymes with *funnel*)
	N: upper edge of a ship's side
	...break in the gunwale of the port side...
WHALE(S)	VB: engage in whale fishing
	...whale in the waters off Japan...
	VB: lash, thrash, strike or hit vigorously
	...began to whale on him...
	VB: defeat soundly
	N: mammal that swims in the ocean
	...took the whale-watching boat...
	N: one that is impressive especially in size
	EXPRESSION

    whale of a... = huge, large
    ...whale of a difference...
    ...whale of a good time...

WAIST	N: circumference of the body between the ribs and the hips
	...*had a tiny waist*...
	N: garment that comes to the waist, blouse
	...*wore a waistcoat*...
WASTE	VB: squander, not take advantage of
	...*waste the opportunity of a lifetime*...
	N: refuse, trash, useless or worthless material
	N: desert, wilderness
	...*was a land of barren waste*...
WASTED	SLANG: drunk
WAIT	VB: stand still, halt
	...*had to wait for over an hour*...
	VB: serve
	...*decided to wait tables to earn money for college*...
	N: length of time spent standing still or halted
	...*wait of well over five hours*...
WEIGHT	N: amount or quantity of heaviness
WEIGHTY	ADJ: important
	...*discussed a weighty subject*...
WALK	VB/N: ambulate, stroll
	...*took a walk to clear his head*...
	N: pathway
	...*put a cement walk near the fence*...
WOK	N: cooking utensil
WANDER	VB: roam, move aimlessly, stray
	...*tended to wander when left alone*...
WONDER	VB: speculate, want to know
	...*often wonder how to handle him*...
	N: marvel, miracle
	...*is a wonder he is even alive*...

WANT	VB: wish or desire
	N: desire
	...has a lot of wants and needs...
WONT	ADJ: accustomed, used to
	...paced as he is wont to do...
	N: habit
	...is his wont to be unable to sleep...
WON'T	CONTRACTION: *will not*
WAR	VB: engage in armed conflict
	N: major armed conflict, especially between nations
WORE	Past tense of *to wear*
	VB: be a worry
	...her drinking problems wore on him...
	VB: have on
	...always wore black...
WARD	VB: turn aside something threatening, deflect (used with *off*)
	...need to ward off evil spirits...
	N: administrative district of a city or town
	...occurred in the Ninth Ward of New Orleans...
	N: division of a hospital
	...in the maternity ward...
	N: section of a prison
	N: person under the legal guardianship of another
	...made a ward of the court...
WARRED	Past tense of *to war*
	VB: combat, fight
	...warred against her desire to drink...
WART	N: small, usually hard, abnormal growth on the skin, caused by a virus
	...had the wart on her thumb removed...

WARE	N: goods, specified kind of merchandise (usually used in the plural) *...selling his wares...*
WEAR	VB: carry on one's person for covering, ornament, defense *...would often wear a heavy jacket even in warmer weather...* VB: impair by constant use or friction (usually used with *away*) *...surface of the tooth would wear away...* VB: hold up in use *...will wear the crown well...*
WEREWOLF	N: human being that has become or is capable of becoming a wolf
WHERE	ADV/CONJ: at or in what place *...not sure where he lives...*
WARILY	ADV: with caution *...warily approached the closed door...*
WEARILY	ADV: tiredly *...wearily continued the negotiations...*
WARM	ADJ: moderately hot *...too warm to stay in the sun...*

WORM	N: maggot, bug
	 N: despicable person
	 ...acted like a worm in the divorce...
	 EXPRESSION
	    worm one's way in = connive to be accepted
	    ...tried to worm his way into the group by bringing food each time...

WARN	VB: give notice in advance *...have to warn her of the danger...*
WORN	Past participle of *to wear* VB: have on *...has worn the responsibility well...* ADJ: tattered, well used, beaten down *...looking worn and tired...*

WARY	ADJ: cautious *...wary of getting involved with her...*
WEARY	ADJ: tired *...weary after the long day on the job...*
WORRY	VB: be concerned *...always worry about their relationship...*
WATT	N: unit of electric power *...need more watts for this light...*
WHAT	PRO/ADJ: question word *...wanted to know what he was doing...*

WAX	VB: treat with polish, shine
	...applied several coats of wax to the floor...
	VB/N: increase, grow
	...moon on the wax...
	N: yellowish substance secreted by bees for making their honeycomb
	N: phonograph recording
	...wax of the old song...
	EXPRESSIONS
	    wax on = talk on and on
	    ...wax on about his war experiences...
	    wax nostalgic = become
	    ...wax nostalgic about the good old days...

WHACKS	N: resounding blows
WAC's	ACRONYM: Woman's Army Corps (World War II era)
WAY	N: manner, method, path, means, direction *...different way to do it...*
WEIGH	VB: find the weight of VB: consider *...needs to weigh his options...*
WHEY	N: watery liquid that separates from milk after it curdles *...Little Miss Muffet was eating her curds and whey...*

WEAK	ADJ: lacking strength *...too weak to continue...* ADJ: deficient in vigor *...very weak argument against the bill...*
WEEK	N: seven successive days
WEAKEN(ED)	Past tense and past participle of *to weaken* VB: make less strong, decline *...was in a weakened state after the surgery...*
WEEKEND	N: Saturday and Sunday
WEATHER	VB: endure, survive *...trying to weather the tough times...* N: condition of the atmosphere
WHETHER	CONJ: indicating a choice or alternative *...do not know whether he can go...*
WEAVE	VB/N: interlace, intertwine *...tried to weave the details of the story together...*
WE'VE	CONTRACTION: *we have*

WEED	VB: pull up something that is not wanted (often used with *out*)
	...will weed the garden this weekend...
	...need to weed out the used ones...
	N: plant that is not valued, usually one that grows quickly
	...sometimes hard to tell the flowers from the weeds...
	EXPRESSION
	    growing like a weed = growing quickly
	    ...growing like a weed and is almost as tall as his dad...

WE'D	CONTRACTION: *we had, we would*
WERE	Past tense of *to be* VB: exist *...were with them when it happened...*
WE'RE	CONTRACTION: *we are*

WET	VB: dampen
	ADJ: damp
	...ground was wet and slippery...
	EXPRESSION
	wet your whistle = get a drink
WHET	VB: sharpen by rubbing
	...used a whetstone on the razor...
	EXPRESSION
	whet your appetite = stimulate
WHEAL	N: welt
	...left him with a wheal on his shin...
WHEEL	VB: roll
	...tried to wheel it into the room on a cart...
	N: circular frame
	...small wheel which was defective...
	EXRESSION
	wheels = car
	...finally got wheels for my birthday...
WE'LL	CONTRACTION: *we will*
WHEEL(ED)	Past tense and past participle of *wheel*
	VB: conveyed by a vehicle with wheels
	...wheeled into the operating room...
WIELD	VB: hold in a threatening manner
	...wield a gun...
	VB: exercise authority over
	...intended to wield his power...
WHICH	PRO/ADJ: indicates a choice
	...don't know which one to choose...
WITCH	N: evil woman with magical powers
	...acted like a witch most days at the office...

WHILE VB: spend time (usually used with *away*)
...while away the time...
N: indefinite period of time
...happened a while ago...
N: time and effort used
...worth your while...
CONJ: during the time that
...happened while I was in Canada...

WILE N: trick or stratagem
...used wile to get results...
N: charm (usually used in the plural)
...used feminine wiles to persuade him...

WINE(D) N: fermented juice of fruit, beverage
EXPRESSION
    wine and dine = treat in high style

WHINE(D) VB/N: utter a low, unusually nasal, complaining sound or cry
...motor began to whine as we turned it on...
...high-pitched whine of the engine...

WIND Pronounced /wind/ (rhymes with *kind*)
VB: coil or twine about something
...needs to wind his watch...
...can wind him around her finger...
Pronounced /wind/ (rhymes with *sinned*)
N: natural movement of air
...strong wind blowing all day...

WISHFUL ADJ: expressing a desire, often one that is not likely to happen
...wishful thinking on her part...

WISTFUL ADJ: melancholic, yearning
...wistful as he stared at the stars...

WIT	N: mind, memory (usually used in the plural)
	...has his wits about him...
	...at my wits' end with her behavior...
	EXPRESSION
	    to wit = namely
	        ...most egregious crime, to wit, murder...

DIMWIT	N: mentally slow person *...real dimwit about computers...*
WHIT	N: smallest part imaginable *...don't give a whit about that...*
WITHER	VB: become dry or sapless, shrivel from loss of moisture *...leaves tend to wither in the fall...* VB: lose vital force and freshness *...watched him wither away...* VB: make speechless or incapable of action, stun *...wither him with a look...*
WITHERS	N: ridge between the shoulder bones of a horse at the base of the neck to just before the saddle
WHITHER	N: to what place *...whither thou goest...*

WOOD	N: hard fibrous substance
	N: dense trees (usually used in the plural)
	...wandered into the nearby woods...
	EXPRESSION
	    out of the woods = out of trouble
	        ...think he is finally out of the woods...

WOULD	VB: helping verb *...hoping he would go with us...*
WORST	ADJ: most corrupt or evil or bad *...is the worst representative of his profession...*
WURST	N: sausage

WRENCH	VB: twist
	...tried not to wrench his back...
	N: tool for twisting and tightening
RINSE	VB/N: wash something from
	...needed to rinse the dishes...
	N: hair coloring
	...added a rinse to her hair...
WRY	ADJ: cleverly and ironically humorous
	...wry sense of humor...
RYE	N: cereal grass
	...ham on rye...

CHAPTER 24
THE LETTER *Y*

YAY
INTERJ: exclamation of support
...*Yay. We did it...*

YEA
N: affirmative response, yes
...*need to vote yea or nay...*
ADV: indeed, truly
...*won, yea routed, their rival...*

YEAH
INTERJ: informal *yes*

YOKE
VB/N: tie, link
...*tried to yoke them together...*
N: wooden frame used to fasten two animals together for an equal load
...*yoke on the oxen...*
N: servitude, bondage
...*yoke of slavery...*

YOLK
N: yellow part of the egg
...*yolk contains all the fat...*

YOKEL
N: naive or gullible person of a rural area or small town
...*acted like a yokel when he got to the big city...*

YORE
N: long ago time
...*in the days of yore...*

YOUR
ADJ: possessive form, second person, used as an adjective
...*gave it your best...*

YOURS
PRO: possessive form, second person, used as a pronoun
...*think it is yours...*

YOU'RE
CONTRACTION: *you are*

YOU'LL
CONTRACTION: *you will*

YULE
N: Christmas
...*celebrate the Yule with family...*

CHAPTER 25
ONE WORD OR TWO?

(*Court Reporting: Bad Grammar/Good Punctuation*, Chapter 29, has a more complete explanation of these words and also contains a few other one-word/two-word combinations.)

ALMOST	ADV: close to, nearly ...*almost had an accident*... ...*had almost secured the loan*...
ALL MOST	PRO + ADV: "everyone very" ...*were all most happy to see him*... ...*all most sincere in our offer*...
ALOT	This is never a correct form!
A LOT	N: much, very much (substandard form) ...*had a lot to do that day*... N: piece of land, parcel, set of merchandise ...*had a lot on the beach that was out of my price range*... ...*bid on a lot of drill bits*...
ALREADY	ADV: previously, before now ...*had already made the decision to leave the company*... ...*has already previewed the book*...
ALL READY	PRO + ADJ: "everyone or everything prepared" ...*are all ready to proceed with the vote*... ...*were all ready to eat when he got there*...
ALRIGHT	This is NEVER a correct form! (Think of *alwrong*)
ALL RIGHT	ADV: okay, totally correct ...*said it was all right to leave our stuff there*... ...*was it all right with her folks*...

ALTOGETHER	ADV: totally, completely, entirely
	...altogether sure that he did it...
ALL TOGETHER	PRO + ADJ: "everyone in one place"
	...were all together for the reading of the will...
	...all together to celebrate Mom's birthday...

ALWAYS	ADV: forever, for all times
	...always tried to do the right thing...
	...was always trying to find a way into the group...
ALL WAYS	ADJ + N: every method, by any means
	...considered all ways to try to solve the problem...
	...was with him in all ways...

ANYBODY	PRO: indefinite person
	...can be done by anybody...
	...did not see anybody inside...
ANY BODY	ADJ + N: any physical body, any governing body
	...was not any body found in the ashes...
	...need any body of the government to make a decision on this...

ANYMORE	ADV: from this point forward, no longer
	...am not doing that anymore...
	...will not attend there anymore...
ANY MORE	ADJ + PRO/ADJ: anything left, anything additional
	...not any more he can say...
	...not taking on any more projects...

ANYONE	PRO: indefinite person
	...haven't seen anyone that can finish it...
	...did not talk with anyone in the group...
ANY ONE	ADJ + PRO: whatever one
	...any one of them can do it...
	...looked at cars. Any one will be okay...

ANYTIME	ADV: whenever, indefinite point in time *...can see you anytime...* *...could do it anytime...*
ANY TIME	ADJ + N: indefinite period of time *...do not have any time to discuss this...* *...does not spend any time with his kids...*
ANYWAY	ADV: in any case, no matter what *...will try to do it anyway...* *...could not participate anyway...*
ANY WAY	ADJ + N: by any method, by any means *...help in any way I can...* *...not any way to do that...*
APIECE	ADV: each, per *...sent them $20 apiece...*
A PIECE	N: one portion, one share, one part *...wants a piece of the deal...* *...eats a piece of pie...*
AWHILE	Though this CAN be one word in certain circumstances, it can ALWAYS be two words. Why bother with one word? ADV: indefinite period of time *...were together a while...* (OR *...together awhile...* but why?)
A WHILE	N: indefinite period of time *...took a while to see it...* *...spent time a while back...*
EVERYBODY	PRO: indefinite person *...saw everybody on Sunday...* *...got help from everybody there...*
EVERY BODY	ADJ + N: physical body, governing body *...every body was autopsied after the fire...* *...need every body in the town government to vote on this measure...*

EVERYDAY	ADJ: usual, normal, habitual (used only as a direct adjective)
	...was an everyday job for me to do laundry...
	...had the everyday responsibility for the operation...
EVERY DAY	ADJ + N: each and every day
	...saw her every day that week...
	...will be paid every day that he comes to work...
EVERYONE	ADJ + PRO: indefinite person
	...everyone was in on the surprise...
	...saw everyone there...
EVERY ONE	ADJ + PRO: all
	...every one of the men has it...
	...considering a new apartment. Every one I saw was too expensive...
INTO	PREP: move to (always implies movement)
	...put them into the safe...
	...walked into the room...
IN TO	ADV + PREP: (part of two different elements in the sentence)
	...went in to cash a check...
	...come in to discuss the matter...
MAYBE	ADV: possibly, perhaps
	...maybe get in tomorrow...
	...will maybe be able to call...
MAY BE	VB: possible, it could be
	...she may be with her friend right now...
	...he may be our only choice...
NOBODY	PRO: indefinite person
	...got nobody to help us...
	...saw nobody on the premises...
NO BODY	ADJ + N: physical body, governing body
	...no body could survive such torture...
	...no body is willing to pass the law...

NOONE	This is NOT a word
NO ONE	PRO: indefinite pronoun, not one
	...no one is here...
	...have seen no one of them that I would read...
ONTO	PREP: move to (always implies movement)
	...drove onto the shoulder of the road...
	...walked onto the wet cement...
ON TO	ADV + PREP: (part of two different elements in the sentence)
	...went on to bigger and better things...
	...moved on to become the manager...
OVERALL	ADJ/ADV: complete, thorough, comprehensive
	...overall assessment of the company...
	...overall, it was a good day...
OVER ALL	PREP + PRO/ADV: above, in charge of everybody
	...picked him over all the candidates...
	...put him in charge over all the accounts...
SOMEBODY	PRO: indefinite person
	...somebody stepped up to help...
	...will get help from somebody...
SOME BODY	ADJ + N: physical body, governing body
	...could be some body that needs to be examined for signs of torture...
	...may be some body of the government that will vote on this...
SOMEONE	PRO: indefinite person
	...need someone to help...
	...saw someone in the crowd...
SOME ONE	ADJ + PRO: whatever one
	...some one of them is going to have to...
	...walked to the employees. Some one of them will...

SOMETIME	ADJ: occasional, fleeting
	...was a sometime friend...
	ADV: indefinite point in time
	...will be with him sometime late in July...
	...date for sometime next week...
SOME TIME	ADJ + N: indefinite period of time
	...need some time to heal from the tragedy...
	...haven't seen her for some time...
SOMETIMES	ADV: occasionally
	...would sometimes spend the afternoon at the park...
	...sometimes saw her on the weekends...
SOME TIMES	ADJ + N: certain occasions
	...were some times that I wanted to just leave...
	...some times that she was really sick...
THEREON	ADV: on that, on that thing
	...based his argument thereon...
	...statements were based thereon...
THERE ON	ADV + ADV: from that point forward
	...did not see him from there on...
UPON	PREP: positioned on
	...placed it upon the counter where we could examine it...
UP ON	ADV + PREP: (part of two different elements in the sentence)
	...went up on a different charge...

ALPHABETICAL LISTING: THE LETTER A

ALPHABETICAL LISTING: THE LETTER *B*

ALPHABETICAL LISTING: THE LETTER C

ALPHABETICAL LISTING: THE LETTER D

ALPHABETICAL LISTING: THE LETTER *E*

ALPHABETICAL LISTING: THE LETTER *F*

ALPHABETICAL LISTING: THE LETTER *G*

Alphabetical Listing: The Letter *H*

ALPHABETICAL LISTING: THE LETTER *I*

ALPHABETICAL LISTING: THE LETTER *J*

ALPHABETICAL LISTING: THE LETTER *K*

ALPHABETICAL LISTING: THE LETTER *L*

ALPHABETICAL LISTING: THE LETTER *M*

ALPHABETICAL LISTING: THE LETTER *N*

ALPHABETICAL LISTING: THE LETTER *O*

ALPHABETICAL LISTING: THE LETTER *P*

ALPHABETICAL LISTING: THE LETTER *Q*

ALPHABETICAL LISTING: THE LETTER *R*

ALPHABETICAL LISTING: THE LETTER S

ALPHABETICAL LISTING: THE LETTER *T*

ALPHABETICAL LISTING: THE LETTER *U*

ALPHABETICAL LISTING: THE LETTER V

ALPHABETICAL LISTING: THE LETTER *W*

ALPHABETICAL LISTING: THE LETTER *Y*, *Z*